When Nations Gather

By Sultan Abdul Latif

Original Cover Art Designed By Melody Lightfeather

Published by
Nadia's House Publishing Company
In conjunction with
Latif Communications Group, Inc.
8 South Michigan Avenue, Suite 1510
Chicago, IL 60603
(312) 849-3456

Photography by Bill Hardin

When Nations Gather

By Sultan Abdul Latif

Copyright 2001 by Sultan Abdul Latif

ISBN 0-9640118-1-6
Printed in the United States of America

Dedication

This book is dedicated to the Native American prophets who warned that the destruction of their nations was the beginning of the end of mankind through world wars and natural catastrophes; to the Hopi people of America and the Dogon people of Africa whose sacred tablets foretold of the time when a divided humanity would one day reunite; to the ancient prophets Zoroaster, Abraham, Moses, Buddha, Jesus, Muhammad, and many others (peace be upon them) who brought mankind the Divine laws; to the spiritual leaders Ahmadu Bamba and the Dalai Lama, who brought enlightenment to the modern era; to the Native American spiritual leaders Crazy Horse, Sitting Bull, Deganawidah, Wovoka, Handsome Lake, and Black Elk whose visions gave them the courage to fight against oppression; to the Divinely inspired messengers who brought guidance and spiritual light to the indigenous people of the Pacific Islands, Australia, New Zealand and other remote regions of the world; to the courageous visionary Marcus Mosiah Garvey of Jamaica, whose international movement uplifted oppressed African people worldwide and reconnected African Americans to the spiritual teachings of their fore parents; and to Hazrat Mirza Ghulam Ahmad of Qadian, India, whose writings verified the teachings of the ancient prophets and visionaries that a Messiah would come in the latter days to gather the nations as one family under God.

Acknowledgements

First I give thanks to Almighty God for His divine Grace in enabling this book to be published.

Thanks to my beautiful wife Naimah Latif for her knowledge, professional skills, contributions and support, without which this book could not have been written.

Thanks to the Black Indian Society for invaluable support and research.

Special thanks to Micah Tair, whose diligence in seeking historical information helped to broaden the scope of this book, and whose consistent hard work and commitment enabled this book to be completed.

Thanks also to my research team of Gerald Watson, Melody Lightfeather, Najma Rafat, Rasheed Ahmad, Munir Hamid, Gilda Hamilton, Robert Porter, Mark Jackson, Nafi Rafat, L.A. Emenari, and Abubakr Salahuddin.

Special thanks to Munir Ahmad, Azim Aziz, Najma Rafat, Byron Artist, Global Millennium Group and Accion Chicago for the financial support which made this book possible.

Thanks to Granville T. Ware and Sean Mullin for technical assistance. Special thanks to Top Artist for their support. Thanks to the many family members and friends for their prayers and encouragement.

Special thanks to my many Native American brothers and sisters who gave personal interviews and entrusted me with the responsibility to bring to the world's attention their stories of hardships and struggles, as well as their dreams and hopes for the future. They are people like Wayne Reels, Zachary Running Bull Brown, Leonard E. Fooshay, M.D., Laurence Martinez, Nancy Red Star, Dr. Lita Mathews, Derek Mathews (founder of the Gathering of Nations), Melody Mathews, Lloyd Thompson, Tall Oak, Jerry Shepherd aka Kana Misitim (Dancing Medicine Horse), Empress Verdiacee "Tiara" Washitaw-Turner Goston El-Bey, and many, many more.

My undying gratitude goes to Hazrat Mirza Tahir Ahmad, Supreme Head of the Ahmadiyya Movement in Islam, whose writings provided such brilliant enlightenment for these modern times.

Contents

Table of Illustrations

Foreword

By Melody Lightfeather

Spiritual inspiration usually comes from personal experiences relating to religious events in one's life during ones youth and gains more meaning later on, prompted by education, growth, relationships and maturity. Sometimes it comes from dreams and visions as this one did, at the time of *The Gathering of Nations 2000 -- the Millennium Gathering*. It was an anxious time because of all the predictions and undercurrents about the first major events during the Spring Solstice 2000. I had had a dream during the twilight hours more than a year before that would not leave me, and for quite a while I had no idea what to make of it.

In the dream, I saw my husband standing on a stage in front of a podium talking to a mass of people of all colors and creeds from many different places and walks of life. Out of the masses came a tall, thin, soft spoken, humble Holy man who wore a white cap on the center of his head speaking in poetic verses of an oral history that related to all people of color. He claimed to know through his research of an unearthed relationship between cultures of centuries past that showed the correlations between them and the shared parallels into their future. It was the symbolism in the words he spoke and the manner it was given that shook my very soul - one which came back to me in a vision which stirred my soul. You will see as this book unfolds how I came to actually meet him this one particular day when nations gather -- at the **Gathering of Nations**.

I am an Artist and Designer born from the Hohokam People of the Salt River Pima Tribe of the Southwest Territory. My father's people came from the islands. While I've lived most of my life without either parents, I had the very good fortune of learning about both sides. This was due to the circumstances of my parents careers and my Grandmother's diligent upbringing in teaching me the old ways, while we lived in a modern age, between two worlds.

Many aboriginal people have no choice in order to survive, which brings me back to the reason why this book is so important in its intent: Spiritual experiences and absorption of knowledge can only serve as valuable to growth in one's life if it directly impacts our "need-to-know" for a purpose. Oftentimes it can be so subtle an experience or there are so many other things going on around us, that we don't recognize its purpose until somewhere down the road in life. It's usually when there's some major changes going on that when we stop to reflect about the reasons things happen the way they do. There, in an instant, it all comes back in that tiny unspoken moment of revelation. We recall in our spirit within, what all of those moments collectively perceived really mean.

I had a chance to meet Sultan Abdul Latif at a Board meeting of the Black Indian Society while on Powwow tour from the Midwest through the Northeastern coast. I kept feeling "deja vu" as though I had known him somehow before we actually met in person. Then my husband showed me his first book called, *Psychic Trauma.*

After reading several chapters, I realized that he was the Holy man from within the vision, holding the keys to the doorways of our shared cultural history. He knew ... This was the reason he had come to the Gathering of Nations, held each year, usually on the third weekend in April in Albuquerque, New Mexico where I now live. I have been an exhibitor with my beadwork and art-to-wear clothing designs since the very first "Gathering" held in the Agricultural annex barn at the University of New Mexico. It has become the largest Powwow in North America since those days.

I'm still amazed how great an event it is, especially for sharing of our culture and history of Native America with song, dance, ceremonial dress and arts and crafts of all people who come together at this incredible event. Many people had come there to meet and greet each other, the tribal elders, friends and their families, which is very reminiscent of family reunions. However, this event embodies reunions of tribes and legions of Native families and their ways, Native foods and their indigenous roots, as well as the beauty of all the handiwork from all reaches of American native people.

Following the Gathering of Nations, it was a warm, sunny Sunday afternoon. We had an opportunity to tour some northern most reservations with Sultan and a few of his dearest companions. I knew then and there that the vision was in the process of becoming a reality. We made several stops and had several conversations that day. But it wasn't until we stopped inside the Hidden Valley of the Picuris Old Pueblo to visit with an elder and a friend did the vision start to take on its true meaning.

When the gift of tobacco was given and a blessing prayer, our Creator came forth with the cries of children from the hills behind us at the Kiva. It was then that I began to truly appreciate what the vision meant, and how it is that I was chosen to open the doorway to you. I am honored both in the symbolism within my art and inherent in my pen, for the gifts I have received through a vision which will unfold right now before you within the pages of this book, *"When Nations Gather."*

A TRIBUTE TO MELODY LIGHTFEATHER

Melody and I had an engaging conversation one day where she mentioned how her grandmother had once told her that her art would be used to bring the true spiritual history of her people back and that it was very important for her to realize that she had a mission. When we discussed this, it had an impact on me to know that someone felt that the work we were doing had tremendous cultural and spiritual significance. Also, that it is important to realize how many times our elders have a far greater vision for ourselves then we could possibly have.

Sister Melody passed away on November 7, 2001 in an unfortunate auto accident. We will greatly miss her. She was an inspiration to us all and a positive force among her people. Her legacy will continue to live on through her family and her artwork. This book is a tribute to Melody Lightfeather as well as her grandmother - whose spirit was reflected in Melody's words.

0A – Melody Lightfeather

Melody Lightfeather was a world renowned, award winning artist, whose highly sought after work is owned by U.S. Presidents, top CEOs of Fortune 500 companies, and a host of movie stars and sports stars. She was the only woman in the world to have been accepted in the International "Le Salon de Nationale" of Paris, France, and was the only woman to win the International Gold Medal of Nations representing the United States. Her paintings have received national and international awards and her work has been featured in such prestigious publications as People Magazine, Vogue and Advertising Age. She was a featured guest on television shows such as Good Morning America, ABC, NBC, and CBS news. Her biography has been listed in 28 published journals including the International Who's Who of Women Executives.

Melody Lightfeather

The Pima People

The tribe known as the Pima, of Southern Arizona, is one of several tribes descended from the ancient Hohokam, or "vanished ones," of the Southwest. They came to be known by the name Pima through a miscommunication with the early Spanish missionaries. The name Pima is said to be based on a phrase of theirs, "Pi-nyi-match," meaning, "I don't know." This was thought to be their frequent response to the many questions the Spanish had for them, possibly due to a language barrier.

The Spanish mistook this response as a statement of who they were and then, through the grapevine, this name came to be included on the maps of the Southwest during that time – and the people came to be known as the Pima. The Pima call themselves Aatam-akimult "people of the river" or Akimel O'odham "river people."

Like their ancestors the Hohokam, the Pima were also farmers and hunter-gatherers and were known as great artisans. As farmers the Pima were known for growing such foods as corn, cotton, tobacco, beans and squash.

The Pima were also a very spiritual people, with a long history of religious practice and culture. The Pima's Genesis account speaks of the Creator or "Earth Doctor," evolving from a dense cloud of darkness, who created the earth and a race of immortal humans. This race eventually came to severely overpopulate the earth so the Creator decided to destroy them and created a new world where its inhabitants would be subject to death.

Like many other people throughout the world, the Pima also speak of a deluge that took place long ago, just like the one mentioned in the Bible and the Quran about Noah and the Ark. Also held in great reverence by the Pima are the Sun, Moon, Coyote and the hero god known as "Elder Brother." At the center of their spiritual life was the importance of maintaining harmony with nature.

Pima society was well structured. Each village had one leader who guided a government led by consensus. The only exception to this rule was during times of war where the village war chief was given absolute authority.

Today the Pima, like every other Native American tribe, are confined to government reservations. The poverty level is high and the schools are less than ideal and a number of social ills plague the community. Much of the traditional lifestyle the Pima once practiced has been replaced due to an overbearing "western" culture. And some of the changes that came with the new "western" way of life have not helped the Pima. For instance, the diet of the Pima has drastically changed. The natural foods of their land that their bodies had grown accustomed to have been replaced with the modern day fatty, processed foods.

Just one of the results of these unhealthy eating habits on the body can be called, ironically, pimelosis – defined as: conversion into fat; fatty degeneration; obesity. The growth of obesity among the Pima is frightening with large numbers of the population from adults to small children being dangerously overweight.

The number one threat, however, to the physical well-being of the Pima is diabetes. Diabetes is so prevalent among the Pima that it has the potential, if unchecked, to bring about the complete annihilation of the tribe by the end of this century. During the 1980s the National Institute of Health chose to focus most of its research on Type 1 diabetes, also known as juvenile diabetes, which affects many White Americans but does not affect Native Americans like the Pima. It is the Type 2 diabetes, or adult-onset diabetes, that is also known as the "Pima Plague." This is the type of diabetes that is most common among Native American people. This is also the most common type among African Americans as well. Both nations are dying slowly because they are no longer living a holistic and natural lifestyle.

The lack of resources given to Type 2 has become a serious problem for the Pima. Now the past rituals of singing and dancing and giving praises to the Creator are slowly being replaced with new rituals of amputation and dialysis. The Pima, once abundant with spiritual sight, are now abounding in physical blindness.

The Pima were once known as healers of mankind, utilizing herbs and natural remedies. Now they are the ones in need of healing. Their plight is shared by Native American nations across the country, all of which experienced the destruction of their culture and the loss of their homelands at the hands of European invaders.

We pray that the Creator will answer our prayers and the prayers of Melody Lightfeather and heal the Pima, Native Americans, and the World.

Introduction

Thanksgiving Day.

In the United States it is celebrated on the fourth Thursday in November as an annual festival to give thanks to God for the year's blessings. School children are taught that this tradition evolved out of a friendship that developed between the native inhabitants of what is now known as "America" and those first European immigrants, called "Pilgrims," who arrived near the end of the 1400s.

As the story goes, the Pilgrims were on the verge of starvation during their first winter because they had no knowledge of how to grow food in this land. The native people came and shared their corn and wild pheasant, and taught them how to grow crops. This act of kindness is recognized throughout North America in the form of an annual holiday feast called Thanksgiving.

But there is another side to this Thanksgiving story, one that does not appear in American history books. It is the story of violence, brutality, slavery, and massive slaughter of the native population.

Immigrants Claim Land Ownership

For nearly 150 years, European immigrants had lived in the "New World" they called the Americas. As long as there were only a few white settlers, the life style of the native people was relatively undisturbed. Then as word spread throughout Europe about this wide open, "unclaimed" territory, more settlers began to trickle in. This new land became a safe haven for outlaws, prisoners, and exiles, along with the political radicals and religious nonconformists. By 1614, a band of English explorers had landed in the area of Massachusetts Bay and saw what looked like free land.

It was the custom in European countries to claim a parcel of land and mark the boundaries with a fence of wood or stone. They had no understanding of the system of sharing and communal ownership of land as practiced by the native people. They couldn't comprehend the idea that land, like air, was free for all to use.

In addition to their ideas about private ownership of land, the Europeans brought along something else to the New World: smallpox. Within a few years of their arrival, the entire Native population of Massachusetts Bay was extinct, wiped out by this deadly disease.

Wayne Reels, Director of Cultural Resources for the Pequot Tribe, during a recent interview, commented on those tragic times:

"Beginning with the time when they first entered our villages was the most devastating - going back to when smallpox first came as gifts of blankets and the devastation that it caused. It hit us in the early 1620s. Then it spread to the Midwest, and all the way to the far west as the years went on.

We had our first war in 1637. Some tribes just had their first war a hundred years ago. We had ours almost 400 years ago. We're from New England. The first colony states were on the East Coast from Virginia up to Massachusetts." (Wayne Reels, 2001 Interview)

There are many different family groups within the Pequot Nation. Wayne Reels is from the Narragansett Tribe of Southern New England. American history books reflect a Eurocentric point of view, portraying what happened as a victory over "Indian savages." However, the Native people express quite a different perspective. The opinion of most Native Americans is that this was the first act of biological warfare and just one of the many terrorist acts committed by the invaders.

When the Puritans arrived from England, exiled because of their religious beliefs, they settled near the ruins of a former Native village of the Pawtucket Nation. The Pawtucket Nation's lone smallpox survivor, a man named Squanto, had learned the language and the customs of the English.

He taught the Puritans how to pick wild corn, how to fish, and how to find the herbs and fruits of the land. At the end of the first year, the Puritans held a great feast following the harvest of their new farming efforts. The feast honored Squanto and his friends, the Wampanoags, who had helped them survive. This was the first Thanksgiving.

The Pequot War

However, as the years passed, the number of Puritan immigrants grew.   These new Puritan settlers, having no concept of tribal living and group sharing, began to claim that the land was theirs for the taking.   They declared the native people "heathen savages" and with Bible passages in their hands to justify their actions, the Puritans began to march inland from their seaside communities.   Joined by British settlers, they seized the land, took the strong, young Natives as slaves to work the land, and killed the rest. Their intention was to take all the land and enslave the people.

However, around 1633, when they reached the Connecticut Valley, the English immigrants were stopped by the powerful Pequot Nation.   When resisting Natives killed two British slave raiders, the Puritans demanded that the killers be turned over.   The Pequot refused, and what followed was the bloodiest war in the northeast, which became known as the Pequot War.

Because of the lack of fighting experience among the British, and because of the vast numbers of fierce Pequot warriors, British commander John Mason elected not to stage an open battle. Instead, his troops sneaked into Pequot territory, approaching one village at a time.   They came during the early hours before dawn, setting the villages on fire while the natives slept – burning them alive.   Women and children over 14 years of age were captured to be sold as slaves.   Other survivors were massacred. The British sold their Native captives into slavery in the West Indies, the Assures, Spain, Algiers and England, everywhere the Puritan merchants traded. They developed quite a lucrative business, regularly sending boatloads of captured and enslaved natives from the New England harbors.

In 1641, the Dutch governor of Manhattan offered the first scalp bounty, a common practice in many European countries. European savagery against the natives increased; a chopped off head of an Indian brought a handsome price.   Puritans broadened the monetary incentive to include a bounty for Natives fit to be sold for slavery. The Dutch and Puritans joined forces to exterminate all Natives from New England. They attacked and burned village after village.

Following an especially successful raid against the Pequot in what is now Stanford, Connecticut, the churches of Manhattan announced a day of Thanksgiving to "celebrate victory over the heathen savages." During the feasting, the hacked off heads of natives were kicked through the streets of Manhattan like soccer balls. The killings took on a frenzy, with days of thanksgiving being held after each successful massacre. Even the peaceful Wampanoags, who had helped the Puritans survive their first year, did not escape the brutal attacks. Their chief was beheaded and his head was placed on a pole in Plymouth, Massachusetts, where it remained for 24 years.

Wayne Reels explains the Native American perspective of Thanksgiving:

"In our folklore, Thanksgiving derived from the conquering of the Pequots - after the Pequots were defeated. We were the first native tribe to be defeated. One of the first Indian wars in this country was the Pequot War - they call it a war, but it was more of a massacre. As the Treaty of Hartford said, "Let there be no more Pequots." And they divided the Pequots up amongst the neighboring tribes who went to war against us. So Thanksgiving to us came along as a sign of defeat and a sign of celebration for the colonists and the allied Indian groups." (Wayne Reels, 2001 Interview)

The beheading of the defeated Pequots was done as a symbol of victory for the colonists and signaled other colonists that they too could conquer territory in the New World. Wayne Reels observed:

"The colonists were showing their dominance over the most powerful Indian group in the territory. That put fear in the hearts of most Indian groups and gave more courage to the colonists that they could in fact start a new world here and conquer it. They did that for fourteen years after the Pequot War. They would not only take the heads, but also the hands. That was a sign if, after the Pequot War, you were to get a Pequot warrior and show signs of him, mainly by the markings on his hands, tattoos and stuff, you would turn them in for ransom, then you would get rewards for body parts of the Pequots." (Wayne Reels, 2001 Interview)

Each town held thanksgiving days to celebrate their own victories over the natives until it became clear that there needed to be an order to these special occasions. It was George Washington, the first President of what became the United States of America, who created an official schedule, when he declared one day to be celebrated across the nation as Thanksgiving Day. It was President Abraham Lincoln who finally decreed it to be a legal national holiday. The irony is that he made this declaration during the Civil War -- on the same day and at the same time he was ordering troops to march against the Sioux in Minnesota. He subsequently ordered 38 Santee Sioux to be hanged for leaving the reservation in search of food -- the supplies promised to them had never materialized and they were forced to search for food because their families were starving.

They were hanged on Christmas Eve that year.

Native Americans share many cultural similarities with African people -- the communal life style, the extended family of tribal kinship, the deep respect for nature. These are the qualities, which Europeans have derisively called "primitive."

African Explorers Come in Peace

Meanwhile, Europeans arrived with war and disease, and imposed a culture of slavery and feudalism upon the New World. In stark contrast to the barbarism brought to America by 15th century Europeans, shiploads of African explorers arrived upon the shores of both North and South America centuries before Christopher Columbus and developed harmonious relationships with Native Americans.

According to historian Ivan Van Sertima, in his book *They Came Before Columbus*:

The Mandingo blacks practiced settled agriculture, and they must therefore have had fixed settlements in South and Central America. But their traders, by the very nature of the occupation, were nomadic, ever on the move...

There were several bases from which African traders spread in the two Americas: from the Caribbean in the Songhay period (circa 1462-1492); from the northeastern South America in the Mandingo period (1310 onward) into Peru; and from a base in

Darien moving along roads marked by the presence of burial mounds into and beyond Mexico, as far north as Canada. These burial mounds provide further witnesses to their presence and the lines of their dispersal. (They Came Before Columbus, Ivan Van Sertima, Pages 103-104).

Contact between Native Americans and Africans can be traced back to ancient antiquity. Egyptian styled pyramids, gigantic black statues with Negroid faces and other ancient monuments found in Mexico present undeniable evidence that African people sailed to America as early as 800 B.C. Van Sertima explains that a new approach to history is needed:

What is needed far more than new facts is a fundamentally new vision of history.

In this new vision the Atlantic is an open sea long before Columbus. But accidental drift voyages by African men, except in those cases where they brought fruit or grain with them alien to America (and this happened in prehistory at least twice) would in themselves have a very minimal effect, if any. Planned expedi-tions, however, or expeditions intended for other destinations in Africa which were blown off-course, would be a different matter. They would bring not only a substantial but a select group of aliens to American shores. This may account for the presence of Negroid women in pre-Columbian America...

One of these women from the early pre-Classic period bears a striking resemblance to the ebony head of the Egyptian queen Tiy, the Negroid mother of Tutankhamen. This racial type - - Negro-Egyptian -- with its peculiar coiffure, facial geography and expression, appears in the Mexican heartland around 800-700 B.C. (They Came Before Columbus, Ivan Van Sertima, Page 29).

This presents quite a contradiction to present day American history books, which assert that most Africans arrived in America as slaves to the Europeans.

Both African and Native American people share a common history of invasion and enslavement following the European immi-gration to America. After centuries of struggle against oppression, both are striving to recapture their own rich cultural heritage and to correct historical misinformation.

Movies Create Negative Stereotypes

My first impression of Native American people, like many African Americans, was a personal one, because of my own family members who were known to be part Native American, or "Indian" as they were called at that time.

My Aunt Minnie, who owned a bakery, was said to be part Cherokee and part African American, or "Negro" as we were called at the time. Her husband was said to be a full-blooded "Indian." But what I remember most about Aunt Minnie was that she made the best cakes and pies and she had the most beautiful smile. As a young boy, I remember a number of my relatives on both my mother and my father's side of the family saying that they had "Indian" ancestors. In the early 1940s there were a number of people in our neighborhood who were of Native American ancestry, some of whom were my playmates. So, my first impression of "Indian" people was a very positive one.

The movies of the 1940s and 1950s created the image of an "Indian savage," a red man who spoke broken English and chased after Whites in order to "scalp" them. In the movies, when "Indians" attacked wagon trains carrying white settlers, we as children cheered when the white soldiers of the U.S. Cavalry came to the rescue. Movie heroes like John Wayne became famous for their roles as tough cowboys who could single-handedly defeat a whole tribe of "Indians."

In the 1939 movie *Stagecoach*, directed by John Ford, the character played by John Wayne captured the imagination of many young boys. For us black boys, John Wayne became our ultimate hero. When we played "Cowboys and Indians" everybody wanted to play John Wayne or the Calvary. Nobody wanted to play the "savage Indian." They were always the losers. The irony is, many of us had "Indian" blood running through our veins.

Hollywood movies have always had a powerful influence on our perceptions of people and cultures. American filmmakers translate the political philosophy of the nation into screen images, which are imprinted onto the minds of millions.

During a television interview, actor Anthony Quinn, who claimed to be a mixture of Mexican and Irish parentage, described how he obtained his first role in the movies, that of an "Indian." He said that when he came in for an audition, the casting director

asked him, "Do you know how to speak "Indian?"" He replied,
"Yes." He held up his hand and said "How, Pale Face." He was
hired.

Speaking "Indian" often consisted of using broken English
and using sentences like, "Me chief, you squaw." Or, "Me want
fire water." These concoctions of white filmmakers of the "Indian"
language became accepted as reality by a vast majority of Americans. Never were actual "Indian" people consulted on their language or culture. Had actual "Indians" been involved in the creation of dialog according to their own language, they would have
informed white film makers of the fact that the word "squaw" is an
insulting, derogatory, vulgar term to use when referring to females,
and that no respectable person would ever call a woman a "squaw."

Few if any real "Indians" were hired in those early films.
In fact, "Indians" were usually played by white actors wearing ill
fitting wigs and brown make-up. Reinforcing U.S. political philosophy that the "Indian" people needed to be removed from the
land in order for whites to bring "civilization," these films always
ended with a resounding victory for white cowboys and Cavalry
men over the savage "Indians." A popular line that has been used
in many films is actually a quote from past U.S. President Andrew
Jackson: "The only good Indian is a dead Indian."

By the 1950s, the television industry had evolved, and
movie screen images could be seen in the privacy and comfort of
ones own home. Hollywood's reality has become the reality for an
entire nation. Television is now the undisputed information source,
therefore fantasy so easily becomes reality, and fiction so easily
becomes fact.

In the popular television series, *The Lone Ranger*, Native
American actor Jay Silverhill played Tonto, the faithful "Indian"
sidekick of the masked hero played by Clayton Moore. Tonto was
considered a "good Indian" because he fought on the side of the
whites against robbers, thieves, and "bad Indians" alongside his
hero friend, whom he called "Quimo Sabe."

I don't know what native language Tonto supposedly spoke
to his friend the Lone Ranger. However, it's interesting that in the
Spanish language, the word "Sabe" means "knows" and the word
"Tonto" means "stupid."

The 1960's and 1970s brought an awakening of political
consciousness which spread not only throughout the African

American community, but also throughout Native American communities. Both were defeated, oppressed people, fighting for self-
determination and respect. Just as voices of protest arose from ur-
ban ghettos, voices of protest also arose from "Indian" reservations, where the descendants of the once great Native American
nations demanded the right to define themselves and remove
stereotypical images of their people and culture.

Correcting Historical Misinformation

The practice of white Europeans of imposing their culture
on every other racial and ethnic group was questioned. History
books which claimed that America was "discovered" by Christopher Columbus were challenged. African American historian Ler-
one Bennett, in his book *Before the Mayflower,* revealed that civilizations existed in America many years before Columbus' journey.
He also revealed that Africans came to the American continent first
as free people and interacted peacefully with the native inhabitants.
Columbus arrived on the shores of America by mistake, as
history books have long admitted. Following the theory that the
Earth was round, he sailed west, hoping to find a new trade route
to India, which was in the east. When he landed in America, he
thought he had in fact reached India.
Although Columbus was mistaken in his naming of the native people "Indians," European invaders persisted in calling them
"Indians," refusing to acknowledge their national identities -
Apache, Cherokee, Choctaw, Hopi, Navajo, Pequot, Sioux, Paiute,
Pima, Algonquin and so forth. During the era of the 1960s and
1970s, "Indians" protested this historically incorrect reference to
themselves. Although the term "American Indian" became an ac-
ceptable title, many preferred the term "Native American" to establish the fact that they were the original inhabitants of this continent
and had established a civilization and a culture long before Columbus' arrival.
In 1972, actor Marlon Brando shocked the entire country
when, during the nationally televised Academy Awards ceremony
he refused to accept his Oscar Award for the film *The Godfather*.
He sent a Native American woman, Sacheen Littlefeather, to tell
the audience that he was refusing his award to protest the treatment
of Native American people.

By the 1970s and 1980s, the film industry had begun to reflect this new social consciousness. The old "Cowboy and Indian" movies had disappeared, and new films expressing a different political philosophy emerged. In the 1972 film *Buck and The Preacher*, African American actor Sidney Poitier portrays an ex-soldier who leads a wagon train of African American ex-slaves across the western frontier, where they are planning to resettle and start a new life. He is joined by a traveling con man/ preacher portrayed by actor Harry Belafonte. The wagon train is being pursued by an armed band of white men, who intend to kill the blacks for refusing to return to southern plantation labor.

After an intense gun battle with the whites, Poitier and Belafonte, with the help of Native American friends, escape with the wagon train as Native American warriors hold off their white attackers at gunpoint. This was the first film to show the historical alliance that had developed between African Americans and Native Americans.

In the 1990 film *Dances With Wolves*, actor Kevin Costner portrays a white soldier in the U.S. Cavalry whose mission was to spy on a Native American community for the purpose of planning an attack. Instead, he ends up becoming a part of the tribe, living among them, changing his name, taking a wife and adopting their culture.

This film presented quite a contradiction to the "Indian savage" image of earlier movies. In *Dances With Wolves*, it was the whites who savagely massacred Native American women and children. Greedy white hunters senselessly slaughtered great masses of buffalo, taking the hides and leaving the carcasses to rot. In stark contrast was an honest, simple culture of peace, respect for elders, and family harmony among the Native Americans.

At the end of the movie, the character portrayed by Kevin Costner had totally rejected his "white" identity and was escaping from U.S. soldiers with his wife, a white woman who had been raised by the Native American people and had also adopted their culture as her own. (Due to his respectful portrayal of Native Americans in the movie, Costner was made an honorary member of the Sioux Nation.)

The history books and documentary films produced by whites tend to show Native American culture as "primitive" and their religious ceremonies are often portrayed as superstitious tribal customs. While ancient ruins point to the fact that advanced Native American culture and civilization existed on the continent thousands of years prior to the coming of the Europeans, never have books or films hinted that these people may be part of the ancient lineage of the very same people identified in religious scriptures. European historians treated the history of Native Americans much the same way as they treated the history of African people – they either claimed it was primitive, or said it just didn't exist.

Today's Native American communities, hidden away on small parcels of land known as "reservations," are mere shadows of the great nations of the past. Unlike the immigrants who arrived en masse from other countries, these are the original inhabitants of the continent. For centuries, they have endured the invasion to their homeland and the destruction of their way of life by outsiders who have never bothered to learn anything about their culture or beliefs.

The Dogon Door

I first became fascinated with Native American spiritual beliefs in 1995. My wife Naimah and I were in Lincoln, Nebraska, as part of a lecture series and promotional tour for our previous book *Slavery: The African American Psychic Trauma*. One evening in our hotel room, I happened to see a television program about the Native American mystic from the Paiute tribe by the name Wovoka, who popularized the Ghost Dance Movement.

I found this bit of history fascinating because this Ghost Dance Movement led up to the Wounded Knee Massacre. This massacre was the United States government's fight to suppress Native American prayers for a Messiah. Scriptures in the Holy Bible and the Quran (often spelled "Koran" by westerners) both predict the coming of a Messiah, a "return of Jesus," whose presence in the latter days will cause a "shaking of the earth" or a total upheaval in the world as we know it. Religious scriptures and traditions from many nations of the world contain prophesies about the return of a Messiah in the latter days, a time which many believe is this present age. I found it fascinating that the Native Americans also share this belief.

Another discovery led me to delve deeper into the spiritual teachings of Native American people. In 1995, while attending an

Islamic conference, a friend from St. Louis, Missouri, Najma Rafat, introduced us to her friend Ishana Gilda Hamilton, who stated that she was initiated as a High Priestess by the Dogon people of Mali, West Africa. The Dogon people are known for their mystic philosophy, their psychic abilities and their astonishing knowledge of the universe.

Gilda told us the story of how they revealed to her an ancient tablet of carvings and symbols, said to contain coded prophecies about the future. According to the spiritual teachings of the Dogon, the tablet, known as "The Dogon Door" is one of a set of four such ancient carvings. The other three are being kept by the other three nations of man. (The Hopi of Arizona are the keepers of the sacred doors for the red nation.) When the four doors are brought back together, mankind would begin to witness a cleansing and healing, and they would begin a reawakening which would lead to the discovery of self and the knowledge of the creating forces of the universe. Then mankind will again be unified in peace.

So I began on this spiritual path knowing that I'm only a humble servant of God. The Creator of the heavens and the earth is perfect in His plan and any mistakes made would be my own. Being imperfect, I recognized that I needed to document all information gathered as thoroughly as possible. Then the reader could understand that the Creator has indeed manifested His signs in support of the prophecies and that it is now time to determine what part we will choose to play in its continuing manifestation.

The twentieth century has seen two destructive World Wars. According to Native American prophecy, a third World War is imminent, unless we change the conditions in the world today. Recent events have caused some to speculate that perhaps this third World War has already begun.

As we enter the 21st century, violence continues to spread across the face of the earth and weapons of war have become more deadly. With the Dogon people possessing one door and the Hopi people possessing another door, it seems that the first step is to bring two of the doors together. The "American Indians," whose history and culture have been ridiculed by the American cinema, and the African people, whose ancestors were forcibly scattered across the globe, have developed a common bond. They may, in part, hold some of the keys to the world's future in their hands.

It is understood that the physical doors themselves, carved with ancient signs and symbols, do not themselves possess any mystical powers. They represent a common spiritual beginning that is shared by all of humanity. If all of mankind, now spread out across the earth, can come together philosophically in a common understanding that we are all one people, under the same Creator, given the responsibility to protect the earth and its inhabitants, then, in a metaphorical sense, the ancient doors have come back together.

One time when I was with Melody Lightfeather at the *Gathering of Nations* Powwow in New Mexico she was approached by some people who knew her family and remembered her as a young girl. These people looked like dark skin Africans but they had straight black hair. They were very noble looking and I was very impressed with how they carried themselves. I said to Melody that they reminded me of Mandinka royalty. She responded by saying that she called them "Pima-Mandinka." I felt that there must be a great and exciting history behind this because some of the early Mandinka tribe of Africa are believed to have came to America in the 13th century. One of the reasons for writing this book is to explore these types of relationships that existed between Native Americans and Africans. I feel that these types of relationships are symbolic of some of the doors being brought together.

My greater purpose for writing this book is to examine ancient religious teachings of the Native American nations and compare them to the teachings found in two of the world's major religions, Christianity and Islam. Somewhere in our past is the key to saving ourselves from a future of self-destruction. Perhaps, through the teachings of the ancient Native American prophets, we will discover the missing pieces to the puzzle of how we can all unite for the sake of world peace.

The drawing on the following page, provided by Gilda Hamilton, is a reproduction of the original Dogon Door and its symbolic carvings. In a way, it represents the door to a hidden past of ancient knowledge and wisdom, a door that has been locked for centuries. So let us now open that door to the past and thereby discover our future.

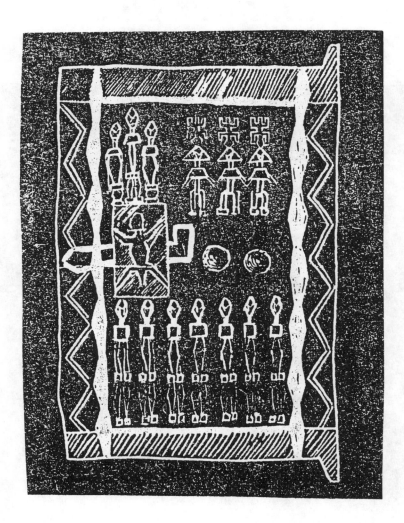

0B - The Dogon Door

This reproduction of the ancient door held by the Dogon people of West Africa is said to contain symbols that predict the future of mankind. The Dogon Tribe is one of the most mystic and secret tribes of our world. One book, by French writer Marcel Griault, describes their philosophy, their psychic abilities, their knowledge of the universe, and their relationship with the planet Sirius. He called them, "The Gods of The Waters."

Chapter One
The Beginning or The End?

1A – Ancient Symbol of Time and of Change
By Melody Lightfeather

"From the old moon into the time of darkness into the new moon of change. He who stands in the darkness of the old moon, fearful of the change of man, to watch the one without fear step into the light of the impending new moon, into a new life, sees their spirits become one as the eagles soar over the mountain together."

Chapter One
The Beginning or The End?

Imagine:

You left home a few years ago and have lived abroad for several years, away from modern civilization, on a remote island where there is no television, no radio, no newspaper. You have lived a simple life among the rural people of the land. You breathed fresh air and drank fresh well water. You learned how to catch fish and cook it over an outdoor fire, using simple utensils. You learned how to grow vegetables. You ate fresh fruit growing from the trees. You learned to make simple, homespun garments. You bathed in fresh water from the river. Now, healthy and robust, you are returning to the modern comforts of life.

After a bumpy ride aboard a small airplane, you arrive at the airport in a major American city. You disembark and look around, horrified by what you see. There is an extremely foul stench in the air. A thick fog of pollution surrounds everything, making it difficult to see more than twenty feet ahead. Your eyes burn from the smoke-filled air. The smell is so foul, you hate to inhale, but you have no choice.

The ground oozes with slime and filth. There is simply no place to put the trash, so the city no longer bothers to pick it up. People on the street look like walking corpses. Their faces and hands are full of open sores, oozing with pus, and bloody gashes which many try in vain to cover with make up. You are told that many people are now suffering from skin cancer, either as a result of AIDS or from over exposure to ultra violet rays. The sun's ozone layer has been destroyed, and direct sunlight has become fatal to those with fairer skin. In disgust, you painstakingly avoid touching anyone.

You stop at a small store to purchase food. All the meat smells strangely rotten, even though it has been artificially colored to make it appear fresh. The fruits and vegetables also have an artificial coloring and are abnormally large. You are told it is a result of genetic engineering.

Disgusted, you decide against buying food and walk on

down the street. In a northern east coast city in the middle of December, it is 98 degrees, unseasonably warm. You pick up a newspaper and read the front page which announces, "Another Earthquake Expected Tonight." Another headline reads "Millions More Die From AIDS." Still another declares "U.S. Prepares Defense Against Bombing Attacks."

As you stand on the corner, reading your paper, suddenly the sky grows dark. You hear a crack of thunder, and at the same time, the ground beneath your feet starts to shake. Right before your eyes, the ground splits open. You hold onto a wall and brace yourself as chunks of bricks from surrounding buildings begin to hit the ground all around you. In disbelief, you see walls crumbling and people falling from top floors of buildings, some of them falling into the open cracks in the street. Electrical wires, shaken loose by the earthquake, begin to hit pedestrians, who scream in shock as they are instantly electrocuted. Buildings catch on fire from the sparks.

Suddenly a loud explosion is heard. You are knocked to the ground. As you lie there, dazed, your eyes strain to see the street before you. Tall buildings are torn to the ground; bricks and lampposts are toppled over on bodies that lie motionless in the street. The smell of smoke from fire is choking you, but there is no sound of fire engine sirens, no motion of people anywhere. Was it a bomb? Was it thunder? Was it an earthquake? There is no way to tell. Everyone around you appears to be dead.

The Purification Plan

Does this story sound far fetched? According to the prophecies passed down from Native American ancestors, this is our destiny in just a few short years. Unless we heed their warnings and change our present course, Earth and its inhabitants will soon be horribly destroyed.

The native people of America, those who have been forcibly removed from the land of their ancestors, have within their religious traditions some ancient prophecies about the fate of the world in these present times. Much of what they predicted has already come true. About the near future they say:

"We are entering a time of purification and can expect to witness chaos and destruction in all the kingdoms of nature. It is a time for the reuniting of the races. Barriers of religion and nationality will begin to fall as all people realize their essential unity. We must heal the damage done to Mother Earth, the source of life, and recognize that all living things are endowed with spirit. In the coming times we will see the return of one or more Great Teachers who will guide us into the future." (Ancient Prophecies for Modern Times, by Bette Stockbauer)

In a time where science and religion have parted company, mankind continues to move rapidly toward what is perceived to be "progress." However, according to Native American prophecies, this society is rapidly moving toward self-annihilation.

To understand the nature of prophecy, one has to first understand the concept of time. The Western nations concept of time is like a line stretching out into infinity. Every event along that line is something new.

However, the Native American concept of time is like a circle. The past will repeat itself in the future. Everything that happens at this point in time occurred at the same point in the last cycle, and will repeat itself endlessly at the same point in the cycles to come.

Western culture, which is presently dominated by European thought and philosophy, is based on the belief that modern man is reaching the apex of his development. Europeans trace their history as beginning some time after the Ice Age, which ended thousands of years ago when the sheet of ice over Northern Europe, Northern Asia and North America slowly began to melt.

According to European anthropologists, primitive human beings appeared on the continent of Europe about 30 thousand years ago, and slowly evolved into modern man. Western scientists promote the idea that real human progress began in the 14th century with the European Renaissance and continues into the 21st century, with technological advancements unimaginable centuries ago.

The native people of this land say that it is this so-called modern society that is primitive, backward and destructive. They say that an age of advanced technology has occurred before, in the distant past. They say that when mankind reached this point of advancement before and had begun to destroy the earth, God destroyed nearly all of mankind. They say it has happened at least three times before...and it's about to happen again.

Can this be possible? To find out the truth, one must go back to the very beginning.

The Beginning of Creation

In the beginning God created the heaven and the earth. And the earth was without form, and void; and darkness was upon the face of the deep. And the Spirit of God moved upon the face of the waters. And God said, let there be light; and there was light. And God saw the light, that it was good: and God divided the light from the darkness. And God called the light Day and the darkness he called Night. And the evening and the morning were the first day. (Genesis, Chapter 1, verses 1-5. Holy Bible, King James Version, Original African Heritage Edition.)

The common theme in all of the world's great religions is the belief in a Divine being who is the force which created the very essence of life. In the Book of Genesis of the Bible, the world is described as being created in six days, which Christian theologians have interpreted literally to mean six 24-hour periods. However, as today's scientists continue to study the universe and the life forms that exist on Earth, it becomes clear that a literal interpretation of creation as occurring in 6 days is a physical impossibility. The universe is estimated by scientists to be about 20 billion years old. The Earth is presently calculated to be 4.5 billion years old.

According to many Christian theologians, Adam, the first man, was created about six thousand years ago. However, new scientific techniques, such as Carbon 14 dating, enable scientists to calculate the approximate age of fossil remains. Human fossils have been discovered which are calculated to be at least two million years old. This presents such a clear contradiction between fundamental Christian theological teachings and scientific discovery that many modern scientists, raised in the European Christian tradition, have become atheists. As a result, today's science is totally disconnected from any spiritual base and has become quite destructive in its mad pursuit of "progress."

Religion is seen by many so-called modern scientists as

mere collections of senseless myths by primitive people, used to explain that which is unexplainable. Today's astronomers, who take an agnostic view of creation, have verified through scientific observation that a sudden great force of energy created this ever-expanding universe. Professors Robert A. Muller of Louisiana State University and Theodore M. Oberlander of University of California, Berkeley state in their book, *Physical Geography Today*:

There was once a time when all the matter and the energy in the universe was compressed into a single nucleus, or "cosmic egg." Pressure within the nucleus was so great that individual atoms -- and hence elements – could not exist. Energy soon heated this primordial matter to a temperature of billions of degrees, and the nucleus exploded into a fireball. As a result of this "big bang" the nucleus began expanding. The primordial matter separated into atomic particles, and the extreme heat caused these to fuse into elements. However, as expansion continued, the temperature decreased considerably and the initial period of element formation came to an end. (Physical Geography Today, Portrait of A Planet, Pages 6-7).

The Big Bang

The theory that the universe began with a big explosion, spreading bits of matter far into space, is known as the "Big Bang Theory." This is a theory, which developed during the 20th century. However, the explosion which created the universe is also described in the Holy Quran, the book of scriptures revealed 1400 years ago to Muhammad Mustapha of Arabia. The entire text of the Holy Quran is said to be direct revelations from God relayed to Muhammad by the angel Gabriel. (Gabriel is said to be the angel who brought the news to Mary that she would give birth to Jesus.)

In the book *Revelation Rationality, Knowledge and Truth* author Mirza Tahir Ahmad explains the Quran's description of the creation of the universe:

It clearly explains the stage by stage process of creation, in a manner which perfectly falls into step with the theory of the Big Bang. The Quran goes further and describes the entire cycle of the

beginning, the end and the return again to a similar beginning.
The first step of creation as related in the Quran accurately describes the event of the Big Bang in the following words:

"Do not the disbelievers see that the heavens and the earth
were a closed up mass, and then We opened them out? And We
made of water every living thing. Will they not then believe?" (21:
31)

(Revelation Rationality, Knowledge and Truth, by Mirza
Tahir Ahmad, Pages 303-304)

If theological teachings from other cultures are studied,
they may provide a more accurate interpretation of the Bible. Regarding Earth's creation the Holy Quran proclaims:

Surely, your Lord is Allah, who created the heavens and the
earth in six periods, and then He settled Himself firmly on the
Throne. He makes the night cover the day, which it pursues
swiftly. And He created the sun and the moon and the stars--all
made subservient by His command. Verily, His is the creation and
the command. Blessed is Allah, the Lord of the worlds.
(Holy Quran, Chapter 7, Al-Araf, Verse 55).

It is interesting that in the Biblical and Quranic accounts of
the Earth's creation, they both use the exact same word "yaum."
Linguists know that there is a close relationship between the Arabic and Hebraic languages. In the Islamic understanding the term
"yaum" means, in general, a span of time or a period in time. This
could then mean anything from a second to a day to a year or even
a duration of a billion years. It is quite possible that in Hebrew it
conveyed the same meaning but, due to translations into English, it
came to be understood as specifically 24 hours. If "days" are understood to mean "periods" then the Biblical narrative becomes
more in harmony with current scientific calculations. Scientists
have studied the patterns created by the movement of water over
the earth and have concluded that earth passed through several
stages of development prior to the emergence of life.

And God said, let there be a firmament in the mist of the
waters and let it divide the waters from the waters. And God made
the firmament and divided the waters which were under the firma-

*ment from the waters which were above the firmament: and it was
so. And God called the firmament Heaven.   And the evening and
the morning were the second day.   (The Holy Bible, Genesis,
Chapter 1, Verses 6-8.)*

The original atmosphere of the earth would continually
change over millions of years. A new atmosphere began to form
as gases released from molten rock escaped to the earth's surface
from the interior. Scientists speculate that the composition of this
second atmosphere was probably similar to the gases present-day
volcanoes release: water vapor, carbon dioxide, sulfurous gases
and nitrogen. Eventually, much of the water vapor condensed and
fell to the ground as rain.

The evolution of the earth continued, as dry land became
separate from water. This was later followed in the next stage (or
on the third "day") by the appearance of plant life.

*And God said, let the waters under the heaven be gathered
together unto one place, and let the dry land appear: and it was
so. And God called the dry land Earth; and the gathering together
of the waters called He seas: and God saw that it was good. And
God said, Let the earth bring forth grass, the herb yielding seed,
and the fruit tree yielding fruit after his kind, whose seed is in itself, upon the earth; and it was so. (Holy Bible, Genesis, Chapter
1, Verses 9-11).*

Fossil records, imprints preserved on rocks in the shape of
living organisms, provide most of information scientists use to determine the history of life on earth. As stated by Professors Muller
and Oberlander:

*The earliest living things of which we have direct evidence
are the simplest plants which flourished about 3 billion years ago.
This early form of vegetation closely resembled the blue-green al-
gae which can be seen today floating on the surface of ponds in the
summer. (Physical Geography Today, Portrait of A Planet,
Page16).*

The appearance of plants 3 billion years ago set new processes in motion that literally changed the face of the earth. The

first plants were confined to the shallow layers of the sea, where water shielded them from the sun's damaging ultraviolet light. The atmosphere was predominately carbon dioxide, nitrogen and water vapor. The green plants used carbon dioxide dissolved in water to produce carbohydrates by photosynthesis, a process that involves capturing energy from sunlight. In the course of photosynthesis, water molecules are split and oxygen is released. Plant cells use some of the oxygen and give off the remainder.

The release of oxygen into the earth's atmosphere led to the formation of ozone. Ozone, which has a molecular structure consisting of three oxygen atoms as opposed to oxygen's two, forms a layer high in the present atmosphere that absorbs much of the cell-destroying ultraviolet radiation given off by the sun. Once a protective layer of ozone surrounding the atmosphere began blocking the lethal radiation, the earth was prepared to support animal life.

And We have made the heaven a roof, well-protected, yet they turn away from its Signs. (Holy Quran, Chapter 21, Al Anbiya, verse 33.)

Scientists, who have examined the earth and the remains of previously existing life forms, have concluded that animal life began in water, evolving from the simplest one-celled amoeba to the most complex organism, moving from water to land and air. According to Professors Muller and Oberlander:

Beginning about 600 million years ago, the fossil record testifies to the sudden appearance of complex, shelled, multicellular marine animals. (Physical Geography Today, Portrait of a Planet, Page 18)

Or, as the Bible states:

And God said; let the waters bring forth abundantly the moving creature that hath life, and fowl that may fly above the earth in the open firmament of heaven. And God created whales, and every living creature that moveth, which the waters brought forth abundantly, after their kind, and every winged fowl after his kind. And God saw that it was good. And God blessed them, saying be fruitful and multiply, and fill the waters in the seas, and let fowl multiply the earth. And the evening and the morning were the fifth day. (Holy Bible, Genesis, Chapter 1, Verses 20-23).

The Green House Effect

Changing climates and ecological conditions have affected the evolutionary development of plants and animals, often in dramatic ways. About 130 million years ago, there was a flourishing population of giant reptiles, descendants of the earlier amphibians. These animals dominated the land until about 65 million years ago. Geologists have determined that after their disappearance, modern mammals appeared, followed by mankind.

And God said, Let us make man in our image, after our likeness: and let them have dominion over the fish of the sea, and over the fowl of the air, and over the cattle, and over all the earth, and over every creeping thing that creepeth upon the earth. So God created man in his own image, in the image of God created He him; male and female created He them. (Holy Bible, Genesis, Chapter 1, verses 26-27.)

The continuous recycling of life on Earth points to an intricate system in which all life is interdependent and ever evolving from one stage to the next. As science has shown, all life forms were created from and are sustained by the very elements contained in the earth itself. At some point all life again becomes part of the earth.

And the Lord God formed man of the dust of the ground and breathed into his nostrils the breath of life; and man became a living soul. (Holy Bible, Genesis, Chapter 2, verse 7).

Many scientists believe that the initial evolution of organic matter, and all life, began when matter combined with water becoming a "primordial soup." It was then necessary for this mud or clay to go through a process of drying. Science has shown how clays can produce certain amino acids, fundamental to life, when put through repeated processes of wetting and drying. The Bible and the Quran speak of mankinds' creation being from mud or clay. The Holy Quran states:

And surely We created man of dry ringing clay, of black mud wrought into shape. (Holy Quran, Chapter 15, Al-Hijr, Verse 27).

Native American spiritual beliefs are rooted in a reverence for the earth, the water and the air as a part of man's creation. It is understood that these elements are the essence of man himself.

Today, the earth is in trouble, largely because of an ecosystem that has been knocked off balance by technology gone awry. According to the prophecies passed down from Native American ancestors, because of man's violence against man and against the earth, this present world is heading rapidly toward a tragic end. They say that it won't be the first time that mankind's actions have led to complete self-destruction.

Keepers of the Sacred Knowledge

Native American beliefs reflect an extensive concept of time. The Hopi people of Arizona, who claim to have roots in the ancient Mayan civilization, tell a story of creation that accurately describes the earth's stages of evolution over the past 4.5 billion years. During the 1986 Continental Indigenous Council meeting in Fairbanks Alaska, Hopi representative Lee Brown gave a talk on North American Indian Prophesies. He began with an explanation of the earth's cycles according to Hopi traditions:

There was the cycle of the mineral, the rock. There was the cycle of the plant. And now we are in the cycle of the animals coming to the end of that and beginning the cycle of the human being.

When we get into the cycle of the human being, the highest and greatest powers that we have will be released to us. They will be released from that light or soul that we carry to the mind. But right now we're coming to the end of the animal cycle and we have investigated ourselves and learned what it is to be like an animal on this earth. (Lee Brown, Continental Indigenous Council, 1986)

The Mayan people, known for their advanced knowledge of astronomy, possess calendars which date back hundreds of thousands of years. They also say that mankind has been on Earth before and has created advanced civilizations, which have all been destroyed. Adrian G. Gilbert and Maurice Cotterell note in their book, *The Mayan Prophesies,*

> *Lost in the jungles of Central America are the remains of a most mysterious people; the Maya. Who were they? Where did they come from? What message, if any, did they leave for our own times? These are some of the questions that have taxed explorers, scholars and writers for over 200 years since the ruins of their most famous city, Palenque, were rediscovered in 1773. This amazing city, which is still not fully excavated and is constantly threatened by the encroaching jungle, is one of the wonders of the New World. Made out of resplendent white limestone and built with a perfection that would have done justice to Renaissance mansions, its pyramids, temples and palaces continue to amaze all who see them...*
>
> *The pattern that is emerging is of a people very different from ourselves...they were expert astronomers. They believed that they were living in the fifth age of the sun: that prior to the creation of modern men there had been four previous races and four previous ages. These had all been destroyed in great cataclysms, leaving few survivors to tell the tale. According to Mayan chronology, the present age started on 12 August 3114 BC and is to end on AD 22 December 2012. At that time the Earth as we know it is again to be destroyed by catastrophic earthquakes... We are beginning to understand that they had knowledge vital not only for their own time but for the very survival of the human race in our own. (The Mayan Prophesies, pp.1- 2)*

The Holy Quran, over 1400 years ago, predicted that the remains of past civilizations would one day be unearthed, revealing that there have indeed been previous ages where technology, even more advanced than the present age, once existed. These civilizations were destroyed, it is said, because the people failed to heed the warnings of the Prophets of their time:

> *Have they not traveled in the earth that they might see what was the end of those who were before them? They were more numerous than these, and mightier in power and left firmer traces in the earth. But all that which they earned was of no avail to them. And when their Messengers came to them with manifest Signs, they*

*exulted in the little knowledge they had. And that at which they
mocked encompassed them. (Holy Quran, Chapter 40, Al-Mu'min,
Verse 83, 84.)*

Archaeologists today continue to make fascinating discoveries that challenge long accepted beliefs about human history. Christian theologians, because of their Eurocentric concept of history and their miscalculation of time, cannot conceive of a technologically advanced civilization existing prior to this present age. Stone tools have been found the world over by many archeologists dating back past 3 million years ago. (Among modern historians, the consensus is that the oldest stone tools are no older than 3 million years and found only in Africa.) Also, archaeologists have recently unearthed many unexplainable objects that appear to be pieces of machinery unknown to this present age. Items from a previous civilization have been recovered from deep below the sea. They appear to be modern lamps, operated by some type of battery. Strange patterns are carved into the ground upon vast areas of land in remote deserts of Northeast Africa. They are known to have existed for thousands of years. Viewed from above, these patterns give the appearance of some type of directions for aircraft. This contradicts the currently held belief is that flight is a recent discovery by 20th century man.

Theories have been offered, suggesting that ancient man had possibly been visited by more technologically advanced beings from outer space. However, the Hopi people say that the answer to these mysteries is contained in their religious teachings, passed down through many generations. They agree with the stories of mankind's previous destruction as recorded by the Maya. Thomas Banyacya, a member of the Hopi sovereign nation from Kykotsmovi, Arizona, explained in a 1992 message to the United Nations:

The Creator made the first world in perfect balance where humans spoke one language, but humans turned away from moral and spiritual principles. They misused their spiritual powers for selfish purposes. They did not follow nature's rules. Eventually the world was destroyed by sinking of land and separation of land by what you would call major earthquakes. Many died and only a small handful survived. (Thomas Banyacya, United Nations Address, 1992)

1B - Precambrian Spheres

Many different artifacts have been discovered during the last century. During the late 1900s, one of hundreds of hollow metallic spheres were found by South African miners. They were found buried in a pyrophylite mineral deposit that was formed by sedimentation around 2.8 billion years ago. The spheres are considered to be made of a type of iron ore, yet they are reportedly unable to be scratched by steel. One of the spheres (pictured above) has three groves running parallel around it. It is unlikely that these spheres could have each formed singularly by way of some natural geological process. Although it is believed that humans did not exist during Precambrian times, it is obvious that an intelligent life form, earthly or extraterrestrial, created these spheres. (Forbidden Archeology, Michael A. Cremo and Richard L. Thompson, p.813)

Atlantis: The Not So Lost Continent

As scientists continue to examine the earth and observe the patterns of the ocean, there is an increasing speculation that a body of land once existed between the east coast of the United States and the west coast of southern Europe and northern Africa. Known as the "lost continent of Atlantis," it has long been considered a myth. However, Hopi narratives of history describe it as part of their ancestral homelands, washed away in a great flood and now lying at the bottom of the Atlantic Ocean.

The Mayan people also have recorded extensive information about human activity on the continent of Atlantis. Their stories are supported by the other written narratives from ancient times. Gilbert and Cotterell write:

The earliest written account of Atlantis that we have is that of Plato, who in two of his last books, Critias *and* Timaeus, *gives a brief outline of the story. This is what he says he told to Solon, the great lawgiver of Athens, when he paid a visit to Sais in Egypt. Critias, one of Plato's characters, narrates the story to Socrates as reminiscent of the Mayan belief in periodic destruction of the Earth. An Egyptian priest explains to Solon that they know far more about the history of the world than the Greeks:*

"You (the Athenians) remember only one deluge though there have been many... You and your fellow citizens are descended from the few survivors that remained, but you know nothing about it because so many succeeding generations left no record in writing." According to Plato's account there was once a great island continent in the middle of what is now the Atlantic Ocean, and it was the Greeks of Athens who checked an invasion of Europe and Africa by people from this island.

"Our records tell how your city (Athens) checked a great power which arrogantly advanced from its base in the Atlantic Ocean to attack the cities of Europe and Asia. For in those days the Atlantic was navigable. There was an island opposite the strait which you call, so you say, the Pillars of Hercules, an island larger than Libya and Asia combined; from it travelers could in those days reach the other island, and from there the whole opposite continent which surrounds what can truly be called the ocean."

Now what is truly astonishing about this account, which

was written around 350 BC, is that it not only presents the earliest known record concerning the existence of Atlantis but also indicates that the Egyptians at least knew of the Americas. It states categorically that there is a" whole opposite continent which surrounds what can truly be called the ocean." Even if one discounts the existence of a former continent of Atlantis, it offers powerful support for pre-Columbian contacts between the Old World and the New, for how else would the Egyptians have known that there was another continent on the other side of the Atlantic Ocean? (The Mayan Prophesies, Page 167)

Plato the Greek

According to the writings of Plato, Atlantis was a very powerful naval empire, which ruled over not only Western Europe, much of North Africa and the islands of the Atlantic, but also parts of the continent of America.

This Atlantean empire was determined to take control of all the countries of the eastern Mediterranean as well, including Greece and Egypt. An alliance was formed to fight the invaders, but it eventually fell to Athens alone to repel the Atlanteans. The Athenians prepared for battle, however, according to Plato,

"At a later time there were earthquakes and floods of extraordinary violence and in a single dreadful day and night all your (Athenian) fighting men were swallowed up by the earth, and the island of Atlantis was similarly swallowed by the sea and vanished; this is why the sea in that area is to this day impassable to navigation, which is hindered by mud just below the surface, the remains of the sunken island."

In Plato's other account of the myth, Critias, *he tells us that 9000 years have elapsed since the declaration of war between those who lived outside and all those who lived inside the Pillars of Hercules. That Plato account was written around 350 BC, we must be looking for a date of at least 9500 BC for the outbreak of this war. Now, that is an incredible date, many thousands of years before the accepted beginnings of either Greek or Egyptian history, when Europe was only just emerging from the last Ice Age. (The Mayan Prophecies, Page 167).*

MAP OF ATLANTIS

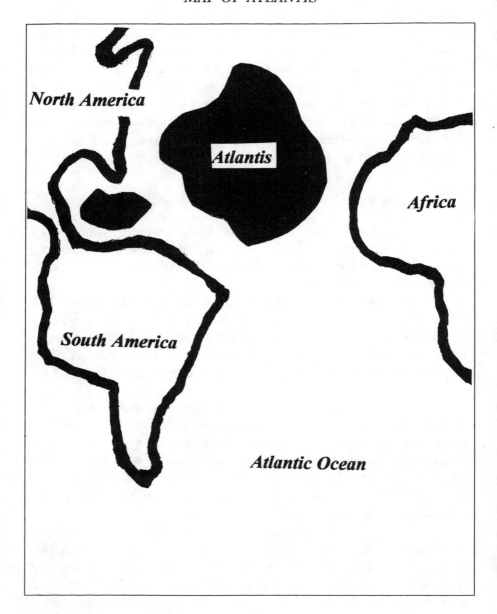

1C - Legend of the Lost Continent
The shaded areas in the above map show some of the various locations where Atlantis researchers have speculated the continent may have existed. The most popular theories place Atlantis in the heart of the Atlantic or in the Caribbean. (Illustration by Sultan A. Latif)

According to Hopi timetables, the sinking of Atlantis marked the end of the first world, leaving only a few survivors to begin civilization anew. Thomas Banyacya continues his narrative of the history of the Hopi:

"Then this handful of peaceful people came to the second world. They repeated their mistakes and the world was destroyed by freezing which you call the Ice Age." (Thomas Banyacya, United Nations Address, 1992)

The last Ice Age ended some 10,000 years ago, which would put the demise of the Hopi post-Atlantis account of the second world around the same time as Plato's account of Atlantis. Our purpose is not to determine which account is more accurate but only to show the similarity between two culture's, on opposite ends of the Atlantic, that share the same historical accounts of the existence of a lost continent and advanced civilization prior to current dogma.

Since Europe does not have written records prior to this time, they insist that no advanced civilization could have begun before the last Ice Age. European Egyptologists tell us that Egyptian civilization only began around 3100 BC with the First Dynasty - this, in spite of the fact that archaeologists have unearthed stone monuments dating back nearly 10,000 years. The Sphinx has been dated as far back as 10,500 B.C.

The Hopi teachings declare that the Ice Age brought a catastrophic end to the second world, again leaving a few survivors to carry on. Thomas Banyacya explains:

The few survivors entered the third world. That world lasted a long time and as in previous worlds, the people spoke one language. The people invented many machines and conveniences of high technology, some of which have not yet been seen in this age. They even had spiritual powers they used for good. They gradually turned away from natural laws and pursued only material things and finally only gambled while they ridiculed spiritual principles. No one stopped them from this course and the world was destroyed by the great flood that many nations still recall in their ancient history or in their religions. (Thomas Banyacya, United Nations Address, 1992)

The Great Flood

Throughout the continents of Africa and Asia, stories about a catastrophic flood and a group of people who escaped in an ark are interwoven into the culture. The Dogon people of West Africa trace their beginnings back to a being named Nommo, who descended to earth in an ark with eight ancestors and a supply of animals and plants. This story has been part of Dogon traditions for thousands of years.

Both the Holy Bible and the Holy Quran narrate the story of Noah, who it is written was directed by God to build a large wooden ark to escape the impending flood. According to the Bible:

And God said unto Noah, the end of all flesh is come before me; for the earth is filled with violence through them; and behold, I will destroy them with the earth. Make thee an ark of gopher wood; rooms shall thou make in the ark, and shalt pitch it within and without with pitch. And this is the fashion which thou shalt make it of: The length of the ark shall be three hundred cubits, the breadth of it fifty cubits, and the height of it thirty cubits. (Holy Bible, Genesis, Chapter 6, Verses 13-15)

The ark saved Noah, his family, and perhaps a small group of believing people. However, most of the people of the time refused to believe that the world would be destroyed by water. They ignored Noah's warning, in fact, they laughed and made fun of him while he worked. They therefore perished. The Holy Quran states:

Noah said, 'O my Lord, help me, for they treat me as a liar.' So We directed him by revelation: 'Make the ark under Our eyes and according to Our revelation. And when Our command comes, and the fountains of the earth gush forth, take thou into it two pairs of every species and thy family, except those of them against whom the word has already gone forth.

And address Me not concerning those who have done wrong; they shall surely be drowned.' (Holy Quran, Chapter 23, Al-Mu'minun, Verses 27-28)

The story of the Great Flood was long considered by religious skeptics to be a myth.   And then in 1955, evidence relating to the wooden ark was found high upon Mount Ararat, the highest peak in eastern Turkey.   It matched the Biblical descriptions exactly.

Some historians are puzzled as to how the Great Flood story is known throughout the world by other nations of people. They theorize that this could only be a result of contact with Judeo-Christian belief.   However, many ancient cultures can recall historical teachings of the flood, which predate Christianity. The Pima of Arizona have passed down through the ages a story of creation, which also includes a disastrous flood, brought about by man's disobedience. This story is known as *The Flood on Superstition Mountain*:

In the state of Arizona, the Pima Indian tribe declares that the father of all men and animals was Great Butterfly--Cherwit Make, meaning the Earth-Maker.

One day long ago, Great Butterfly fluttered down from the clouds to the Blue Cliffs, where two rivers met, later called the Verde and Salt rivers.

There he made man from his own sweat.

From that day on the people multiplied, but in time they grew selfish and quarrelsome. Earth-Maker became annoyed with their behavior and decided it might be best to drown all of them. But first, he thought to warn them through the voices of the winds.

"People of the Pima tribe," called North Wind. "Sky Spirit warns you to be honest with one another and to live in peace from now on."

Suha, Shaman of the Pimas, interpreted to the people what North Wind had warned them about.

"What a fool you are, Suha, to listen to the voices of the winds," taunted his tribesmen.

On the next night, the same warning from Earth-Maker was repeated by East Wind, who added, "Chief Sky Spirit warns that all of you will be destroyed by floods if you do not live nobler lives."

Again, the Pimas mocked the winds and ignored their warnings. Next night, West Wind spoke, "Reform, people of the Pimas, or your evil ways will destroy you."

Then South Wind breathed into Suha's ear, "Suha, you and

*your good wife are the only people worth saving. Go and make a
large, hollow ball of spruce gum in which you and your wife can
live as long as the coming flood will last."*

*Because Suha and his wife believed the warnings and were
obedient, they set to work immediately on a high hill, gathering
spruce gum and shaping it into a large hollow ball. They stocked
it with plenty of nuts, acorns, water, and bear and deer meats.*

*Near the appointed time, Suha and his good wife looked
down sadly upon the lovely green valley. They heard the songs of
the harvesters. They sighed to think of the beauty about them that
would be destroyed when the flood came because of the people's
selfishness.*

*Suddenly, a bright lightning flash and loud thunder rocked
the Blue Cliffs. It was a signal for the flood to begin. Suha and his
wife went into the gumball ark and closed the door tightly. Swirl-
ing, dark clouds surrounded them. Torrents of rain poured down
everywhere. For many days, the ark rolled and tossed about on
the deepening sea. After many, many moons, the downpour of rain
stopped.*

*The ark settled upon the land again, high on a mountaintop.
Suha opened the door and stepped forth to see a tuna cactus growing near his feet. He and his wife ate some of the red fruit of the
cactus plant.*

*Below them, they saw water everywhere. That night they
retired again to the ark. They must have slept a very long time,
because when they awoke the water had disappeared, the valleys
were green, and the bird songs rang forth again.*

*Suha and his wife descended from Superstition Mountain, a
name later given to the mountain upon which the ark had landed.
They went down into the fertile valley and lived there for a thousand years. The forthcoming people prospered, becoming known
as the Pima tribe. (Native American Lore, 1996 StoneE Productions, www.ilhawaii.net/~stony/lore72.html)*

The Pima had preserved this story, as had other peoples,
and had passed it down to the present generation. The Pima didn't
learn about the Great Flood from Christian missionaries. They
learned about it from their own ancestors.

The Hopi explain that this flood was actually the third time
mankind has been destroyed. Banyacya states:

The Elders said again only a small group escaped and came to this fourth world where we now live. Our world is in terrible shape again even though the Great Spirit gave us different languages and sent us to the four corners of the world and told us to take care of the Earth and all that is in it. (Thomas Banyacya, United Nations, 1992)

The Holy Quran corroborates the Hopi accounts that there have been several episodes in which humanity as a whole has been destroyed.

And We destroyed many generations before you when they did wrong; and there came to them their Messengers with clear Signs, but they would not believe. Thus do We requite the guilty people. Then, We made you their successors in the earth after them that We might see how you behave. (Holy Quran, Chapter 10, Yunus, Verses 14-15.)

The Hopi prophecies explain that this present age of man is but another cycle, another opportunity to obey the divine command to live in peace and take care of the earth. Previous floods and earthquakes had broken the earth's land mass into pieces. According to Hopi teachings mankind was divided into separate groups and spread out across the globe.

Hopi representative Lee Brown explained the prophecies concerning this present age at the 1986 Continental Indigenous Council meeting:

At the beginning of this cycle of time, long ago, the Great Spirit came down and He made an appearance and He gathered the peoples of this earth together they say on an island which is now beneath the water and He said to the human beings, "I'm going to send you to four directions and over time I'm going to change you to four colors, but I'm going to give you some teachings and you will call these the Original Teachings and when you come back together with each other you will share these so that you can live and have peace on earth, and a great civilization will come about."

And He said, "During the cycle of time I'm going to give

each of you two stone tablets. When I give you those stone tablets, don't cast those upon the ground. If any of the brothers and sisters of the four directions and the four colors cast their tablets on the ground, not only will human beings have a hard time, but almost the earth itself will die." (Lee Brown, Continental Indigenous Council, 1986)

The Guardianship

To "cast their tablets on the ground" is interpreted to mean to discard the Divine law that had been revealed to them. This story expresses the idea that all of humanity is interconnected, and failure to adhere to the Divine commandments by any one group will jeopardize the existence of everyone. Lee Brown explains,

And so He gave each of us a responsibility and we call that the Guardianship. To the Indian people, the red people, He gave the Guardianship of the earth. We were to learn during this cycle of time the teachings of the earth, the plants that grow from the earth, the foods that you can eat, and the herbs that are healing so that when we came back together with the other brothers and sisters we could share this knowledge with them. Something good was to happen on the earth. (Lee Brown, Continental Indigenous Council, 1986)

The Natives of North and South American and the Aborigines of Australia, both of whom can be included as part of the "red people" are known for their special affinity to the earth. Many possess knowledge of the healing qualities that come from natural herbs. Many holistic medicines come from America. The natives of Australia were perfect keepers of the land, using natural fertilization techniques to insure the continuous growth of the rain forests.

To the South, He gave the yellow race of people the Guardianship of the wind. They were to learn about the sky and breathing and how to take that within ourselves for spiritual advancement. They were to share that with us at this time. (Lee Brown, Continental Indigenous Council, 1986)

When one studies the martial arts, such as Kung Fu, Karate and Tai Chi and meditation practices which require controlled breathing techniques - all of theses practices originated in the lands of the Far East, among the "yellow race." These ancient forms of meditation and self defense required knowledge of how the breath of life controlled the body's energy. Much of eastern philosophy and theology centers on meditation and self control through breathing exercises.

To the West He gave the black race of people the Guardianship of the water. They were to learn the teachings of the water which is the chief of the elements, being the most humble and the most powerful. (Lee Brown, Continental Indigenous Council, 1986)

In ancient times, intercontinental travel required mastery of the seas. Ancient pyramids and great stone monuments in North and South America stand as evidence of an African presence in the Americas since antiquity, proof of great skill in sea travel. Water also makes up 98% of the human body. Water in Native American symbolism is the element that controls human emotions, and in many religions water is symbolic of spiritual cleansing. Through powerful rhythms and sounds, the black race transmits spiritual inspiration through music that influences cultures world wide.

To the North He gave the white race of people the Guardianship of the fire. If you look at the center of many of the things they do you will find the fire. They say a light bulb is the white man's fire. If you look at the center of a car you will find a spark. If you look at the center of the airplane and the train you will find the fire. The fire consumes, and also moves. This is why it was the white brothers and sisters who began to move upon the face of the earth and reunite us as a human family. (Lee Brown, Continental Indigenous Council, 1986)

The white race is known for its use of fire in the creation of modern modes of transportation. It is also known for its use of fire as a weapon, such as in the creation of bombs.

It should be remembered that even though certain groups of people were given specific guardianships, it should not be under-

stood that they alone hold a monopoly over their specific guardianships. It is not to say that the people of Europe, Africa, and Asia
have not at one time or another lived in relative harmony with nature; or that other cultures besides the black race have not created
great art and music to stir the soul; or that the "white race" is the
only group to make use of fire in their technology. History shows
that this is not the case.

The Hopi spiritual belief is that each "race" was given a
special concentration of sacred knowledge. Each has a special gift
or talent which is to be shared through positive interaction, thereby
enhancing other members of the human family. This is also expressed in the Holy Quran, where it states:

*And of His Signs is the creation of the heavens and the
earth and the diversity of your tongues and colors. In that, surely,
are Signs for those who possess knowledge. (Holy Quran, Chapter
30, Al-Rum, Verse 23)*

The Sacred Stone Tablets

According to the Hopi teachings, each of the races of mankind were given sacred stone tablets containing symbols, which
were to be a special sign for future generations. Lee Brown continues:

*And so a long time passed, and the Great Spirit gave each
of the four races two stone tablets. Ours are kept at the Hopi Reservation in Arizona at Four Corners Area on 3rd Mesa. I talked to
people from the black race and their stone tablets are at the foot of
Mount Kenya. They are kept by the Kukuyu Tribe. I once had the
honor of presenting a sacred pipe at the Kukuyu Tribe carved from
the red pipestone of Mount Kenya. I was at an Indian spiritual
gathering about 15 years ago. A medicine man from South Dakota
put a beaded medicine wheel in the middle of the gathering. It had
the four colors from the four directions; He asked the people,
"Where is this from?" They said, "Probably Montana, or South
Dakota, maybe Seskatchewan." He said, "This is from Kenya."*

*It was beaded just like ours, with the same color. The stone
tablets of the yellow race of people are kept by the Tibetans, in Tibet. If you went straight through the Hopi Reservation to the other*

side of the world, you would come out in Tibet. The Tibe

for "sun" is the Hopi word for "moon" and the Hopi word for

is the Tibetan word for "moon."

The guardians of the traditions of the people of Europe a
the Swiss. In Switzerland, they still have a day when each family
brings out its mask. They still know the colors of the families; they
still know the symbols, some of them. I went to school with some
people from Switzerland at the University of Washington and they
shared this with me. Each of these four peoples happen to be peo-
ple that live in the mountains." (Lee Brown, Continental Indige-
nous Council, 1986)

These tablets verify that the Hopi spiritual teachings are far
more than just legend. They actually exist among all four groups,
all four "races" of mankind. From among each of the four "races,"
it is the simple mountain people who have been entrusted with the
sacred tablets. They have passed these traditions down through
generations.

But what about the rest of the world, embroiled in wars
over territory, wealth, and control? Why are they not in harmony
with those who are the keepers of the stone tablets? Why does
each race look upon the other as an enemy? How did the people
become so divided that they cannot see themselves as one human
family?

The Holy Quran agrees with the Hopi teachings that, prior
to the gradual evolution of mankind into four colors or "races," at
one time mankind was indeed one people:

Mankind were one community, then they differed among
themselves, so Allah raised Prophets as bearers of good tidings
and as warners, and sent down with them the Book containing the
truth that He might judge between the people wherein they dif-
fered. But then they begin to differ about the Book, and none dif-
fered about it except those to whom it was given, after clear Signs
had come to them, out of envy towards one another. Now has Al-
lah, by His command, guided the believers to the truth in regard to
that which they differed; and Allah guides whomsoever He pleases
to the right path. (Holy Quran, Chapter 2, Al- Baqara, Verse 214)

ngs by researchers in the field of genetics seem
Biblical and Quranic accounts of mankind's
acial" groups. According to an article pub-
er 10th, 2000 edition of the *Chicago Sun-*
human beings can be traced to one female
continent of Africa. Oxford Ancestors, a
group at Oxford University in Oxford, England,
that this Ice Age "Eve" had children that branched off over
thousands of years into 33 clans. *Sun-Times* science reporter Jim
Ritter writes:

*Each of us descends, on our mother's side, from one of
these clans. Oxford researchers call the female founders of these
Ice Age clans the "Daughters of Eve." Researchers have given
names to Eve's daughters and imagined what their lives were like.
Eve's daughters gave rise to every race and ethnic group on every
continent. (Chicago Sun-Times, December 10, 2000, page 34A)*

Giving the "Daughters of Eve" names like "Lubaya," "Ai-
yana," "Malaxshmi" and "Velda," Oxford Ancestors have traced
their migration to the continents of the world. They have determined that every human being descends from one of these 33 female ancestors. The article continues:

*All of us descend from a small ancestral population in Af-
rica --Eve's clan. About 150,000 years ago, the theory goes, this
population split into different branches. Modern human beings
began walking out of Africa and colonizing the world about 50,000
years ago. They replaced Neanderthals and other archaic human
species. (Not all scientists accept this view of a relatively recent
origin of modern humans. A competing theory states that humans
originated 2 million years ago in Africa and spread across the
world as a single species.)*

*Oxford Ancestors analyzes fragments of DNA taken from
mitochondria, cellular structures outside the nucleus. You inherit
mitochondrial DNA from your mother, who got it from her mother.
(Chicago Sun-Times, December 10, 2000, page 34A)*

Mitochondrial DNA provides a direct and undiluted link to
ones maternal ancestor. However, it does not reveal paternal an-

cestry. Using the data from the matrilinial DNA, researchers have tried to reconstruct mankind's family tree. Of the 33 world clans Oxford Ancestors has identified, 13 are found mostly in Africa, 11 are in Europe, eight are in East Asia and the Americas and one spans Eurasia and the Americas.

Those continents which the "Daughters of Eve" are said to have migrated to could very well be the "four corners of the earth" described in the Hopi prophecies. If so, the people of the "black race" would be the descendents of those who remained in Africa, the people of the "red race" are the descendents of those who traveled to America, the "yellow race" are the descendents of those who came to settle in East Asia, and the "white race" are those who had traveled to the lands of Europe.

According to the Hopi prophecies, after living separately on the earth for a long time, the red man, the black man, the yellow man an the white man would meet again. The Hopi were determined to remain steadfast and hold on to their teachings. They would not be swayed from the belief that there was only one Creator and all of mankind was linked to Him and to each other. Lee Brown recalls:

So we went through this cycle of time and each of the four races went to their directions and they learned their teachings. We were given a sacred handshake to show when we came back together as brothers and sisters that we still remembered the teachings. (Lee Brown, Continental Indigenous Council, 1986)

The Native American people waited, knowing that the other races of man would one day appear on the shores of their continent, just as prophesized. The question was, would they come in peace, indicating that they had remembered their sacred teachings? Or would they come in search of material gain, bringing conflict and war?

The Hopi prophecies say that if they came in peace, mankind would live together as brothers and sisters. But if they brought war, the earth would suffer and mankind may once again be destroyed by the Great Spirit, ending yet another cycle. So when the strange ships from other lands set sail across the Atlantic, the wise Hopi elders were on the other side, anticipating their arrival... and waiting to see what the fate of man would be.

Chapter Two
The Descendents of Atlantis

2A - Hopi Ceremonial Spirit Dance (1984)
By Melody Lightfeather
"Here the Hopi are on the mountain in the Spirit Dance. The spirits make them transparent so that we can see right through them. We have a spirit that we don't use in our world today for fear of it making us transparent. The only thing that makes us transparent is when the world takes over and the spirit cannot become clear."

Chapter Two
The Descendents of Atlantis

History: A recorded narrative of past events, especially those concerning a particular period, nation, individual, etc. (Funk and Wagnalls New Comprehensive International Dictionary of the English Language, Deluxe Reference Edition, Publishers International Press.)

A Not So Lost History

Native American History remains an obscure subject for most of today's western world, probably for the same reasons that African and Asian history is also relatively unknown to western society. American schools reflect a Eurocentric view of history, a view that basically asserts that nothing existed until Europeans became aware of it. Western civilization teaches a vague notion that the ancestors of Native Americans arrived in the Americas as wandering nomads approximately 20,000 years ago via the Bering Straits from northeast Asia.

However, in his book *Mitakuye Oyasin "We are all related"*, author Ehanamani Emaciyapi (also known as Dr. Allen Chuck Ross) examines the oral histories of 33 native tribes of North America. While searching for his own roots, he discovered that ancient Native American oral historians claim a history in North America that existed many thousands of years earlier. They again point to a previous civilization on the sunken continent of Atlantis, which present day European historians still claim to be no more than a myth. However, Ehanamani Emaciyapi notes:

Researching Atlantis more fully, I uncovered information about a petroglyph, which was thought to be 50,000 years old. It was found in Inca, Peru and displayed a map, which identified North America, South America, and a very large island in the Atlantic Ocean. Is this evidence of an island that used to exist in the Atlantic that might have sunk? (Mitakuye Oyasin "We are all related", America before Columbus, based on the oral history of

33tribes, by Ehanamani (Dr. A.C. Ross), Pages 61 & 62).

A petroglyph is a prehistoric carving or inscription on a rock. It is highly unlikely that a fictitious body of land would be carved in stone. Ehanamani Emaciyapi continues:

> *Poring over the books on Atlantis, I could see that many of the writers felt the people of Atlantis had migrated east and west from Atlantis to civilize the world. Some went to Europe, others to America. They came out from Atlantis in two directions. In my way of thinking, if this was true, there should be similarities on both sides of the Atlantic that would corroborate this migration pattern.*
>
> *I perused* America B.C. *by Barry Fell, a linguistics specialist. He learned that the Micmac Indians of Canada are related linguistically to the Egyptians. The Algonquin-speaking peoples are related to the Celts and Basques. The Zunis have a linguistic relationship to the Lybians, and the Pimas to the Iberic-speaking peoples...*
>
> *Charles Berlitz, who speaks 33 different languages and is the grandson of the Berlitz who started the Berlitz School of languages, stated in "The Mystery of Atlantis" that people of the Siouan linguistic stock were related linguistically to the Rumanian and Turkish-speaking people. The strongest evidence for the existence of an Atlantis was the linguistic studies reported in his book. In* America B.C., *Barry Fell wrote of the discovery of ancient hieroglyphics of the Micmac Indians of Canada which, when compared with Egyptian hieroglyphics, were very similar and in some cases, identical. (Mitakuye Oyasin, "We are all related", by Ehanamani (Dr. A.C. Ross), Pages 62 & 63).*

Native American historical accounts verify the existence of continents, now under water, which played a major role in the migration of their ancestors to America. Ehamani Emaciyapi states:

> *The tribe I am a member of, the Mdewakantowan, has an oral history that says we came from an island in the east...The literature about Atlantis estimated that the island sank about 10,000 years ago. Before it sank, however, the people on the island were warned. Those who heeded the warning left and came to North*

America to join their red brothers...I recalled a book entitled The Sioux Trail *by John Upton Terrell, who had traced the roots of the Siouan linguistic peoples. In his book, he presented evidence of those peoples originating in North Carolina approximately 15,000 B.C. They slowly migrated northwestward until eventually they reached the Dakotas. (Mitakuye Oyasin, "We are all related", by Ehanamani (Dr. A.C. Ross), Pages 72 & 73).*

Accounts of Atlantis also exist on the other side of the Atlantic. The Greek philosopher Plato (427 B.C.-347 B.C.) speaks of Atlantis in his works, *Timaeus* and *Critias*, adding support to the Native American account. Based on Plato's writing, a general history of Atlantis has been formed:

"Atlantis was an island continent that lay westward beyond the Pillars of Heracles (the Straits of Gibraltar.) It was ruled by a coalition of kings descended from the sea god Poseidon. The chief king was descended from the sea god Poseidon's oldest son, Atlas, who gave his name both to the island and the surrounding Atlantic Ocean. Once the Atlanteans had been almost godlike in their purity of heart, but as the divine bloodline in them faded they became corrupt and greedy. They already ruled a vast empire, stretching as far as central Italy in Europe and to the borders of Egypt in Africa..." (Ancient Mysteries, Peter James and Nick Thorpe, Page 18-19)

Edgar Cayce: Visionary or Charlatan?

Navajo historical traditions state that their people came from an island in the west. Ehanamani consulted author Edgar Evans Cayce, whose book *Edgar Cayce on Atlantis* revealed extensive research on the subject of the sunken continent of Atlantis.

Edgar Cayce (1877-1945), was widely known as a spiritual healer and a psychic. Before his death he made a prediction that the lost continent of Atlantis would "rise again" between 1968 and 1969 in an area in the Caribbean around the Bahamas. (Coincidently, during those years oceanographers did discover a number of man-made structures beneath the ocean in those areas.) Cayce claimed to receive this information from communication with people who were from his "past lives." Regardless of the legitimacy of his many psychic claims, it is worth mentioning some of his specific claims, as they are in sync with the traditions of many Native American tribes concerning Atlantis.

According to Edgar Cayce, there was also an island in the Pacific, known as Lemuria, or Mu, which sank into the ocean about 28,000 B.C. Before it sank, people were warned, and those that survived escaped to North America.

According to Cayce, in 3,000 B.C., the remaining people of the lost tribes of Israel reached America by boat from Lemuria. In his book *Understanding Mu*, author Hans Sefan Santesson writes about a British colonel named James Churchward, who had lived in India for twenty years. During one of his visits to Tibet, he came across a map located in one of the libraries of the ancient monasteries. The map identified an island in the Pacific named Mu. Churchward's map of this island was published in 1926.

Author Ehanamani Emaciyapi states that Hopi oral history traces its people's origin to seven islands, believed to have once been located in the Pacific. He reasoned that if there was an ancient continent or island in the Pacific and if people migrated east and west from it, then there should be linguistic, cultural, and architectural similarities on both sides of the Pacific.

The Yupik Eskimos of Asia have been identified as being linguistically similar to the Inupik Eskimos in America. The Manchu-tungus speaking peoples of China have a tone value in their language that is similar linguistically to the Navajo. (In these languages, the same word said in a different tone has an entirely different meaning.) The Turkic-speaking peoples are linguistically like the Hokan-speaking peoples in the Pacific northwest. And the Middle Eastern Aramaic-speaking people were found to be linguistically similar to the Mayans. (Mitakuye Oyasin, "We are all related", by Ehanamani (Dr. A.C. Ross), Page 83).

According to Edgar Cayce, five races of man appeared on the earth at the same time: the white man appeared in the Caucasus and in the Carpathian Mountains; the red man appeared in North America and Atlantis; the brown man appeared on the island of Mu and in South America. The yellow man appeared in Mongolia; and the black man in the Sudan and Upper West Africa.

Both Atlantis and Mu sank beneath the oceans and all that

is left are the mountaintops. Cayce believed that during the time when the two great islands of Atlantis and Mu existed, there was extensive trade between the two. Ehanamani Emaciyapi reflects on the significance of this connection:

> *The idea of trade between two ancient continent islands that no longer exist fascinated me. Contemplating this possibility, I remembered having known about a giant stone head found in ancient Mexico, on the eastern coast. Anthropologists had no idea where this figure had come from because the face had Negroid features. To me, if this part of Mexico was a trade route between Atlantis and Mu, then the appearance of a Negroid face there made sense...I studied more about the island of Mu and became aware that the aborigines of Australia were a mixture of the brown people from Mu and the black people from Africa. (Mitakuye Oyasin, "We are all related", Ehanamani Emaciyapi (Dr. A.C. Ross), pages 86- 87).*

The disappearance of these two major bodies of land seems to corroborate the Hopi story of mankind's journey through time. The Hopi believe that when man was created during the first world, mankind eventually became wicked, and then the Creator destroyed that world bringing a few into the next era. This cycle repeated itself in the second world, and again some of mankind survived. In the third world, man misused technology and a flood destroyed that world. Presently, according to the Hopi, we are living in the fourth world.

Endless volumes of stories could be written about the episodes of human activity on the continents of North and South America twenty thousand years ago. However, Native American history, language, customs, and spiritual beliefs were not the subject of any deep study or consideration by the European invaders who arrived only 500 years ago.

Had they inquired, the Europeans may have discovered that the native people upon whom they sought to force "civilization" were hardly "primitive." The native people had made a conscious choice to live in harmony with nature. Perhaps other so-called "primitive" people on other continents have also chosen to reject modern technology and instead have chosen to peacefully coexist with nature, as a result of the hard lessons learned by their ancestors. Ehanamani Emaciyapi reflects:

I recalled that in our oral history, previous ages are referred to as a time when we had technology. We misused it and mankind destroyed himself. Is that when the traditional Native Americans developed the philosophy of respect for Mother Earth and all living things on her? I wondered, "Is the destruction of previous ages through misuse of technology the reason why the traditional people at Taos Pueblo don't have electricity and modern plumbing?" The traditional people in Wallis Village on the Hopi Reservation have no electricity or modern conveniences for that reason. (Mitakuye Oyasin, "We are all related", Ehanamani Emaciyapi (Dr. A.C. Ross), Page 100.)

Navajo and Hopi Oral History

Both the Navajo and the Hopi believe that man has evolved through four worlds. The Hopi's oral history states that during the second world, when mankind became greedy and the Creator destroyed the world with ice, the Hopi went underground to escape the ice. In the third age, man had developed a high level of commerce, trade and technology, and even had the ability to fly.

An artifact with the appearance of a bird was located in Egypt. Anthropologists are reexamining these artifacts, realizing that they may be symbols of ancient aircraft. On the plains of Nazca in Peru, archaeologists have discovered giant etchings on the desert floor, several of which appear to be ancient landing strips. (Similar to those found in North East Africa mentioned earlier.)

In Baghdad, Iraq, archaeologists have found an ancient electrical battery, which they estimate to be nearly 5,000 years old. In California, ancient spark plugs were uncovered, estimated at 50,000 years old. At the University of Ica, Peru, surgeon and professor Dr. Javier Cabreara Darquea discovered ancient petroglyphs that he determined to be nearly 50,000 years old. One of the carvings portrayed a Native American with a feathered headdress scanning the heavens with a telescope. Another showed three individuals with feathered headdresses performing a heart transplant.

Yet another petroglyph portrayed ancient Native Americans performing a brain transplant - something not yet even attempted by modern science, yet it was depicted on an artifact dating back 50,000 years. It is highly unlikely that such scenes would be carved in detail in rock if they never existed.

16th century Europeans fancied themselves as the epitome of civilized man, creating stories about the rest of humanity that placed everyone else's existence at a lower level of evolution to their own. This concept is now recognized as false, as anthropologists uncover more ancient carvings and artifacts that demonstrate how the other races of man shared their advancements in science and technology on a global scale.

Olmec and Egypt: Twin Civilizations

Until recently, European historians refused to acknowledge that Ancient Egyptian civilization, from which Europe borrowed much philosophy and science, was dominated by the Nubian people for a significant span of its history. These Negroid people were the same Negroid people who 16th century Europeans would later seek to convince the world were primitive savages.

So determined was Europe to rewrite history in order to justify its capture and enslavement of African people, that the faces of Egyptian statues were often disfigured so as to hide their true racial origin. Napoleon, during his attack on Ethiopia, took his cannons and blew off the telltale Negroid nose of the great Sphinx along with many other relics of the great African Pharaohs. In spite of the attempted cover-up, African civilization left its indelible mark on the world – even in North America. In his book *They Came Before Columbus*, author Ivan Van Sertima states:

Let us consider, first of all, the pyramids. They have a very long history in the Mediterranean world. The type found in America—the step-pyramid--may be traced to ancient Babylon and Egypt. It is also known by the name of ziggurat. The ziggurat, step pyramid or stepped temple is as distinctive a type of religious architecture as a Chinese pagoda or a Mohammedan mosque. It has been found no-where in the Old World without clear and contestable proof of diffusion. It goes back three thousand years before Christ. The very first American pyramid, or stepped temple, appears at la Venta, the site of the colossal Negroid heads and the stele on which is carried the Mediterranean type figure with beard

2B – Olmec Stone Head

The massive Olmec stone heads date back at least 5 thousand years during the time when the Nubian dynasty ruled the kingdom of Egypt. Many stone heads like the one pictured above are found throughout Mexico..

2C – Egyptian Sphinx
There is much similarity between the helmet style of the Egyptian Sphinx and the helmet styles of the Olmec stone heads. This suggests that there was some interaction between these two cultures.

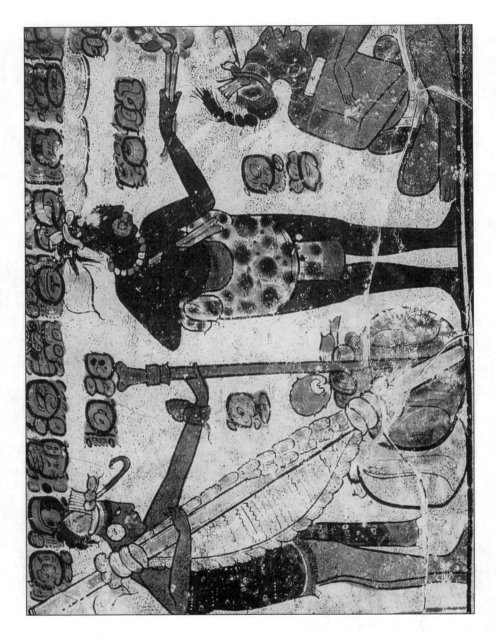

2D - Mayan Hieroglyphics

The Mayan system of writing is very ancient. Notice the similarities in style that exist between the Mayan hieroglyphs and the hieroglyphs of the Egyptians on the following page.

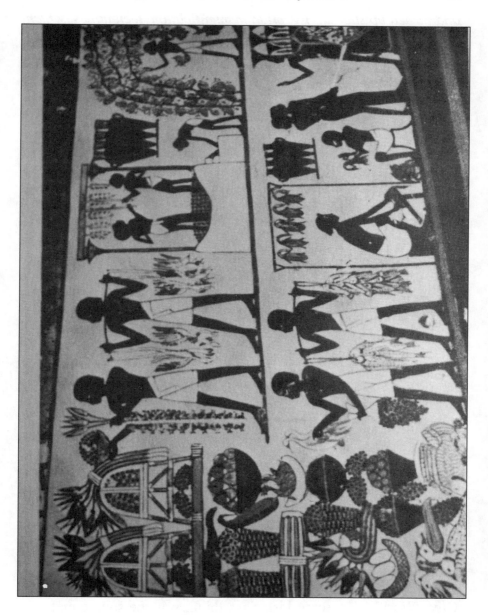

2E - Egyptian Hieroglyphics

Egyptian Hieroglyphic go back at least 5,000 years. Some say that they may be even 10,000 years old. Shared similarities with the Mayan hieroglyphics suggest either a cultural exchange between the two or a common heritage of both to an even more ancient culture.

and turned up shoes.... Egyptian mummification techniques (which originated in pre-dynastic Black Africa and were developed and refined in the dynastic period) are most in evidence in Peru. There, in the desert sands, we find very specific and ample evidence of the Egyptian influence...The Indian tribes of Virginia, of North Carolina, the Congarees of South Carolina, the Indians of the Northwest coast of Central America and those of Florida practiced this custom as well as the Incas... (They Came Before Columbus, Ivan Van Sertima, pages 155 & 157)

Ivan Van Sertima notes a number of indications of heavy contact between ancient Egyptian and ancient Native American peoples. He observed that the Egyptian surgical procedure of trephining was also found in both ancient Mexico and Peruvian civilizations. Trephining is the removing of a piece of bone from the skull, to relieve pressure. This was performed on the skulls of Egyptian-Nubian soldiers to relieve the pressure caused by violent blows to the skull. It involved removal of plaques of bone from the skull, and in many cases the operation was remarkably successful. Doctors in ancient Egypt, Mexico and Peru performed this procedure, which is recommended by Greek physician Hippocrates in his essay *"On Injuries of the Head."*

An examination of patients' skulls, in Egypt, as well as those in Mexico and Peru, show square and circular holes drilled into the skull bone.

Archeologists have concluded that extensive contact occurred between the ancient inhabitants of the Americas and Africans. Then, around 1200 B.C., the Mediterranean area became embroiled in devastating warfare.

This was due to invasions by a mysterious coalition led by "The People Of The Sea" as they were known to the people of ancient Kamit, later known as Egypt. (Kam, translated in the Bible as "Ham" represented the land of the dark or black people.) This Great World War, some historians think, was the source material for the greatest epics in ancient world history, such as the Iliad, the Norse Ragnarok sagas, the Philistine tales in the Old Testament, the story of Atlantis, and the Ethiopis, which featured the legendary story of Memnon, the great Black warrior.

The Great Memnon

In his book *Shades Of Memnon*, author Gregory L. Walker (Brother G), notes that in ancient times, the people of Europe were called Tamahu. In the Kamitic language, Tama means "people" and hu means "white":

Various Tamahu peoples dwelled near the Mediterranean Sea, living in relative peace with their Kushite neighbors until the Great World War circa 1200 B.C. At this time, nearly all of these civilizations were destroyed by a coalition led by northern Tamahu called the People of the Sea. (Shades of Memnon, The Africa Hero of the Trojan War and the Keys to Ancient World Civilization, by Brother G, Seker Nefer Press).

This account of a cataclysmic World War that destroyed much of civilization resurfaces in African history, lending credence to the ancient Native American stories.

Like the Native Americans, inhabitants of Africa also strived to live according to a spiritual law which was intended to maintain harmony. In the land of Kush (south of Kamit, home to the Kamitians before they settled further north) the people followed a set of Universal Principles much like those observed by Native American nations. Author Gregory L. Walker notes:

The Ancient Kushites' pattern of behavior inspired awe among the ancient Greeks, who called them "Blameless Ethiopians" and referred to them as "the most favored of the gods." This was due to a code of spirituality and ethics which the Kushites propagated to the world. Here is that list, compiled from the traditions of the Kushites themselves and what witnesses such as the Greeks said about them:

1. Covet no land or riches that the Supreme Being does not naturally grant you.

2. Respect the opposite sex as your equal and your compliment.

3. Give unto the world what you would have the world give unto you.

4. Always seek balance in all things, for only in harmony can there be growth.

5. Honor your ancestors, especially those who sought justice and

balance in their time upon the earth.
6. Seek not simply to do good, but encourage others to do good as well.
7. Always seek higher wisdom in all of life's endeavors.
8. Honor and safeguard the children, who have come to forge the future of the world.
9. Seek to be part of a brotherhood, sisterhood, or group, for we accomplish more together than alone.
10. Have no tolerance for evil and injustice, so that you will forever be known as blameless.
(Shades of Memnon, The Africa Hero of the Trojan War and the Keys to Ancient World Civilization, page 36).

Common spiritual principals, cultural practices, and technological advances point to common roots between African and Native American people.

In the ancient region of trading cities and countries known as Tamana, (located in what is now the Sahara Desert) one can observe the remnants of tremendous engineering feats like stone tunnels hundreds of miles long beneath the north African sands and giant megaliths in Morocco. When the Sahara dried up, the people of Tamana migrated. Gregory Walker observes that the Xiu people were Taman migrants who left the drying Sahara, settling in ancient China, Iran and Mesoamerica:

The Xiu were Western Kushites, linguistically and culturally related to the Manding people who still lie in West Africa today. In Iran they built "ziggurats" and left many artifacts, while in Mexico they built pyramids and carved huge stone portraits. The Native American Maya called them "Tul Tul Xiu" and remember them as teachers. (Tul Tul in Manding means "supporters or teachers of the High Order"). Today they are called Olmecs, mother civilization of America, and referred to as the "Shi Dynasty" by Chinese anthropologists.

In China they left African physical remains and dozens of pyramids (many still standing) in that country's Shensi province, while artifacts and statues from settlements in Mexico indicate that the Xiu had Kushites and Asians among the population. This hints at an empire, or at least trade relations that may have stretched from China to the Americas. (Shades of Memnon, The Africa

Hero of the Trojan War and the Keys to Ancient World Civiliza-tion, page 31).

The Descendents of Kedar

Jews, Christians and Muslims all trace their history back to one man, The Prophet Abraham. He is also known as "Father Abraham," because he was the father of many nations. These na-tions are not just spiritually related but in many cases are biologi-cally related due to common ancestry. The Bible records that some of the ancestors of the branch of Ishmael were from the lands of Egypt, those areas also known as Kamit and Kush.

And Sarai, Abram's wife, took Hagar her maid the Egyp-tian after Abram had dwelt ten years in the land of Canaan, and gave her to her husband Abram to be his wife. (Holy Bible, Gene-sis, 16:3)

The Prophet Ishmael, son of Abraham and Hagar, would also marry an Egyptian like his father.

And he dwelt in the wilderness of Paran: and his mother took him a wife out of the land of Egypt. (Holy Bible, Genesis, 21:21)

The descendents of these unions became the Arab people. Biblical maps show that the Wilderness of Paran and the Desert of Paran are both located in that region that would later be known as Arabia. It is interesting to note that no other group other than the Arabs have ever claimed to be the descendents of Ishmael.

The reason for mentioning this ancestral line of the Prophet Abraham is because of those people who were of the same ances-try as Hagar and Ishmael's wife. They were of Egyptian, Kamitic or Kush origin, and would produce descendents who would one day become an Arabian tribe known as Kedar (as will be explained shortly.) As mentioned earlier, in *Shades of Memnon*, it states that the Xiu were western Kushites who migrated from the Sahara to the lands of what is now North and South America. This link shows that these two groups of people are related. This may also show why there are similarities between these cultures, like archi-tecture, hieroglyphics, and biological make-up.

2F – Children of North Africa in 1920
This photo taken of children in Morocco appears to show a wide range of ethnic diversity. The varying types of facial features clearly show that many different cultures had visited the area. Although this was taken of Moroccans, it looks like it could have been taken of the Mayan people. Some Native American legends state that their people sailed east across the Atlantic. (Illustrated Africa, Boyce, 1920)

In general, Christians don't find much reason to acknowl-edge the ancestral line of Ishmael as anything of much importance, whereas most Arabs, because of their Islamic faith, feel this ances-tral line is of great importance.   There are some Christians who even consider Hagar's marriage, and her son, as illegitimate. This is just one of many differences that exist between the Islamic and Christian interpretation of events that took place in Abraham's family. In his Commentary on the Holy Quran, Hazrat Mirza Na-sir Ahmad explains the conflicting opinions:

The Quran and the Bible are at variance as to which of his two sons – Ishmael or Isaac – Abraham, in pursuance of God's command, offered for sacrifice. According to the Bible it was Isaac (Gen. 22.2). The Quran, on the other hand, declares that it was Ishmael. The Bible contradicts itself in this respect. Accord-ing to it, Abraham was commanded to offer his only son for sacri-fice, but Isaac was at no time his only son.

Ishmael was senior to Isaac by 13 years and for these many years was Abraham's only son... It stands to reason, there-fore, that Abraham must have been required by God to offer for sacrifice his nearest and dearest thing which was his only and first-born son who was Ishmael. Some Christian evangelists have vainly tried to show that, 'Ishmael being of the handmaid, was born after the flesh while Isaac, being born of the free woman, was by promise' (Galatians, 4:22-23)

Apart from the fact that Hagar, Ishmael's mother, belonged to the royal family of Egypt and was no handmaid, Ishmael has repeatedly been mentioned in the Bible as Abraham's son, exactly as Isaac has been mentioned (Gen 16:16, 17:23,25.) The vision (of Abraham) had already symbolically been fulfilled in Hagar and Ishmael having been left by Abraham in the Valley of Mecca which at that time was an arid and barren waste.

That brave act, had in fact, symbolized the sacrifice of Ish-mael. The Divine command to Abraham first to sacrifice his son and then to abstain from carrying it into actual fact showed also that it was intended to abolish human sacrifice, a most inhuman practice which was prevalent at that time among most nations. (Holy Quran with commentary, Hadrat Mirza Nasir Ahmad, 1981, p. 968)

Despite attempts to label Hagar's marriage and her off-spring as illegitimate and therefore devoid of God's blessings, the Bible records otherwise. God is stated to have said to Abraham:

And I will bless the son of the maidservant and make him into a mighty nation, because he is your offspring. (Holy Bible, Genesis, 21:13)

And again in Genesis God states,

As for Ishmael, I have heard thee. Behold, I will surely bless him. I will make him fruitful and will greatly increase his number. He will be the father of twelve princes. And I will make him into a great nation. (Holy Bible, Genesis, 17:20)

These twelve princes were the twelve sons of Ishmael recorded in the Bible (Genesis 25:13.) One of Ishmael's sons was named Kedar, which means "dark-colored, dusky." One of the Arab tribes, known as Kedar, had this name in honor of Ishmael's second son. Islamic genealogists trace some of the Prophet of Islam, Muhammad Mustapha's ancestors through this tribe.

So as can be seen, the promise God made concerning the son of Hagar is the same promise He made to Sarah concerning her son (Genesis 17:16.) Just as those descendents of Isaac would eventually become a great spiritual nation through the Prophet Moses, likewise would the descendents of Ishmael also become a great spiritual nation.

A Message For All Nations

In the year 580 Christian era, a young Arabian merchant by the name of Muhammad Mustapha had left his wife Khadijah at home and gone into seclusion in a cave to pray fervently for the upliftment of his people.

The Arabs at that time were quite barbaric, prone to frequent tribal wars and violent feuds between families. It was during this time of intense prayer that he felt a presence in the cave with him. He looked up and a being of light, an angel, appeared to him in the form of a man, and commanded him, "Read! Recite, in the name of your Lord!"

Stunned, Muhammad told the angel, "I can't read." The angel insisted that he repeat the words spoken to him, saying, "Recite! Recite what God taught man by the pen what man knew not!"

Muhammad, quite shaken by this experience, returned home to his wife and began to try to explain what happened. Khadijah then took him to her cousin, who was a devout Christian, to get a possible explanation of this spiritual experience. Khadijah's cousin informed them that Muhammad had been the recipient of Divine revelation, and had been visited by the angel Gabriel (or Jibreel in Arabic.)

Days later, when Muhammad returned to the cave and began praying he was again visited by the angel Gabriel, who recited more verses to him which Muhammad committed to memory. These verses told of previous prophets, who had come to warn their nations and tell them to reform their behavior in order to avoid destruction by God. The verses also told of historic events as contained in the Bible regarding Abraham, David, Moses, Jesus, and other significant people whose mission it was to bring spiritual guidance to their people.

The Arabic verses recited by the angel Gabriel revealed to Muhammad that he had been chosen as a messenger to bring God's universal law, which would reform and unify all of mankind. These collected verses, known as the Quran, also established that throughout mankind's existence, all civilizations and nations of the world were recipients of divine guidance.

And We did raise among every people a Messenger with the teaching, 'Worship Allah and shun the Evil One. Then among the people were some whom Allah guided and among them were some who became deserving of ruin. So travel through the earth and see what was the end of those who treated the Prophets as liars! (Holy Quran, Al-Nahl 16:37)

Verily, We have sent thee with the Truth, as a bearer of glad tidings and as a Warner; and there is no people to whom a Warner has not been sent. (Holy Quran, Al-Fatir 35:25)

The essence of the teachings of Islam is that humanity is all one family, descendents of a common ancestor. According to Islam, all people have been given spiritual laws and guidelines to

follow, through a prophet raised up by God from amongst themselves. Thus, Islam verifies the legitimacy of the prophets and
holy men of other nations and cultures, whose spiritual teachings,
if uncorrupted, would be in harmony with those contained in the
Holy Quran.

Contrary to Western portrayals of Islam as a religion spread
through violence and war, Islam appealed to people on the African
continent because of its teachings of brotherhood and peace. Islam
spread to Morocco, North Africa and paved the way for the establishment of the great Moorish Empire. Islam became a dominant
force in the establishment of powerful kingdoms in West Africa
including Timbuktu and Jenne.

The religion of Islam lays special emphasis on the seeking
of knowledge and wisdom. This inspired its followers to establish
schools, libraries, and other institutions of higher learning. Wherever Islam spread, the pursuit of knowledge increased. The Holy
Prophet Muhammad is reported to have said, "Seek knowledge,
even if you have to crawl on your hands and knees to China."

International Trade

African Muslims sailed the seas in pursuit of knowledge.
Their explorations led them to the shores of America; however,
their encounter with the native people was vastly different than that
of the Spanish who arrived centuries later.   The Africans came to
the natives in peace, extending a hand of brotherhood and offering
to share knowledge. As a result, the natives recognized them as
people who had not forgotten the sacred laws of the Great Spirit.
Historical accounts of the African Muslims who traveled to America indicate that there was a sharing of cultures and traditions, and
intermarriage among the people. Many traces of African culture
exist throughout America as a result of these earlier encounters.
According to this article on "Islam In Latin America," printed in
the San Francisco, California publication, *The Islamic Bulletin,*

*Muslims have exerted a great and largely unrecognized
impact on American society, beginning with their exploration of
America more than 300 years prior to the "discovery" of the "New
World" by Christopher Columbus.*

The Muslim explorers accessed the interior of the continent by using the Mississippi River. The traces of their early presence may be found in the architecture and calligraphy of towns such as St. Augustine, Florida (America's oldest town), in the names of islands such as Islamadora, and in the customs of the American Indians. Some little known but very intriguing statistics follow:

In 1178, a Chinese document known as the Sung Document records the voyage of Muslim sailors to a land known as Mu-Lan-Pi (America). This document is mentioned in The Khotan Amirs, published in 1933.

Abu Bakari, a Muslim king from the Malian Empire, leads a series of nautical voyages to the New World in 1310. In 1312, African Muslims from Mandinga arrive in the Gulf of Mexico and explore the American interior via the Mississippi River. 1513, Piri Reis completes his first world map, including the Americas, after researching maps from all over the world. The map is unsurpassed in its practicality and artistry. (The Islamic Bulletin)

Africans made a number of journeys across the Atlantic. They established harmonious relations with the native people of America, affecting the language and culture. Traces of their arrival have been examined to determine the scope of their explorations throughout the Americas. *The Islamic Bulletin* article continues:

New Zealand archaeologist and linguist Barry Fell in his work "Saga America" points to evidence of a Muslim's presence in various parts of the Americas. In addition to drawing several cultural parallels between West African peoples and certain "Indian" peoples of the southwest, Fell points out that the southwest's Pima people possessed a vocabulary which contained words of Arabic origin.

The presence of such words among the Pima is compounded by the existence of Islamic petrogyphs in places like California. Fell informs us that in Inyo county, California, there exists an early American petrogyph (rock carving) which states in Arabic: "Yasus ben Maria" ("Jesus, Son of Mary"), a phrase commonly found within the surahs of the Holy Qur'an. Fell is convinced that this glyph is many centuries older than the U.S.

Fell also identifies the Algonquian language as having words with Arabic roots, especially words which pertained to navigation, astronomy, meteorology, medicine and anatomy. The presence of such words again illustrates significant cultural contact between the American "Indians" and the Arabic-speaking peoples of the Islamic world. Such Islamic peoples evidently came primarily from the African continent as additional evidence suggests. (The Islamic Bulletin, San Francisco, CA).

In his book *They Came Before Columbus* Ivan Van Sertima points out evidence of ancient and early African contacts in the American continent. He points out that many Native American names such as Ges, Zamoras, Marabitine, and Marabios are African Muslim surnames. The names "Marabitine" and "Marabios" relate to "Marabout" (Murabit), meaning the "Holy Men and Women" of the Moorish Empire. The Marabouts were the protectors of African Muslim frontiers. They are often remembered for having acted as buffers against Catholic/European encroachment.

Columbus admitted in his papers that on Monday, October 21, 1492 CE, while his ship was sailing near Gibara on the northeast coast of Cuba, he saw a mosque on the top of a beautiful mountain. The ruins of mosques and minarets with inscriptions of Quranic verses have been discovered in Cuba, Mexico, Texas and Nevada.

Dr. Barry Fell (Harvard University) introduced in his book *Saga America* solid scientific evidence supporting the arrival, centuries before Columbus, of Muslims from North and West Africa. *The Islamic Bulletin* article explains:

Dr. Fell discovered the existence of Muslim schools at Valley of Fire, Allan Springs, Logomarsino, Keyhole Canyon, Washoe and Hickison Summit Pass (Nevada), Mesa Verde (Colorado), Mimbres Valley (New Mexico), and Tipper Canoe (Indiana) dating back to 700-800 CE. Engraved on rocks in the old western US, he found texts, diagrams and charts representing the last surviving fragments of what was once a system of schools - both elementary and higher levels.

The language of instruction was North African Arabic written with old Kufic Arabic script. The subjects of instruction included writing, reading, arithmetic, religion, history, geography, mathematics, astronomy, and sea navigation... The descendants of the Muslim visitors of North America are members of the present

Iroquois, Algonquin, Anasazi, Hohokam, and Olmec native people.
("Timeline of Muslim Exploration of the Americas, 1178 CE Mus-
lim Explore America?" The Islamic Bulletin, P.O. Box 410186,
San Francisco, CA 94141-018-6415-552-8831, Fax 415-552-4737,
info@islamic-bulletin.org)

The Great White One

Major excursions across the Atlantic to the Americas continued right up until nearly two centuries before the sail of Columbus. Historical accounts from the old kingdom of Mali, West Africa, state that in the year 1310, King Abubakari the Second,
grandson of Sundiata, decided to send 200 master boats and 200
supply boats on an exploratory trip across the Atlantic Ocean.
The supplies would last voyagers for at least two years.

He called the captains of the boats together and issued this
order; "Do not return until you have reached the end of the ocean,
or when you have exhausted your food and water."

After a long absence, only one of the ships returned, with
the report that the other ships had been pulled out to sea by a
strong current and disappeared. He was afraid, and did not enter
the current, but turned around and headed back.

King Abubakari was determined to discover the extent of
the ocean. The following year, 1311, he had a special boat built for
himself and assembled a fleet of 2000 ships. He conferred the
power of the regency on his brother Kankan Musa, with the understanding that if he, Abubakari, did not return within a reasonable
time, Kankan Musa would assume the throne.

Dressed in a flowing white robe and a jeweled turban,
Abubakari left Mali with his fleet of ships, heading west across the
Atlantic. He never returned.

There is evidence that both of these expeditions from Mali
landed in America. In his book, *Deeper Roots: Muslims In the
Caribbean Before Columbus to the Present*, author Abdullah Hakim Quick states that traces of Mandinka cities of stone and mortar
were seen by early Spanish explorers and pirates. One of them, a
native of Minas Geres, showed a sample of the Mandinka script
and described the Mandinka cities in a written document.
Abdullah Hakim Quick explains:

In this document, written in 1754, we are told that a city in Minas Geres near a river was well laid out and had superb buildings, obelisks and statues. On the statue of a young man, naked from the waist up without beard, underneath the shield were characters meaning "ahn na we fe nge" ("He is of the maternal aunt, the pure side," or in other words, "He is heir to the throne.")
(Deeper roots: Muslims In the Caribbean Before Columbus to the Present, by Abdullah Hakim Quick, page 15)

This statue appears to be a sign of king Abubakari's arrival to the Americas. Other signs indicate that Mandinkas explored many parts of North America. In Arizona they left inscriptions showing that they also brought a number of elephants to America with them. Writings and pictographs indicate that the Mandinka explorers interacted peacefully with the native people.

In Mexico, the appearance of Abubakari was thought to be the fulfillment of an ancient Aztec prophecy about the return of a half-man, half god named Quetzalcoatl.

According to the beliefs of the people of Mexico, Quetzalcoatl was a kind of reappearing Messiah. The Mexican people, as descendants of the ancient Mayan civilization, divided the passage of time into cycles of 52-year periods. The return of Quetzalcoatl was prophesized to occur during one of these cycles.

According to the legend, Quetzalcoatl was bearded and white. However, this description presents some confusion as to whether he was white skinned or wearing white clothes. Sculptures of Quetzalcoatl portray him as native, or Asiatic or Negroid. In *They Came Before Columbus*, Ivan Van Sertima reflects on the many images of Quetzalcoatl:

No one definition can embrace Quetzalcoatl. He had several representations or aspects. He was the feathered serpent king and rainmaker god in Central America.   Quetzal (bird or plume) and coatl (serpent) signified a connection between bird and snake.
The snake was supposed to be a kind of evil dragon guarding the well of life. He contained or imprisoned the life giving moisture.   An eternal conflict existed between him and the great bird who nested in the tree of life and would wrestle and devour the snake, thus releasing the rains, the fertile waters necessary for men and crops.   The origin of this serpent-devouring bird lies in

Africa. (They Came Before Columbus, by Ivan van Sertima, page 72 & 73).

Ivan Van Sertima notes that only one bird in the world, the Secretary Bird of Africa, with its powerful webbed feet and sharp talons, is a successful hunter of serpents. Stories of this strange African bird were prevalent in ancient Egypt and there is evidence that this bird and serpent traveled in ancient times to America.

Just as the Jews waited for a messiah, so did the people of Mexico await the cyclical return of the legendary Quetzalcoatl. This expectation led them to presume that perhaps he had reappeared in the person of Abubakari the second, who arrived in Mexico in 1311, exactly six cycles after the disappearance of the last Quetzalcoatl by way of the sea from among the Toltecs (A.D. 999). Ivan Van Sertima reflects on how the Mexicans may have perceived Abubakari's arrival:

The year was 1311. The strangest things had begun to happen. The diviners had said there would be another messenger coming from the lands of the sun god that year.

The vessel that bore him was the first to approach the shore. They saw him standing like a king under a canopy that had been mounted on a stepped dais in the center of the boat. He was clothed from head to foot in long flowing white robes. He looked like a true child of the sun, burned dark by its rays. His black hair and beard stood out against the whiteness of his vestment. Surrounding this white, bearded figure was a great company of boats. The men all looked marvelously black, as if they had been bathed in the sacred fire. Surely they had come from a land burning in the white heart of the sun.

Against the blue canopy under which he stood they could see quite clearly the outlines of a great golden bird, the serpent-slaying eagle, they thought, that was an ensign of Quetzalcoatl. Truly this was he come back again, as he had promised, "by way of the sea where the sun rises" and with many white capped, white robed companions. It was exactly six cycles since he had disappeared from among the Toltecs at Tula. (They Came Before Columbus, by Ivan Van Sertima, page 71 & 72)

2G – Traditional Garment of Mali Muslim Rulers

The above is a photo taken in 1920 of a Muslim ruler from Mali. It was a common practice among some of the Muslim rulers of Mali to wear white. Spiritually it was symbolic of purity and it also served as a status symbol, especially the huge white turban. In this context one can understand how a dark complexioned African could be described as "white." (Illustrated Africa, Boyce, 1920)

King Abubakari's strong impact on the native culture is evident in the many houses of worship established throughout South and Central America. Over 40,000 such buildings, called "Kabas" appear in Mexico and Central America, presumably named so after the "Kaba" in Mecca, which according to Islamic tradition is known as a very ancient house of worship built by the very first prophet, Adam. It was later reestablished by the prophet Abraham and his son Ishmael.

A variety of buildings were architecturally designed in relation to the cosmos. Hunbatz Men, in *Native American Prophesies*, explains the purpose of the Uxmal Center, located in Yucatan:

"Uxmal was a special place for women. Kabah is a place for men to make rituals. That is the reason you see at a center different architecture. Each architecture (design) is for specific work. But all the pyramids incorporated sacred geometry." (Native American Prophecies, Scott Peterson, page 9,)

Abubakari, raised in the Islamic faith, had been schooled in the principals of peace, justice and equality. As a Muslim, it was part of his faith to respect other cultures and their religious teachings. As a king, he was responsible for regulating his society according to the divine law as taught in the Holy Quran. He also understood the concept of diplomacy and knew how to initiate peaceful foreign relations.

The Mandingo people showed respect for the native way of life and formed a mutual "give and take" relationship. Of the 2000 plus ships that King Abubakari brought with him, half of them carried supplies, like gold, for the purpose of trading.

This relationship existed for some time because Abubakari and his entourage made a one-way trip - they never returned to Africa. Instead, these Muslim travelers, also known as Moors, continued to explore the Americas, all the way up to Canada, and intermarried with the native population.

This contact between Native Americans and these Moors is also found in the legends of other tribes. In an interview at the *Schemitzuh 2001 Powwow* at Foxwood Resort in Mashantucket, Connecticut, Lloyd Thompson of the Cherokee Nation Bird Clan told of a meeting long ago between Moorish travelers and the Cherokee Nation:

They ended up in the Yucatan peninsula (Mexico) and they spread from there and intermarried with the Native American people. There are many stories like these - like the story of the Cherokee when they first met the Moors. When the Moors came to the camps, the natives didn't fight them because they had the same dark skin like the Cherokee. The Cherokee thought they were relatives, so they eventually adopted their way of dressing. Seeing them was like seeing their people come across the water and realizing that that's where are children went, and now they've come home. That's in Cherokee legend. (Interview: Lloyd Thompson, Cherokee Nation, South East Cherokee Confederacy)

The meetings between these two cultures had a great impact on the Cherokee. History records that in 1866, right after the Civil War, there was a Cherokee Chief named Ramadan Ibn Wati (*Muslims in America*, page 45.) Being a chief with an obvious Islamic heritage, he would probably not have been the only one among his people to have been influenced by the teachings of Islam.

A modern day "collage" of these cultures can be found in Cherokee Blackfoot Mahir Abdal-Razzaaq El who, in an article in *Message Magazine*, comments on the early relationships between Native Americans and Muslims:

My name is Mahir Abdal-Razzaaq El and I am a Cherokee Blackfoot American Indian who is Muslim. I am known as Eagle Sun Walker. I serve as a Pipe Carrier Warrior for the Northeastern Band of Cherokee Indians in New York City.

There are other Muslims in our group. For the most part, not many people are aware of the Native American contact with Islam that began over one thousand years ago by some of the early Muslim travelers who visited us. Some of these Muslim travelers ended up living among our people. (Digging for the Red Roots, by Mahir Abdal-Razzaaq El, Message Magazine July 1996)

According to Van Sertima, the Mandingo explorers from the Mali Empire practiced agriculture, and had fixed settlements in South and Central America. They were also traders, and as such, were nomadic and ever on the move. While traveling they built temporary bases for their defense. These bases, built on elevated mounds, strongly resemble West African stockades.

In the eighth century, the Moorish empire of North Africa had spread into Spain, bringing the light of knowledge to a people steeped in darkness and barbarism. Through superior military force, the Moors of Africa conquered Spain, and brought advancements in education, science, language, geography, and the arts. They introduced the silk industry and brought new agricultural products to Spain such as rice, sugar cane, dates, ginger, cotton, lemons, and strawberries into the country. While the rest of Europe was virtually illiterate, in Moorish Spain there were colleges and universities and many royal palaces surrounded by beautiful gardens. One of these great learning centers was in the city of Cordoba.

History shows that the Moors ruled Spain for almost 800 years. Then in 1492, they lost the empire with the fall of the Moorish city of Cordoba. The Moorish rulers' defeat caused a shift in power that would come to have a long-lasting impact on both Africa and the Americas. What would follow would be a new philosophy towards foreign relations – one that justified the conquering of other people under the banner of religion. This new philosophy would be led by the Spanish Conquistadors under the doctrine of the Inquisition.

Chapter Three
The Spanish Empire Expands

3A – Keeper of the Sacred Path (1994)
By Melody Lightfeather
"This is the ancient Indian symbol of the crossed paths, a sign for faith of things unseen. A warrior of light, on his horse, is carrying the warrior staff - symbolic of the keeping of the sacred path. No matter what direction you come in it symbolizes those things of the spirit that all become one from all people and all nations."

Chapter Three
The Spanish Empire Expands

"We knew that one day a strange people would appear in our midst, who would create man in his own image. Given his language and his knowledge, our own people will become the instrument by which he will try to rule over us and carve the rest of us into his image. His creation will be of our own people. Since they will be his tools he will make certain they do a good job.

But if we are strong and firmly rooted we will not be deformed, whereas they will slump for they will be rootless. So we must have strength to preserve ourselves." (Hopi newspaper Techqua Ikachi, Issue #3):

Columbus Follows Moorish Maps

The Inquisition, a court of the Roman Catholic Church, was formed to discover, examine and punish those guilty of "heresy." All non-Christians and any citizens that were political dissidents or otherwise non-conformants were targeted for attack. The Inquisition, active in central and southern Europe, became the power by which the Roman Catholic Church gained full political control. Citizens accused of heresy were put on trial and executed. Jews and Muslims were forced to either convert or suffer imprisonment, torture and death.

The marriage of King Ferdinand V to Queen Isabella, head of a rival leading family in Spain, united the previously feuding royal houses of Aragon and Castile. This gave Spain the political unity it needed to oust the Moors from power after 800 years of rule. King Ferdinand established the Inquisition at Seville and began expelling Jews and Muslims. Known as Ferdinand the Catholic, King Ferdinand saw his mission of spreading Christianity and expanding his kingdom as one and the same thing.

Therefore, when a young seaman named Christopher Columbus came to King Ferdinand and Queen Isabella with a proposal to spread the Spanish kingdom to the East Indies, the king and queen of Spain were more than willing to invest in his idea.

Italian navigator Christopher Columbus studied in Spain with Moorish scholars, and discovered that maps existed showing a round earth. Africans and Asians had continued to sail the seas and conduct international trade. As it slowly emerged from its Dark Ages, Europe was in a race to catch up with other nations in the world trade market. Here Columbus thought he might find an advantage if he could discover a new trade route to India and acquire gold.

So, as history records, in 1492 he traveled west across the Atlantic Ocean to get to the east in search of India, and landed by mistake on what are now known as the Caribbean Islands in Central America.

In 1492, when Christopher Columbus arrived in the New World, he was strongly influenced by the geography of the 13th-century Arab scholar, Al-Idrissi, who served as an adviser to King Roger of Sicily. Columbus had with him a copy of Al-Idrissi's works mentioning the discovery of a new continent by eight Muslim explorers. He also had some Muslim crewmembers with him for translation and other services. (Muslims in America: Seven Centuries of History (1312-2000), Amir Nashad Ali Muhammad, page 3)

Columbus had heard the stories of a continent that was supposed to exist on the other side of the Atlantic, which he thought might have been India. This idea of sailing west to get to the East came from the knowledge he acquired from those people whose forefathers had already sailed to those lands beyond the Atlantic. Columbus himself, upon arrival to the New World, saw the signs of those who had previously sailed there. Columbus, being from Spain, was familiar with Islamic culture – including Islamic architecture:

On October 21, 1492, Columbus admitted in his papers that while his ship was sailing near Gibara on the northeast coast of Cuba, he saw a Mosque on the top of a beautiful mountain. Ruins of Mosques and minarets with inscriptions of Quranic verses have been discovered in Cuba, Mexico, Texas and Nevada. (Muslims in America: Seven Centuries of History (1312-2000), Amir Nashad Ali Muhammad, page 3)

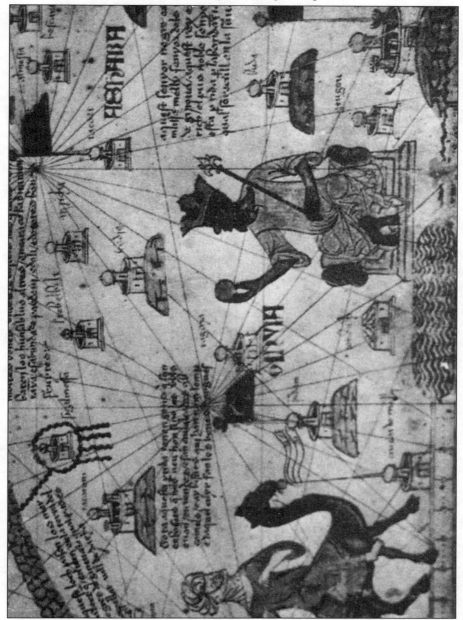

3B – Map of the Fabled Empire of Gold
This map depicts the Catalan Atlas, circa 1375. In the center it shows King Mansa Musa, nephew of King Abubakari, holding a gold nugget. To his left is an Arab trader on camel back. (Europe in the Wider World in 1492, page 254)

Immersed in the brutal practices of the Spanish Inquisition, Columbus and his crew embarked upon a mission to take over the land, subjugate the native people to the authority of the Spanish crown, and to convert them, by force if necessary, to Christianity. For the people of the Americas, the arrival of Christopher Columbus was the fulfillment of a dreadful prophesy.

The European concepts of ownership of land and the enslavement of human beings were so outrageous to the native people that it was simply incomprehensible to them. In his book, *Along The Trail, A Story of One Little "Indian"*, Elmer M. Savilla explains the culture of his people, The Quechan, of Arizona.

> *The Quechan people had a profound respect for all things belonging to In-ti-yah, Mother Earth. They understood that Pipah, the people, could really own none of those things, which was Hers. The water which gave them fish and quenched their thirst was Her blood; the pure desert air which was necessary for life was Her breath, and the soil which grew the delicious watermelons, maize, squash and white beans was Her body. They owed their very life to Her and they knew that one day they would have to give it back.*
>
> *The sun which warmed the earth and all its plants, birds, and animals was called Anya, Father Sun. Giving thanks to In-ti-yah each day for these things was their form of religion; this was their way of life. (Along The Trail, The Story of One Little "Indian", by Elmer M Savilla, page 31).*

The Quechan followed the simple rules laid down by Mother Earth. They enjoyed a bountiful life, after which they expected to join their ancestors, in a place known to non-native people as "Heaven." They lived happily for centuries, until one day a huge strange looking canoe with large wind catchers arrived at a far away eastern shore of the land. Strange looking men with pale skin and hair on their faces, wearing shiny metal coats arrived, riding animals they called "caballos," or horses. Some of the men wore heavy robes. They said that they came from someone they called "God" and told the Quechan people that they had come to save something called their "soul." Elmer Savilla reflects:

> *There were no Quechan words for, or understanding of, "invasion," and so the strange looking people were welcomed and*

treated like relatives. In In-ti-yah's teachings, all men and women were "family," and these newcomers were just the funny looking ones with strange ways. Every family knows that kind.

These newcomers tried to explain to the natives, who were now called "Indians" because of the mistaken belief of the captain of that first sailing ship that he had reached a place called India, that they, the pale looking ones with hairy faces, had "discovered" the Quechan and their ancestral lands, and that they were now the owners of this new and beautiful land and that they now made the laws by which the Quechan must live...

The Quechan did not understand the concept of owning the earth or things of the earth and so did not, at first, argue against the claim of discovery and subsequent ownership. (Along The Trail, The Story of One Little "Indian", by Elmer M. Savilla, page 33 & 34).

The Quechan knew nothing of these white men's violent and bloody history in their own homeland, so they were willing to share the land and its blessings with these strangers, who called themselves Spaniards. They knew nothing of the struggle between the Spanish, French, Dutch, and English over "ownership" of their lands. The European nations had determined that the natives were "people able to reason and capable of conversion to Christianity." The Spanish missionaries felt it their duty to convert the natives, while the Spanish Conquistadors wanted to use them as a source of labor.

First Contact

In his book *500 Nations: An Illustrated History of North American Indians*, author Alvin M. Josephy, Jr. reveals the attitude of Columbus and his crew toward the native people he first encountered, the Arawaks:

To Columbus, the Arawaks (some of whose groups were known as Tainos) were "artless and generous with what they have, to such a degree as no one would believe but he who had seen it. Of anything they have, if it be asked for, they never say no, but do rather invite the person to accept it, and show as much lovingness as if they would give their hearts...These people are very unskilled

in arms...with fifty men, they could all be subjected and made to do
all that one wished." (500 Nations, An Illustrated History of North
American Indians, by Alvin M. Josephy, Jr., copyright 1994, Alfred
A. Knopf, Inc., Pathways Productions, Inc. Page 115 & 116).

So, in stark contrast to the simple, honest hospitality of the
Arawak people, the Spaniards knew only cruelty and greed. On
October 12, 1492, the very first day of his arrival, Columbus wrote
in his diary, "I took some of the natives by force." He recorded
that he found the native inhabitants "peaceful" but resolved that
they "must be made to work...and adopt our ways."

As was their culture, the Arawaks continued to treat the
Spaniards as guests in their land. Since Columbus and his crew
were foreigners, the Arawaks helped them through times of difficulty and came to their aid on many occasions. They followed
their spiritual belief that all human beings should be treated as
family. They were unaware of the sinister plot of the Spaniards to
subjugate them. Alvin Josephy continues:

In December 1492, Columbus reached the heavily popu-
lated island he named Espanola, or as it became known by its
Latin name, Hispaniola. On Christmas Eve, while making its way
along the coast, the Santa Maria ran aground on a coral reef. The
ship was destroyed, but with the help of the friendly Arawak chief
Guancanagari and his people, the crew and most of the supplies
were saved.

Guacanagari proved a warm and trusting friend of Colum-
bus, and the latter, in turn, was deeply impressed by the chief's no-
ble bearing and his large village. As a token of gratitude, Colum-
bus presented Guancanagaru with a red cape, which the Indians
regarded as an object of prestige.

Interpreting the gesture as the opening of trade between
leaders of equal importance, Guacanagari gave Columbus a mask,
plates, a belt, and other objects of gold, revealing to him also that
the source of the gold lay nearby. To Guacanagari, the exchange
of objects was a fair trade--a symbol of mutual respect and recog-
nition. To Columbus, one of the gifts, a golden head ornament,
was a crown. It represented authority, and the giving of it meant
submission. He believed that Guacanagari was delivering his land
and people to Spain.

The golden gifts marked a turning point for Columbus and his attitude toward the island Arawaks...Columbus' heart hardened...On the way home, Columbus prepared a letter to the Spanish monarchs, conveying the news of a "New World" of gold and docile Indian natives--some two dozen of whom he had captured and was taking back to show off in Spain. "They are fit to be ordered about and made to work, to sow and do aught else that may be needed," he noted in his letter, adding darkly that among the sources of wealth that he could ship from the new lands for the profit of the sovereigns were Indian "slaves, as many as they shall order." (500 Nations, An Illustrated History of North American Indians, by Alvin M. Josephy, Jr., Page 122.)

Mandinka Traders

The native people, visited by shiploads of Africans centuries earlier, had no reason to suspect that these explorers from Europe would take advantage of their hospitality. Based on their positive experiences with the Africans, the Arawaks were simply following universal rules of diplomacy among civilized people. When Columbus arrived in the New World, he found that the Africans had in fact arrived before he did, and were conducting regular trade with the native people.

Prior to Columbus' second voyage in 1496, he was informed by Portuguese king Don Juan that boats from Guinea, West Africa had navigated to this new world, this chain of islands which Columbus had claimed to have "discovered" and had brought back merchandise. Ivan Van Sertima, states in his book that:

The Indians gave proof that they were trading with black people. They brought to the Spanish concrete evidence of this trade. The Indians of this Espanola said there had come to Espanola a black people who have the tops of their spears made of metal which they call guanin, of which he, Columbus had sent samples to the Sovereigns to have them assayed, when it was found that of 32 parts, 18 were of gold, 6 of silver, and 8 of copper.

The origin of the word guanin may be tracked down in the Mande languages of West Africa, through Mandingo, Kabunga, Toronka, Kankanka, Bambara, Mande and Vei. (They Came Before Columbus, Ivan Van Sertima, page 11)

3C – Signs of African Presence in America
From carved monuments to inscriptions on rocks, hundreds of archeological finds have been found from North to South America suggesting an early African presence in the Americas. The above artifact was found in ancient Mexico.

Even though Columbus realized that other nations had established trade relations with the native people, he continued to believe he had reached some unknown part of the Indies. He continued to call the native inhabitants "Indians." Although he did record in his diary that he had discovered evidence of a previous African presence, he failed to discover the trade route used by the Africans from Guinea to reach what he believed were islands in the Indies. He had hoped to gain an advantage over other nations engaged in international trade. Historian John G. Jackson notes:

Columbus had been hailed as the discoverer of America; but Columbus himself never succumbed to any such delusion. According to Harold G. Lawrence:

Proof of this is evidenced by the fact that Columbus was informed by some men, when he stopped at the Cape Verde Islands off the coast of Africa, that Negroes had been known to set out into the Atlantic from the Guinea coast in canoes loaded with merchandise and steering toward the west. The same Christopher Columbus was further informed by the Indians of Hispaniola when he arrived in the West Indies that they had been able to obtain gold from black men who had come from across the sea from the south and southeast. It must also be added that Amerigo Vespucci on his voyage to the Americas witnessed these same black men out in the Atlantic returning to Africa [African Explorers of the New World, p. 6, by Harold G. Lawrence].
(Introduction to African Civilization, John G. Jackson, page 241)

Inquisition Brutality

The Spanish objective was simple: Conquer, enslave, and exploit. It was of no importance what the people called themselves, who their ancestors were, what religion they practiced. They were mere commodities, to be subdued and trained to perform wealth-producing labor. The natives needed to first be "civilized" or, in other words, remade in the image of the European - language, clothing, religion, everything.

Shootings, hangings, maimings, beheadings and burnings, as were practiced in medieval Europe, were effective techniques to subjugate those the Europeans sought to enslave. In November of

1493, Christopher Columbus returned to Hispaniola with a fleet of seventeen ships, some twelve hundred colonists, and thirty-four horses. On his way, he stopped briefly at the island now known as St. Croix, where, without provocation, members of his expedition attacked four Native American men and two women in a canoe, cutting off the head of one of the men with an ax and taking the others aboard ship as captives to send back to Spain as slaves.

This reflected the arrogance and cruelty with which the Europeans, led by Columbus, dealt with the natives. Columbus enthusiastically embraced the business possibilities of wholesale enslavement of the native people on the American continent. He first shipped ten chained Arawak men and women to Seville, Spain. He later loaded 1,100 Taino men and women aboard four Spanish ships and sent them across the stormy Atlantic. Only three hundred survived. But Columbus convinced King Ferdinand and Queen Isabella that a profitable slave trade could be generated from America.

At first Spanish priests denounced the horrors of slavery, calling it a mortal sin. In 1511, Dominican Friar Montesinos said Christians could not justify cruelty and tyranny over the "Indians." A few years later, Bishop Fray Bartolome De La Casas, denounced the Spanish for their greed and willingness to kill for the acquisition of gold. Author Alvin Josephy quotes De La Casas:

(The Spaniards) made bets as to who would slit a man in two or cut off his head in one blow, or they opened his bowels. They tore the babies from their mothers' breasts by the feet, and dashed their heads against the rocks...they spitted the bodies of other babes, together with their mothers and all who were before them, on their swords... (They hanged the Indians), and by the thirteens, in honor and reverence for our Redeemer and the twelve Apostles. They put wood underneath and with fire, they burned the Indians alive...I saw all the above things...All these did my own eyes witness.

Fray Bartolome De Las Casas,
History of the Indies 1552
(500 Nations, An Illustrated History of North American Indians, by Alvin M. Josephy, Jr., Page 114.)

The native people were dying off by the thousands from

slavery and European diseases.   Forced to labor in Spanish mines under harsh conditions, the average worker died before age twenty-six.   In the century following Columbus' landing, millions of Native Americans died from a combination of European diseases, harsh treatment and murder.   The 80 million Native Americans alive in 1492 became only 10 million left alive a century later. (This is just referring to the regions of the Caribbean and South America combined, not including Central and North America.)

The 15th century European was coming from a land steeped in internal warfare between various ethnic tribes - the Goth, the Celtic, the Dane, the Viking, the Swede; the German, the Irish, the French, the Italian, the English, and the Dutch.   There was slavery, feudalism, public floggings, imprisonment, burnings at the stake and beheadings.   From this violent, oppressive society came the "white" man, bringing a war-like spirit across the seas, aiming to seize the lands of the "red" man, the "yellow" man, and the "black" man and claim it as his own.

Both Spain and Portugal were vying for riches overseas. The Portuguese had begun to explore the African continent for new sources of wealth and were also planning to colonize the Americas in the hopes of finding precious gold. Italian seaman Amerigo Vespucci, a countryman and contemporary of Christopher Columbus, had entered the race to claim the "New World" in the west, which King Ferdinand and Queen Isabella had set their sights on colonizing for Spain, notes Ivan Van Sertima.

Their orders went forth to the would-be colonizers: Take two thousand Spaniards with you! Plant a colony! Build a church! Build a city! Let's have forts, farms, and towns! Above all, pursue vigorously the search for gold! (They Came Before Columbus, Ivan Van Sertima, page 11)

Was this new world an island or a whole continent? Christopher Columbus asserted the idea that his "Espanola" (which is now present day Haiti and the Dominican Republic) was part of an entire continent, ripe for conquer by the Spanish.   But it is explorer Amerigo Vespucci to whom European history gives the greatest credit.   While Columbus is said to have "discovered" the new world for Europe, it is Amerigo Vespucci for whom the north and south continents have been named.

The Great Aztec Empire

The Spanish began their quest for riches. Starting with the Islands of Central America, they made every conceivable effort to enslave the native people and force them to mine for gold. Their tactics for "persuasion" amounted to cutting off the hands and feet of those who refused. Many escaped slavery and torture by fleeing to the hills, where they remained in hiding. Others suffered under the relentless cruelty of the Spaniards until they died. These attempts at enslavement drove the native population to near extinction.

Spain sought to expand its empire to the mainland. The rise of the Aztec empire changed the face of Mexico and set in motion a series of events, which eventually led to Mexico's fall under the Spanish. The Aztecs were a warrior nation who arrived in the valley of Mexico during the 13th century AD. According to tradition, they came from a place called Aztlan, believed to be in northern Mexico and from which the name Aztec is arrived, though they called themselves Mexica. The Mexica had been led to the valley of Mexico by a seer named Tenoch. He had been told in a dream that he and his people must continue their wandering until they came to a place that he would recognize when he saw an eagle fighting with a serpent.

When Tenoch and his people arrived in the valley of Mexico, they found it to be occupied by five other tribes. The five tribes got together and decided to offer the Aztecs an uninhabited island in the middle of the lake. The island was infested with poisonous snakes, but the Aztecs considered snakes to be a great delicacy. When Tenoch and his followers went out to the island, they saw a large eagle grappling with a serpent in its beak. This was the sign he had been seeking, and there the Aztecs settled. They built a new city, called Tenochtitlan after its founder. They grew to become a dominant tribe in the Valley of Mexico.

The Toltecs, another warlike people whose capital city of Tula was only 25 kilometers northwest of Tenochtitlan, practiced a religion, which demanded bloody human sacrifice. Using knives, they cut open their victims' chests and tore out their still-beating hearts as an offering to the sun god. They believed that by doing this they were feeding it with its favorite food, the human life force, which would ensure that the sun would keep on rising.

The Aztecs adopted these superstitious beliefs and over several generations, took them to absurd limits. Human sacrifice and the removal of human hearts became a focus of their religion and it is estimated that for the consecration of Tenochtitlan's main temple alone, some 20,000 victims were sacrificed. At least 50,000 perished each year. The Aztec empire grew, and the army's task was to keep the priest supplied with victims to sacrifice. The Aztecs were hated and feared by the people of Mexico, who anxiously awaited the return of the legendary god-king named Quetzalcoatl, who, according to prophecy was to return from across the sea to free his people and reclaim his kingdom. He would end Aztec rule and usher in a new era of peace, prosperity and justice.

It was during the reign of King Montezuma that the prophecy of the impending demise of the Aztec empire was revealed. In *Native American Prophecies*, author Scott Peterson explains:

Before the arrival of the Spanish in central Mexico, ominous signs appeared that many Native Americans interpreted as the foretelling of impending doom. The first of these was a comet, or "smoking star," that Aztec emperor Montezuma Xocoyotzin (Moctezuma II) observed from the roof of his royal palace in Tenochtitlan. It appeared in the east, as bright as the dawn, and then stretched across to the very center of the heavens.

Such 'tongues of flames" were always considered evil omens by the Aztecs, or Mexicas as they called themselves. But this one was particularly frightening to Montezuma in light of the startling warning by Nezahaulpilli, the wise astronomer-king of the allied city-state of Texcoco that a sign would soon appear in the heavens signaling the beginning of the end. (Native American Prophecies, by Scott Peterson, pages 29, 30)

Throughout his brief reign, the thirty-year-old Montezuma had been on guard for signs of Quetzalcoatl's return. Nezahaulpilli had warned him,

"In all our lands and provinces there will be great calamities and misfortunes, not a thing left standing. Death will dominate the land! All our dominions will be lost and all this will be done with the permission of the Lord of the Heights.... You will bear witness to these things since it will all happen in your time."

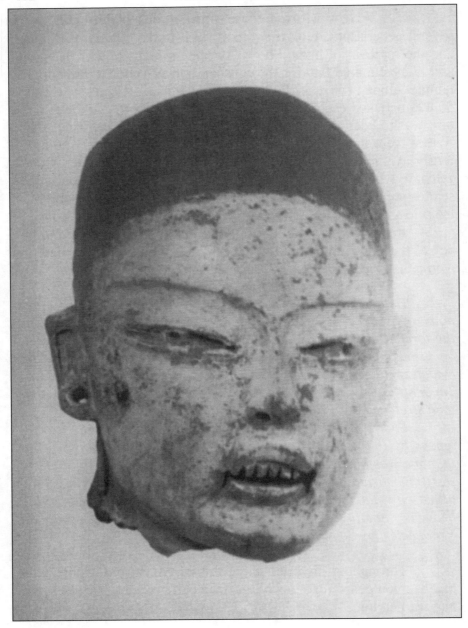

3D - Aztec Girl

This sculpture of a young Aztec girl comes from the Tlatilco, Upper Valley of Mexico. It is estimated to have been created between 1300–700 B.C. The features hint of a possible African presence in pre-Columbian Central America.

Montezuma, in vain hopes to forestall the end of the age, offered the hearts and blood of countless human beings to the Sun. However, other fateful signs appeared over the next ten years. The Temple of Huitzilopochtli spontaneously burst into flames that no amount of water could extinguish. Then, a second "smoking star" appeared in the western sky during the day, and split into three parts, provoking great alarm in the hearts of the people.

Cortez and the Aztecs

In the year Ce Acatl (1519 A.D.) it was reported that strange and powerful beings had arrived upon the eastern shore. The apprehensive ruler, fearful that this was the return of the god-king Quezalcoatl, dispatched emissaries with gifts. Unknown to him, this was not the enlightened Quetzalcoatl, but a cunning Spanish rebel by the name of Hernando Cortez. The gifts from Montezuma merely sparked his curiosity and fueled his greed.

On March 4, 1519, Hernando Cortez, with 11 ships, 600-foot soldiers, 16 horses and some artillery landed on the coast of Mexico and immediately took possession of the town of Tabasco. Before going inland, he founded a colony called Vera Cruz.

The Aztecs expected Quetzalcoatl to return "by way of the sea." The Spanish first settled in the La Venta region - the area of the Olmec Empire (where pyramids stood until 1959 when the Mexican Government destroyed them all to build an International Airport). Many native people believed that perhaps Cortez was Quetzalcoatl returned. Also, his arrival in 1519 was precisely four cycles after the appearance of Abubakari in 1311.

After promoting himself to the rank of Captain-General, Cortez set out for the Aztec capital of Tenochtitlan. Hungry for gold and sword in hand, he mounted a campaign that lasted little more than two years.

On August 8, 1519, four months after landing on the coast, Cortez leads a garrison of 150 men and sets off to confront an empire of millions. He has just 300 soldiers and 800 native allies. Although the Aztecs have an army of over 400,000 warriors, Cortez vows to conquer or die.

This single-minded obsession with conquest came from his boyhood dreams in the hills of Spain. He was born in rural Extre-

*madora in 1484. Growing up, young Cortez's imagination was
fired by exotic legends of the Crusades. He yearned to be a holy
warrior. Then in the space of one year, two momentous events
rocked Europe. The Moors who occupied Spain for over 700 years
were finally driven out.*

*Reunified under a powerful monarchy Spain was acquiring
an empire. Then, shortly after, Christopher Columbus brought
amazing news to the Spanish court: his discovery across the Atlantic, in 1492, of the New World. (Conquistadors Miniseries, The
Learning Channel, 2001)*

By August 13, 1521, Cortez had completely destroyed the
Aztec empire. And as much as the Spanish were responsible, the
defeat of the Aztec Empire would not have been possible without
the help of Natives who sided with the Spaniards and provided important information to Cortez, enabling him to achieve his goal.

*The reality is, Indians conquered the Aztecs, not Spaniards.
It was an Indian victory over Indians, but the Spaniards ended up
taking all the spoils. (Conquistadors Miniseries, The Learning
Channel, 2001)*

With the defeat of the Aztecs, Cortez ordered the wholesale
destruction of their capital, Tenochtitlan, removing all traces of the
Aztec's ancient, bloody rituals of human sacrifice. He reduced the
natives to serfdom and put them to the arduous task of reconstruc-
tion. In a short time the population was decimated through over-
work, disease and casual slaughter.

Under the threat of death, the people of Mexico were
forced to convert to Catholicism and were forbidden to write in
their own language. They were forced to learn Spanish, and all
written records of the old days prior to their conquest were destroyed. During the Spanish occupation, both Church and state
actively discouraged scholars from publishing anything that might
indicate that Mexico prior to the invasion of Cortez had any sort of
civilization or history to speak of.

Upon his return to Spain, Cortez was pardoned by the King
for disobeying his original orders to not try and attempt to conquer
the natives. Perhaps it was the gold sent home, by the tons, that
'softened' the kings heart. The king made Cortez the Marquee of

the Valley of Mexico, disregarding all the rights to the land that the native people had ruled for so long. This would give him 1/12 of all the treasures taken from the fallen Aztec Empire, making him one of the richest men in Europe during that period. This set in motion an expansion policy that changed the course of American history forever. The mercenaries that came after Cortez followed in his brutal and relentless footsteps.

The Inca

Although most historians have long used the name Inca to indicate all inhabitants living within the area of the Inca Empire, the name Inca actually comes from the royal family name of those people who first ruled. The Inca were a small tribe among many tribes in Peru who were constantly at war with each other.

The rise of the Inca Empire began in 1438 with the Sapa Inca, or emperor, Pachacuti. During his reign and the reign of his son, Topa Inca, they would create one of the largest empires ever known on earth. Pachacuti is given credit for politically unifying the various tribes that existed during that time. At its height, the empire would encompass all of the lands of modern day Ecuador, Columbia, Peru, Bolivia, Chile and northern Argentina – a coastal distance stretching over 2,500 miles along the Andean Mountains. The Inca would call their empire Tahuantinsuyu, meaning, "Land of the Four Quarters."

The conquering of the other tribes by the Inca started from Cuzco, which was their capital. Cuzco became the center of Incan political life and remained the wealthiest city of the empire. It was during the reign of emperor Pachacuti that the majority of the awe-inspiring temples and stone monuments we still see today were built. From Cuzco, Pachacuti first conquered the peoples of the Lupaca and Colla, who lived in the area around Lake Titicaca. That was followed by the defeat of the Chanca tribe who lived west of Cuzco. Eventually, the majority of the tribes of the northern regions were brought under Incan rule.

As each tribe was conquered, the Inca integrated the local leaders into the fold of the new government. Each Inca citizen labored on assignment by the government and was paid in the form of food and clothing. Although gold and silver were abundant throughout the empire, it was not used as currency.

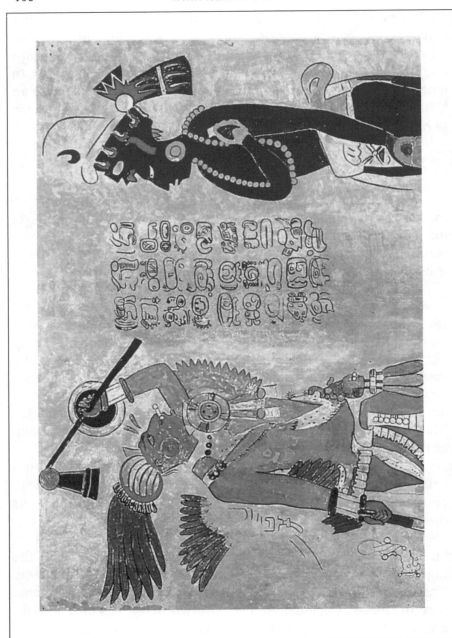

3E – Mayan Marriage Ceremony
*In this illustration we see two different looking members of the Maya, who are
the predecessors of the Inca, in a marriage ceremony. (America 1492, page 68)*

With such a vast empire that integrated so many different tribes, a universal language had to be created in order to effectively govern the empire. This language was called Quechua (pronounced kech-wun.) Today, there are a few among the descendents of the Inca who still speak this language fluently.

The majority of the Inca Empire lay in the Andes Mountains. Also known as the Andean Cordillera, it is second in rank to the Himalayas in terms of altitude. Today's mountaineers are baffled at how the average Incan was able to live a full life at such high altitudes (15,000 feet.) The cold weather and lack of oxygen at those extreme heights is too much for most people to deal with without the help of the most advanced mountaineering gear.

To navigate through the mountains, the Inca built a 14,000 mile-long, crisscrossing road system. One road they built would almost run the entire Pacific Coast of South America. The wheel did not exist in Inca society, so all traveling was done on foot or on the backs of Alpaca (llamas.)

It was along these roads that the chasqui would run. The chasqui were messengers who would literally run up and down along the mountain roads relaying messages from one part of the empire to the other. The chasqui were trained from a young age to perfectly memorize each message. Each one would memorize the message being sent and run about a kilometer to another chasqui waited. The message would be passed on, from chasqui to chasqui, until it reached its final destination.

The great empire that ruled over South America was short-lived, however, ending less than a century later in 1532. Once again, the arrival of the Spanish Conquistadors proved to be an unstoppable force for the Native Americans. Even with a military numbering in the millions, the Inca Empire fell to another group of people who were determined to conquer the land and its inhabitants by any means necessary. The Spanish Conquistadors understood the principle of divide and conquer, and used it to their advantage. Little did the Inca know that this, plus fire arms and disease, would be their downfall.

Pizarro and the Golden Kingdom of Peru

In 1527, off the Pacific coast of South Americas, a Spanish ship intercepts a native raft laden with fine textiles, silver and gold. This chance encounter proves the leader of the expedition, Francisco Pizarro, right and confirms rumors of a rich empire somewhere in the unexplored heart of South America - an empire the Spaniards believe must contain a mythical city of gold, an El Dorado. (Conquistadors Miniseries, The Learning Channel, 2001)

The ruler of the Inca Empire in 1532 was named Atahualpa. Upon hearing the news that a peculiar group of travelers had arrived in the land, a meeting was arranged. Although weary, Atahualpa thought it was to be a peaceful meeting with the Conquistadors. However, when the Conquistadors saw the emperor and his subjects arrive unprepared for any real military confrontation, they seized the moment.

Pizarro and his men managed to take Atahualpa hostage. They planned to ransom the emperor for all the gold and silver they could get. Atahualpa's men, far from being docile, managed to corner Pizarro and his troops into a section of the kingdom. But eventually, in order to gain his freedom, Atahualpa was left with no choice but to comply with Pizarro's demands:

Atahualpa promises to fill a room 8 feet high, 17 feet wide and 22 feet long with gold; and two other rooms with silver, in exchange for his freedom. (Conquistadors Miniseries, The Learning Channel, 2001)

Atahualpa never entertained the false hope that this would somehow result in the Spanish departing. He had hoped that this would buy him more time. The gold and silver had to be brought in from other cities of the empire. It was going to take a few weeks and in the meantime his army could also regroup and assemble more soldiers.

Also, this allowed Atahualpa to send word to have certain political adversaries executed, like his brother Quazcar, who he feared might attempt to take advantage of the situation and seize the throne. Over 50 million in gold, by today's standards, would eventually be gathered from all over the empire. Also, more than 80,000 Inca soldiers would amass outside of where the Conquistadors held their emperor hostage.

Pizarro found himself in a tight spot. Lucky for him, in April of 1533, a fellow Spanish Conquistador by the name of

Diego de Almagro, arrived with a reinforcement of 150 men. Although partners, greed was the guiding principle for all these explorers, and Pizarro was equally unhappy about his "friend's" arrival as he would then expect a cut of the gold.

Although Pizarro recognized that having Atahualpa as a hostage was the only thing that kept the Inca army at bay, at the same time he felt that keeping him alive was only allowing the situation to further sway in the emperor's favor.

It became plain that without Atahualpa, he could even more easily manipulate an unstable situation within the empire. He could play off, internally, the factions within the Inca themselves without Atahualpa around. So he became surplus to immediate requirements - and they decided to kill him. (Conquistadors Miniseries, The Learning Channel, 2001)

Pizarro and his men made it out alive and eventually made it to the Inca capital of Cuzco. Along the way they were quite astonished to find out that they had supporters. These tribes had been previously conquered by the Inca and forced to join the empire.

Had the Inca not mistreated their fellow native brothers, the empire would have been more united against the Spanish. This divine principle of unity exists among all nations and cultures.

It is said there is only one Great Spirit, our maker, and that we, as His children, should be one happy family. But instead of equality, we practiced cast systems and class struggles, glaring at each other in greed. (The Hopi Survival Kit, by Thomas E. Mails, p. 321)

Surely all believers are brothers. So, make peace between brothers, and fear Allah so mercy may be shown to you. (Quran, 49:11)

When people fight among themselves, they become vulnerable to foreign invasion and domination. The fact is that the Spanish were able to take advantage of the internal conflict that already existed within the Inca Empire. This conflict enabled them to conquer the Inca and gain complete control. Just eight years after the Spanish invasion, the Inca Empire was no more.

Although the military technology of the Spaniards was a great factor contributing to the downfall of the Inca Empire, more devastating than that were the diseases that the Conquistadors brought along with them from Europe. The smallpox virus swept through Peru and up into the mountains of the Andes where the Inca lost two-thirds of their population.

During this time the Spaniards sent large amounts of gold and silver back to Spain – some to the king, some to the Pope. This helped the Conquistadors insure positions of influence for the future and gave them the approval they needed to continue with their current mission to conquer in the New World.

The Q'ero Shamans' Prophecies

Today, the descendents of the Incas are the Q'ero, who lived relatively unknown to the outside world until 1949. This small tribe, with less than a thousand members, lived in the highest regions of the Andes Mountains. They fled up into the mountains long ago to escape the Conquistadors and remained there, isolated from the modern world, up to the middle of the 20th century.

In 1949, an earthquake struck near Cuzco. As a result, an ancient Incan temple of gold was discovered buried underneath a monastery in the area. According to the Q'ero shamans, this was a sign of the fulfillment of the Mosoq, or "the time to come."

For the prophecies of Mosoq, a number of signs would occur and when they did the Q'ero were to go out and share their ancient knowledge with the world. During the last century the signs of the time of Mosoq were fulfilled. Their prophecies foretold of the lakes in the mountains where they lived going dry. They were told of the vanishing of the condor, a vulture with a white downy neck (The condor in that region is on the verge of extinction.) And they were told of the rediscovery of the Golden Temple.

According to the prophecies, after these events took place it would then be time for the great gathering or "mastay" to occur where the peoples from all over the earth would really come together to bring about a massive spiritual awakening. They call this great change, pachacuti (like the name of the Inca king.) Pachacuti can be translated as "transformer of the earth." When the next pachacuti comes, there would be great suffering and chaos in the world. Following the collapse of the great nations, the way of the "earth people" would return and a new age of spiritual enlightenment would begin.

As understood by some, Pachacuti is the perfect example of spiritual enlightenment and exaltation. He is a specific individual who represents mankind's greatest spiritual potential. He is reminiscent of the prophets of other religions who also act as spiritual guides and role models for people to follow. So, that person who is pachacuti would be that individual who best embodies the meaning of that word *pacha* meaning "earth" or "time" and *cuti* meaning "to set things right." Many believe that when Pachacuti returns he will be a leader, like the king of old, who will take back the land from the non-natives and restore the native people to their former glory. According to others, the return of Pachacuti is only symbolic of a general transformation that will take place in the minds and hearts of people, resulting in a new era of peace and prosperity.

The purpose of this "Second Coming" is to create a change in the minds and hearts of their people. In this sense it is possible that both literal and symbolic interpretations of the return of Pachacuti are applicable.

To this day the Q'ero continue to spread the message contained in their prophecies, hopeful of the day when the Eagle of the North and the Condor of the South will soar through the skies, side by side, once again. This will mean that the earth and its inhabitants are physically and spiritually healing.

The Warning of the Hopi

It was indicated in the prophecies of the Hopi's stone tablets that the first brothers and sisters to return to them would come as turtles across the land. Lee Brown relays this prophecy:

We were also given a sacred handshake to show when we came back together as brothers and sisters that we still remembered our sacred teachings... So when the time came close the Hopis gathered at a special village to welcome the turtles that would come across the land. and they got up in the morning and looked out at the sunrise. When they looked out, they could see the Spanish Conquistadors coming, covered in armor, like turtles across

3F – The Armor of the Conquistadors
The style of armor worn by the Spanish when they arrived in the Americas re-sembled a turtle in its shell. This was a sign of the fulfillment of one of the prophecies of the Hopi of Arizona.

the land. They went out to greet them, expecting that sacred hand-shake, but a Spanish man dropped a trinket into the Hopi's hand. (Lee Brown, Continental Indigenous Council, 1986)

This meant that the Spaniards had only come with greed and deception, which brought about the Native American phrase, "white eyes speak with forked tongue." According to the prophecy, this act was a sign there would be great violence and suffering for the Native people in the future.

"And so word spread throughout North America that there was going to be a hard time, that maybe some of the brothers and sisters had forgotten the sacredness of all things and all the human beings were going to suffer for this on the earth. So tribes began to send people to the mounds to have visions to try to figure out how they could survive. At that time there were 100,000 cities in the Mississippi Valley alone, called the mound civilization: cities built on great mounds. Those mounds are still there. If you ever go out to Ohio or the Mississippi Valley, they're tourist attractions now." (Lee Brown, Continental Indigenous Council, 1986)

One can't help but wonder what kind of civilizations were part of these one hundred thousand cities. According to Western historians, North America was comprised of a bunch of disjointed Indian tribes with no real culture and no real organized government. But according to Lee Brown, these were organized governments that communicated with each other. They sent out ambassadors to different Native American nations across North America to warn them that the white men had came and difficult times were ahead. We know that in Mexico city the whites destroyed the great temples of the Aztecs and built churches and forts for the Spanish. It seems like the only thing that the invaders left in America were the great mounds in Ohio and the Mississippi Valley.

Chapter Four
The Invasion of North America

4A – Looking Through the Kiva Wall (1986)
By Melody Lightfeather
"I had a vision of the ancestors in the Kiva walking toward the light singing prayers from long, long ago. The ancient mud bricks of the Kiva walls became as clear and transparent as the spirits that once sang there and told stories of histories passed on from one generation to the next of the Pueblo People."

Chapter Four
The Invasion of North America

"Time passed on, people passed on and prophecies of things to come were passed from mouth to mouth. The stone tablets and the rock writing of the road plan were often reviewed by the elders. Fearfully, they waited as they retold the prophecy that one day another race of people would appear in our midst and would claim our land as his own.

We now call those people Bahanna. He would try to change our patterns of life. He would have a sweet tongue, fork tongue, like a snake, and many good things by which we would be tempted. He would use force in an attempt to trap us into using weapons, but we must not fall for this trick. For then we would be conquered and brought to our knees, from which we might not be able to rise. Nor must we ever raise our hand against any nation." (Dan Katchongva, Hopi Traditional Village Leader, from his book "Hopi, A Message For All People," reprinted in "Native American Prophesies" by Scott Peterson, page 260, 261.)

African Imports

As African nations engaged in wars over control of the empire, Europeans found opportunities for a lucrative business in the sale of human flesh. At first they purchased prisoners of war from victorious African chiefs. Then they began to hire kidnappers to capture their human cargo, a business that evolved into a major international enterprise. Companies were formed to finance the building of ships, and the hiring of staff to capture, secure and transport Africans abroad. In his book *Introduction to African Civilizations*, author John G. Jackson explains:

Soon after the onslaught on the trading centers of the East African coast; European invaders inaugurated a systematic traffic in slaves in West Africa. A few Africans were reduced to slavery and transported to Europe early in the fifteenth century; but the African slave trade did not begin in earnest until about a century later.

> *This evil enterprise was the outcome of the Spanish con-*
> *quest of Mexico and Peru. The natives of Peru and Mexico were*
> *reduced to slave status and forced to work in mines. Their death*
> *rate was so high that their European masters were impelled to look*
> *elsewhere for slave labor, but the question was, where?*
>
> *Bartolome de las Casas, Bishop of Chiapa in 1517 came to*
> *their rescue by proposing that each Spanish gentleman be permit-*
> *ted to import twelve African slaves. This advice was adopted by*
> *the king of Spain, who issued a patent to one of his friends giving*
> *him the authority to import four thousand black slaves annually to*
> *Cuba, Hispanionla, Jamaica, and Puerto Rico. This patent was*
> *sold soon after to Genoese merchants, who allotted a share of the*
> *business to the Portuguese; and in a short while nearly all of the*
> *nations of Europe were participants in the traffic. (Introduction to*
> *African Civilization, by John G. Jackson, Citadel Press, pages*
> *304-305)*

European immigrants were thirsty for the wealth and power that land ownership would bring. The Native American population was quickly being depleted due to disease and warfare and exploitation. Thus, Europe looked to Africa as a viable source for more labor. In his book *Black Indians*, William Loren Katz observes;

> *Africans arrived on these shores with valuable assets for*
> *both Europeans and Native Americans. They were used to agricul-*
> *tural labor and working in field gangs, something unfamiliar to*
> *most Indians. As experts in tropical agriculture, they had a lot to*
> *teach both white and red people. Further, Africans had a virtual*
> *immunity to European diseases such as smallpox, which wiped out*
> *Native Americans.*
>
> *For Europeans seeking a source of labor that could not es-*
> *cape, Africans were ideal because they were three thousand miles*
> *from home. They could not flee to loved ones, as Indians could.*
> *The African man and woman who fled could always be identified*
> *by skin color, and black became the badge of bondage. (Black In-*
> *dians, by William Katz, page 28)*

In 1510 King Ferdinand lifted all restrictions on sending Africans to the Americas. In 1511 Governor Ovando forgot his opposition to importing Africans as slaves. "One black can do the work of four Indians," he marveled.

The European's desire to "create man in his own image" was also transported to the African continent, where African men, women and children were captured, chained, stripped naked, and packed into the bottoms of specially designed ships to be transported to the Americas.

National identities were removed and centuries of cultural traditions were erased as white slave traders changed the names of their captives to European names and outlawed the speaking of African languages.

Africans gradually took the place of Native Americans as the labor force in the New World. In 1527 there were 10,000 Africans enslaved in the Americas. By the end of the century, the figure had risen to 90,000.

Native Americans would rediscover the common bond with their African brethren. Besides their struggle against a common foe, which became the first basis for a renewed alliance, the two groups recognized their shared cultural traditions, many dating back thousands of years.

William Katz notes some of the cultural similarities:

Family was of basic importance to both, with children and the elderly treasured. Religion was a daily part of cultural life, not merely practiced on Sundays. Both Africans and Native Americans found they shared a belief in economic cooperation rather than competition and rivalry. Each race was proud, but neither was weighed down by prejudice. Skill, friendship, and trust, not skin color or race were important. Since Indians willingly adopted people into their villages, Africans found they were welcome. (Black Indians, by William Katz, page 28)

Both Native Americans and Africans expressed a profound respect for their ancestors. In spiritual ceremonies, both expressed their prayers through song and sometimes through dance. Both respected traits such as bravery in battle to defend one's family.

Africans studied their white captors and quickly learned their language and their weaknesses. Native Americans taught the Africans how to survive and live off of the land. They truly embraced them as brothers.

4B – Tlingit Warrior Dress

The drawing was done by artist Tomas de Suria who journeyed with a Spanish expedition to the Pacific Northwest in 1791. It shows a warrior of the Tlingit tribe dressed in body armor made from cedar slats. (500 Nations: An Illustrated History of North American Indians)

4C – Art from Benin

This is a photo of a wood carving. The people of Benin are known for their master sculptures. Notice the similarity of the ensemble worn by the figure in the sculpture with that of the Tlingit warrior.

Sometimes Africans escaped with muskets, machetes, and valuable gunpowder and teamed up with Native Americans to fight the white slave holders. In spite of some white historians' attempts to paint both the African and Native American as docile non-resisters to European domination, there were quite a few violent uprisings and wars of resistance in which the Africans and the Native Americans were the victors.

Victorious Rebellion In Hispaniola

On Christmas Day in the year 1522, African and Native American slaves on a plantation owned by Diego Columbus (a son of Christopher Columbus) rose up and in battle killed their masters. Nearby Native Americans joined the rebels, and the sprawling sugar plantations of Hispaniola were shaken by the first recorded wide spread rebellion. The freedom fighters had purposely waited until Christmas Day, when the planters and their families would be too bloated with food and liquor to offer much resistance. Three days later, Spanish troops caught up with the rebels and opened fire, but the fugitives escaped into the woods. Europeans, unfamiliar with the terrain, were unwilling to pursue them.

Recognizing that the powerful alliance between Native Americans and Africans could dismantle their slave system, Europeans established a policy of "divide and conquer." Governor Diego Columbus hired Native Americans for the task of tracking fugitive slaves. Africans realized that their success depended upon maintaining a close friendship with the Native Americans. Friends do not hunt friends.

It was in Mexico that Europeans made their strongest effort to keep Africans apart from Native Americans. One Spanish law prohibited Africans and Native Americans from intermarrying. Another Royal Order forbade the "trade, commerce or communication" between the two peoples. However, in spite of the laws, the spirit of rebellion spread like wildfire across Columbia, Panama, Cuba, Puerto Rico, and Mexico. In 1537, a major rebellion terrified officials and brought a temporary halt to the importation of Africans. Viceroy Antonio de Mendoza reported that Africans "had chosen a King and had agreed to kill all the Spaniards." The Native Americans had also joined them.

Outlaw communities, made up of former slaves, began to grow. These Maroon colonies, as they were called, were sometimes begun by a single African or Native American. Others were the result of several slaves fleeing together. They were a great testimony to the resilience of the African and Native peoples. William Katz observes:

These maroon colonies, as they were called, were considered a knife poised at the throat of the slave system...Men and women who lived in them saw their settlements as the fulfillment of an American dream--a sheltered home in freedom. They were a place for families to educate their young, develop their agriculture and trade, practice religion, justice, and government. As outlaw communities, they operated in remote, difficult-to-find and hard-to-defeat locations. Maroons considered each day of survival a small miracle, and were thankful for each new dawn as free men and women.

The planning of defense and agriculture in most Black Indian settlements drew largely on African models and experience. However, no type of influence was discarded, and these colonies grasped aspects of Indian, African and even slave life considered vital for survival. The African influence was strongest in tropical maroon locations, and there African methods of planting, irrigation, and harvesting held sway under African- type governments ... A leading defense technique--planting sharp sticks in a pit and covering it with thick grass--was African. It not only inflicted terrible damage, but terrified any invading army with the thought that sudden, painful death could occur at any moment ...

Men and women, who were once starved and beaten by masters, grew strong and vigorous in these hidden communities. (Black Indians, by William Katz, pages 37, 39 & 40)

Maroon settlements were an effort to recreate a free society by people who had once lived free. Africans, so far from home, made a special effort to preserve their ancestral ways and pass them on to their children. Women were often in short supply, so many maroon raids sought to bring back African or Native American wives. Women played a crucial role in maroon life and were considered for leadership. Leading a maroon colony took a rare combination of wisdom, toughness and skill. For some colonies, trade became a vital part of economic life, and men and women ventured out to exchange their farm produce for guns and ammunition. Some became prosperous communities, rivaling those of the neighboring Europeans.

The history of the Saramaka people of Surinam, South America, began as a maroon community. In 1685, African and Native Americans escaped and banded together to form a society. They repelled attacks from Dutch armed forces for eight generations. The European abandoned their wars in 1761. Today, the Saramaka community is twenty thousand strong.

The Seminole Nation

The State of Florida became the home of one of the greatest "Black Indian" communities. Florida's thickets and marshes were ideal hiding places for escaped slaves. Dense jungles, high grasses, deadly reptiles and tropical diseases served as deterrents for European would-be slave catchers.

During the time African settlers arrived in Florida, refugees from the Creek Nation also settled there. They called themselves "Seminoles" meaning "runaways" and they were comprised of a variety of Native American ethnic groups -- Yuchi, Hitchiti and Alabama. The Seminole people readily accepted the Africans as part of their group. They forged a strong alliance.

The Seminole Nation created a strong army to repel Georgia slaveholders who invaded Florida in search of runaways. Red and black Seminoles fought for their right to live in peace in Florida. Under General Andrew Jackson, U.S. troops were dispatched to Florida to wage an armed struggle against the Seminoles, with the objective being to kill the natives and force the blacks back into slavery. For years, the U.S. government waged what became known as "the Seminole Wars."

The easy mixture of races in the Seminole nation infuriated U.S. officials. To disrupt their racial alliance, U.S. officials promoted slavery among the Seminoles, hoping that these Native Americans would involve themselves in the slave trade, as had other Native American nations. William Katz states:

Wealthy Creeks, who owed their riches to slave labor, were sent to persuade Seminole chiefs to become slave masters. Whites and Creek Indians were encouraged to raid Seminole villages for slaves. Free Seminole men, women and children were carried off and sold in southern slave markets... Seminole law making it impossible to sell a slave remained firmly in place. Seminole chiefs still married black women and had black military and diplomatic advisors. But U.S. policy had begun to erode a strong friendship and trust and to bend equality. In the face of their changing relations some Black Seminoles left to form their own settlements, and in 1822 the U.S. Secretary of State reported that in Florida there were "five or six hundred maroon Negroes wild in the woods." (Black Indians, by William Katz, pages 56 & 57)

These armed Black Seminoles especially enraged U.S. slaveholders. They owned horses, cattle, hogs, chickens and tended their own gardens. These were not slaves -- they were people who kept their African names, dressed in fine Seminole clothing and turbans, adopted Seminole stomp dances and sang Seminole and African songs. Slave masters saw them as a grave threat.

The United States continued to send soldiers to battle the Seminoles. The government even coerced Seminole chiefs to sign treaties agreeing to leave Florida for reservations in Arkansas and Oklahoma, in the hopes that the Black Seminoles would be forced back into bondage, a threat which the Seminoles actively resisted. According to William Katz:

In December 1835, King Philip led black and red Seminoles in a raid on a U.S. plantation. Chief Osceola led a band that murdered a government agent. Another Seminole column wiped out U.S. Major Francis Dade's entire relief force in the famous Dade Massacre. Florida was again in flames. Before this conflict was over, the U.S. had fought its most costly Indian war, spending over $40 million and losing one thousand five hundred soldiers and many civilians. They battled an enemy one U.S. officer called "bold, active and armed" and Black Seminoles "More desperate than Indians..."

Under their own leaders, Negro Abraham and John Horse (or Cohia), and in concert with Chief Osceola and Wild Cat, Black Seminoles pursued their own strategy: Wear down U.S. military might until compromise was possible. (Black Indians, by William Katz, pages 60-61)

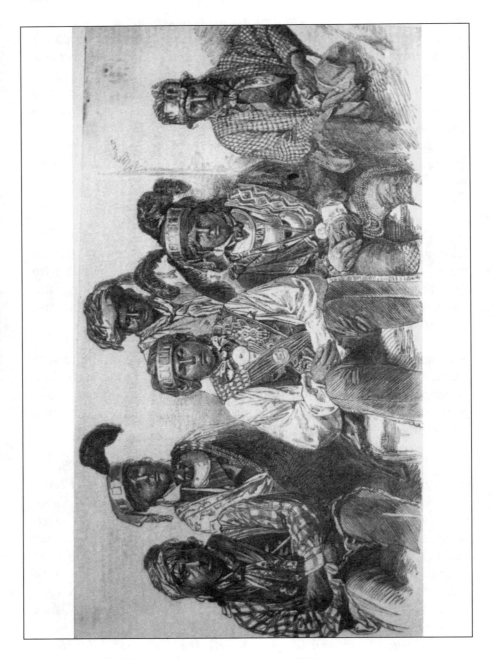

4D – Seminole Delegation to Washington D.C.
This delegation that went to the capitol in 1825 represents the diversity of the Seminole tribe. At top center is a man named "Negro Abraham" who acted as an interpreter for the delegation.

In the final months of his Florida effort, General Jessup resorted to hostage seizures. In the fall of 1837, he had captured King Philip and his Black Seminole son, John Philip. This brought forth King Philip's key son, Wild Cat, to negotiate for his father and brother's release. Wild Cat, and his friend John Horse along with twenty other Seminoles were captured and imprisoned in Arkansas, but later broke out and escaped to the woods.

Dozens hid in the tall grass and trees and there they waged guerilla warfare against Colonel Zachary Taylor, whose forces included 70 Delaware Indians, 180 Tennessee volunteer sharpshooters and 800 U.S. soldiers. In the ensuing battle, 28 U.S. soldiers were killed, and 112 wounded. Only ten Seminoles died in battle. The Seminoles eventually retreated, realizing they were no match for hundreds of soldiers. Still, the strongest country in the new World had received a stunning defeat at the hands of a small band of "Black Indian" guerilla fighters.

Realizing the precariousness of their freedom in the United States, some Seminoles escaped to Islands in the Caribbean, where slavery had been abolished since 1834. Others remained in Florida and today some of their offspring claim that the peninsula belongs to them, the descendants of the inhabitants who never surrendered.

Ben Franklin Learns From The Iroquois Confederacy

As the black and red man banded together in the Seminole wars, other wars were being fought across the United States over control of land and culture. This was a period when the nations of Europe were battling for control of territories in the New World. England and France were bitter rivals, and both sought to negotiate with the Native Americans to gain greater advantage. In his book, *Native American Prophecies*, author Scott Peterson explains:

On his second assignment as a diplomat, Benjamin Franklin was sent to Albany, in the Province of New York by King George II of Great Britain. There, along with several other royal commissioners, Franklin was to reaffirm the alliance with the Indians of the Iroquois Confederacy -- or League of Six Nations -- in order to undermine the influence of Britain's archrival France in North America. But a number of other important developments also occurred at the Albany conference. Not the least of these was how it became evident that Franklin's theories of government had been deeply influenced by an Indian who may have been dead for some three hundred years.

The year was 1754. Franklin was forty-eight years old...Surrounding him and other royal commissioners at the conference were representatives of most of the other colonies as well as some 150 Indian men, women, and children. The leader of the Indian delegation was the Iroquois sachem, or chief, Hendrick Peters. Hendrick at the time was about seventy years old. He was a majestic figure, a born leader, with a prominent tomahawk scar running across his left cheek...The conference got underway according to strict and traditional Iroquois diplomatic protocol. (Native American Prophesies, by Scott Peterson, page 68.)

Scott Peterson noted that the Iroquois Confederacy, founded around the early 1400s, bounded together the nations of the Mohawk, Onondaga, Seneca, Oneida, Cayuga and Tuscarora. The Confederacy provided a blueprint for the structure of what was to become the United States of America. It was created by a man known in Native American history as perhaps the greatest prophet ever born in the Americas. His name was Deganawidah.

Deganawidah, The Peacemaker

The story of Deganawidah has been passed down through countless generations before finally being recorded on paper. This great man, known as the Peacemaker, is said to have been born during a time of savage wars and blood feuds among the people near present day Kingston in the Canadian province of Ontario. Amidst the beautiful, lush green landscape, a cycle of violence, pain and death enveloped the people. Every family was involved in a battle of hatred and vengeance. Deganawidah's mother and grandmother lived alone, poor and despised, on the outskirts of the Huron village. All of their relatives had been killed off in the ongoing warfare.

The birth of Deganawidah is the story of a miracle. Deganawidah's mother was a virgin, yet, she became pregnant. Deganawidah's grandmother was alarmed that her daughter was about to give birth and had not married. She scolded her daughter for bringing scandal upon their family.

Then, one night, the grandmother had a prophetic dream, in which a divine messenger told her that she had committed a great wrong toward her daughter for not believing her daughter was truthful about being a virgin. In the dream, she was told that her daughter was to bear a male child whom they must name Deganawidah, meaning "he who thinks." He would grow up to live among foreigners and raise up a great Tree of Peace. In the dream, she was also warned that the child would someday be the cause of Huron's demise.

It is said that, upon awakening, Deganawidah's grandmother told her pregnant daughter about the dream, and at first the two women sadly concluded that since the child was destined to destroy the Huron nation, he should be put to death in infancy. After he was born, the mother and grandmother took the infant out to the frozen stream, cut a hole in the ice and threw him in the frigid waters.

As the story goes, they sadly returned to their lodge. When they awoke the next morning, there was Deganawidah, lying between them, unharmed and fast asleep. Twice they tried to drown him in the freezing waters and twice he turned up the next morning, safely asleep inside the house. Finally they decided that it was the Will of the Master that the boy should live.

Deganawidah grew up an outcast among the Hurons. As other teenage boys honed their fighting skills, he showed no interest in warfare. Instead, he was a thinker.

When he came of age, Deganawidah left the land of the Huron and journeyed south through the Adirondack Mountains, where he reached the land of the Mohawks. It was there that he met one of the last surviving Mohawks, Hiawatha.

At this point, Deganawidah began his legendary career as the Peacemaker. The Mohawks had been in a long, brutal war with their neighbors, the Onandagas. Hiawatha's wife and seven daughters had recently been murdered by the Onandaga war chief Ododarhoh, and Hiawatha was filled with hatred. But when Hiawatha encountered Deganawidah, he was touched by the purity in Deganawidah's face. They engaged in conversation, and Deganawidah shared his vision of peace and a new philosophy of living. That philosophy is known as new Gayaneshagowa, or the Great Law of Equity and Righteousness.

Intelligent and handsome young man that he was, Deganawidah suffered a major impediment in a culture that valued elo-
quent speech. He stuttered. However, in spite of this flaw, he had
a powerful presence, and inspired Hiawatha to join him. Scott Peterson states:

*Upon hearing Deganawidah's ideas, Hiawatha underwent
a truly tremendous personal transformation. His overwhelming
sorrow and hate were literally swept away by the prophet's bold
vision of peace. By burying the hatchet and forming a federal union of nations, Deganawidah insisted through his coarse-tongued
stutter, they could bring an end to war and suffering.*

*Then and there, the story goes, Hiawatha made the deci-
sion to follow Deganawidah and started calling him the Peacemaker. If Deganawidah had enlisted anyone else for such an important role, his plan might never have worked. But Hiawatha was
a handsome man who possessed that invaluable trait known as
charisma. While the prophet at times had a hard time communicating at all, Hiawatha was capable of eloquence, wit, and persuasion. Hiawatha became Deganawidah's partner and voice...*

*Through Hiawatha, Deganawidah told the Mohawks that
"he had been sent by the Master of Life from whom we all descended to establish the Great Peace...He spoke about establishing
a union of all nations. He told them that all the chiefs must be virtuous men and must be very patient...*

*Over a five year period, due in large part to everyone's
weariness of war, the Mohawk, Oneida, Cayuga and Seneca nations were won over by Deganawidah's vision of a Great Com-
monwealth. (Native American Prophesies, Scott Peterson, Pages
74, 75 & 76.)*

Even Odoðarhoh, the brutal war chief of the Onondaga,
was converted by Deganwidah. Ododarhoh was said to be a mad-
man. As the story goes, Deganawidah, followed by a crowd of
people including members of the Council of Nations, the Onondaga people and their chiefs, walked to the door of Ododarhoh's
lodge and performed a great miracle of healing.

When Onandaga, face full of anger, emerged, Deganawidah
begin to sing the Song of Peace. When he finished the song,
Onandaga was transformed. Deganawidah, once a stuttering out-

cast, had founded the new Iroquois nation. He had proven to be a political genius, the creator of the League of Five Nations (Tuscarora became the 6th member in 1724). And just as today people of the fifty states are citizens of the federal republic of the United States of America, the Seneca, Mohawk, Onondaga, Oneida and Cayuga were welded into citizens of the League in the same way.

The Five United Nations

In the government Deganawidah created, each of the five nations debated proposals first at the local level. Once the village chief had ascertained the views of the majority of men and women, the proposal would be debated by all the chiefs.

Once a consensus was reached at this level, (what might be called the "state" level), the question was put before the federal level or the Grand Council of the League. Matters of overriding foreign policy, including declarations of war, were reserved exclusively for the federal Grand Council. Deganawidah was centuries ahead of his time, giving women the right to vote and participate in the council meetings.

In his remarkable achievement, Deganawidah never lost sight of his reverence for the earth. He instructed federal chiefs that whenever they assembled for the purpose of holding a council, they shall "...make an address and return thanks to the earth where men dwell, to the streams of water, the pools, the springs, and the lakes, to the maize and the fruits, to the animals that serve as food and give their pelts for clothing, to the great winds and the lesser winds, to the thunders, to the Sun, the mighty warrior, to the Moon, to the messengers of the Creator who reveal His wishes, to the Great Creator who dwells in the heavens above, who gives all things useful to man, and who is the source and the ruler of health and life."

Although there were struggles between the individual nations, Deganawidah's dream of peace was maintained for generations among the Five Nations. As he had envisioned, the Iroquois found great strength and prosperity in their union.

It is unknown how much Benjamin Franklin may have been influenced by the story of Deganawidah. Although he did not mention the Peacemaker in any of his writings, it was obvious that he had great respect for Iroquois ideas. On June 28, 1754, months after his conference at Albany with the Iroquois Nation, Ben Franklin presented his *Short Hints Toward a Scheme for a General Union of the British Colonies on the Continent.* It was nearly a duplicate of the federal form of government that had been used by the Iroquois for perhaps three hundred and fifty years. Ben Franklin biographer Carl Van Doren noted that Franklin, "admired the Iroquois confederation and plainly had it in mind in his earliest discussion of the need of union among the colonies."

At that time, the British colonies were disunited factions, with Connecticut squabbling with Pennsylvania over boundaries and New York struggling to maintain dominance. But the aim of the British crown had been to negotiate an agreement with the Iroquois nation to prevent France from gaining a political advantage. However, the Iroquois were angry at the way the British had treated them, and there was a strong pro-French element among the League of Six Nations.

Ben Franklin's first proposal for a Plan of Union was intended as a structure under which the colonies could form a single North American government, under British authority, which would enable them to negotiate with the Native American nation as a unified body. It was by no means an early Declaration of Independence. In fact, the proposal was ignored by New York, rejected by Massachusetts, and voted down by the Pennsylvania Assembly.

Still, the Iroquois and other Native American nations had a tremendous impact on European philosophy. Stories of their societal structure traveled across the water to England and France. In 1690, English philosopher John Locke published his *Two Treaties on Civil Government*, a book that radically attacked the divine right of kings and declared that all men are equal.

In 1753, French philosopher Jean-Jacques Rousseau published his *Discourse on the Inequalities of Men*, in which he asserted that only men who have retained their primitive simplicity have stayed virtuous and strong. Scott Peterson observes:

> *Where had the Europeans gotten these ideas? From the New World, of course...The Iroquois Confederacy was a society without jails, where the leaders were the servants of their people and unlawful entry into private homes was forbidden. These were revolutionary notions to Europeans emerging from feudalism, and evidence of a culture in many ways more highly advanced*

than their own. (Native American Prophesies, Scott Peterson, Pages 92 & 93).

John Locke, praised by Europeans as the intellectual ruler of the eighteenth century, expressed the same ideas as those proposed by Deganawidah nearly two hundred years earlier. However, Locke's ideas were not accepted in Europe in the late 1600s, while the Iroquois had enjoyed living in a democratic state for centuries.

Fur Business Becomes War

While English settlers came to seek their fortunes in America, so did the French and the Dutch. Native Americans were excellent fur trappers as the Europeans soon discovered, and soon the fur trade became quite a profitable business for members of the Iroquois nation. The Dutch became regular trading partners, willing to pay in guns, whisky and other valuable commodities in exchange for beaver pelts.

The lucrative nature of the fur trade gradually changed the culture of the Native American. Before, animals were captured only according to the needs of ones family and no more than that. But the willingness of Europeans to pay high prices for furs caused many Native American communities to abandon their regular agricultural pursuits in preference to building a fur trading business. The farmer who labored to feed his family off of the land suddenly found himself in demand as one who could capture the highly prized fur animals.

Greed for the trinkets paid by European fur traders caused many to temporarily forget the native philosophy of respect for nature. Men who had once followed the spiritual law that said that a life must be taken only to provide what was necessary to survive, were now recklessly hunting beavers, foxes, bears, raccoons, and other animals to near extinction. Gone was the sacred native custom of asking the animal's permission before taking its life. Gone was the prayer of thanks for the animal who gave its life to provide sustenance for another.

Trappers, caught up in their sudden prosperity, slaughtered their prey as quickly and efficiently as they could. When European fur traders moved on to new locations in search of new animal populations to hunt, they left the native communities in a state of near starvation. In despair, many began to turn to alcohol. With increase alcohol use came the usual accompanying social problems -- violence, irresponsibility, immorality. The old ways were gradually disappearing, being replaced with a destructive culture of greed.

Battles over hunting territory became fierce. The Iroquois, a group consisting of five allied Native American nations, captured a virtual monopoly on the beaver pelt business. They established a nearly exclusive relationship with the French, fighting off other natives who sought to hunt and trap on their land. For five years they waged a fierce battle against the British and other Native American nations over control of hunting in the Midwest territory. This armed struggle became known as the "Beaver Wars." In his book *Native American Prophecies*, author Scott Peterson elaborates:

Early in the seventeenth century, Samuel de Champlain arrived to develop New France. He sailed up the St. Lawrence River, exploring and trading furs, and then made a fateful mistake by joining Huron and Algonquian warriors in a battle against their archenemies, the Iroquois, at Ticonderoga. The name Iroquois is, in fact, a French slur, bastardized from an Algonquian word meaning "venomous snakes." Champlain is said to have personally killed two Mohawk war chiefs. The mighty Iroquois braves fled, terrified by the European firearms.

The French would come to regret Champlain's actions. His involvement ignited more than one hundred years of enmity by the Iroquois. Emissaries from the Five Nations soon learned that the Dutch were willing to trade anything for furs. Even rifles. The Iroquois quickly incorporated those weapons into their war machine and became more fearsome than ever.

During this period, the French and English began a heated competition in North America for furs. The entire seventeenth century encompassed the struggle for control of this lucrative trade. Native peoples were drawn into the colonial economies by the Europeans' willingness to trade such items as copper kettles, steel knives, and cotton cloth for pelts. The beaver was particularly prized. While the forests overflowed with them, a relative peace reigned. But when the beaver, mink, and fox began to be depleted, the competition grew increasingly violent. (Native American

Prophecies, by Scott Peterson, pages 87 & 88.)

As profitable as the fur business was, it was also short lived. Once the animal population was depleted, the fur traders moved on to areas where animals were more plentiful. Meanwhile, the farmer who had neglected his farm in favor of fur trapping found himself suddenly without a means of livelihood. His abandoned farmland had gone to waste and the animals he once trapped had all but disappeared.

Many found that they had hunted themselves into starvation, killing animals for fur instead of food, until the local food supply was depleted. And when the European fur traders moved on, they left an impoverished community of once self-sufficient farmers and hunters. The local natives had come to depend upon the fur trading business and suddenly it was no more.

Meanwhile, European society had expanded along the eastern and southern coasts of America. By the mid 1700s, England had established 13 colonies, and European culture was firmly entrenched on American soil. Along with its languages, dress styles, religious beliefs, and social customs, Europe had also transplanted its economic system to the New World. Slaves and indentured servants toiled in European owned shops or under the hot sun on European owned farms and plantations. The goods produced were shipped out to England and France from shipping ports along the coasts.

Africans who were forcibly brought to America and made to work as slaves for the colonialists discovered a kinship with the native people just as had the previous Africans who had traveled to America on exploratory expeditions. Wars among the native people often left communities devastated by the loss of so many young, able-bodied men. Native women often found, among the Africans who came to America, men whose culture was harmonious with their own. Among the Africans brought to America, males greatly outnumbered females, therefore many sought out women with whom they could share a common bond.

One way Native Americans survived was by uniting with Africans, a group of people who shared the same struggle. Native Americans taught African runaway slaves knowledge of the land that was essential for their survival. Africans provided "man power" that was, in return, of great assistance to the Native tribes.

4E – Native Inhabitants of California

These depictions of some California natives show signs of marriage between Indians and Africans. It is based on a watercolor done by Louis Choris in the 1800s. (500 Nations: An Illustrated History of North American Indians)

4F – Feathered California Indians
Drawn in 1806 by Wilhelm von Tilenau, this picture shows Natives who seem to possess some earlier African ancestry.

Paul Cuffe the Wampanoag

There are many stories in American history that give examples of how Native Americans and African Americans unified. One of the more famous stories is that of a man named Paul Cuffe.

Paul Cuffe, a Dartmouth Indian with African parentage, became a wealthy merchant and ship owner in early Massachusetts. He married Alice Pequit of his mother's Wampanoag nation. But his great interest was in protecting fellow Afro-Americans from discrimination in the U.S. and he became the first black man to sponsor a migration of U.S. blacks to Africa. In 1815, he personally paid for and led thirty-eight settlers aboard his ship, Traveller, to Sierra Leone. Cuffe became the father of black back-to-Africa movements in this country. (Black Indians, by William Loren Katz, page 10)

Paul Cuffe is one of the more famous personages of African American history. Although his mother's background is known, his father's background is not commonly known. It has been discovered that Paul Cuffe's father, Saiz Kufu, was born in Ghana, into what some believe was the Ashanti tribe in the 1700s. While a young man he was captured and sold into slavery and brought to Massachusetts. At an early age, his name was changed to "Cuffe."

Saiz met and married a Native American woman from the Wampanoag nation named Ruth, whose people lived near the New England colony. They had ten children together, including Paul.

The Kufu family raised their children to believe in God, to work hard, and be honest, frugal and prudent - values which were part of the Muslim tradition of Saiz Kufu's family in Ghana. They were also in harmony with Native American values, which stressed cooperation within the family, dignity, and respect for others.

Sometime during the 1740s, Saiz was freed. The Cuffe family then moved to the "Indian" community of Massachusetts. Cuffe and his wife made sure their children learned skills which would enable them to survive as free people. He eventually saved enough money to buy a large farm in Dartmouth. Many slaves during that time were able to save enough money to buy their own property. His father's work ethic greatly influenced the most ambitious of the children, Paul.

Paul Cuffe, became the first "Black Indian" industrial giant. He designed and built ships and defied all obstacles in his quest to establish a successful international shipping company. He had trading interests from British Canada to the Caribbean and from Portuguese East Africa to Sweden.

History tells us that he went to Sierra Leone and worked with the Mandingo there, recalling the Muslim teachings of his father. He apparently felt very at home in the Sierra Leone community. This led to Paul's desire to use his economic resources to help the people of Sierra Leone.

Paul recognized that the first hindrance to African independence was the colonial practice of keeping the African elite supplied with rum. After all, it was rum that helped to sustain the slave trade.

Those Africans whose religious beliefs did not forbid the use of alcohol were most likely to succumb to its destructive effects. Paul Cuffe continued to preach against its consumption, recognizing it as a powerful tool in the hands of colonizers whose aim was to keep the natives intoxicated, weak and disorganized.

Part of Paul Cuffe's vision was first to bring an end to the slave trade on the African continent. Secondly, he hoped to revive black industry in those areas under colonial domination. And thirdly, he wanted to uplift those still in slavery on the American continent. Paul Cuffe also continued to use his wealth and influence to support Native American efforts economically, socially and politically.

There was a growing conflict between the slave and free territories in America. A number of those who became the "Founding Fathers" of the United States of America were themselves wealthy slave owners.

Those blacks that were born in bondage and whose parents did not have a vision of freedom were made to believe that black people had always been and would always be slaves. These blacks were kept isolated, and were told to stay away from free individuals like Paul Cuffe, whose existence defied all stereotypes of the capabilities of people of African descent. Enslaved blacks were also kept away from the native people, whose ancestors knew of and often intermarried with those Africans who arrived in America long before Columbus.

Whites did not openly acknowledge the Native American side of Paul Cuffe's heritage. As a Wampanoag, he could have become a Native American role model for overcoming European domination. The success of his parents' intermarriage could have encouraged feelings of brotherhood between blacks and Indians. However, such unions were discouraged by the American colonialists. European whites could only succeed in oppressing both the Natives and the Africans if the two groups were prevented from uniting to form a strong military alliance.

Six Nations Split Over War of Independence

In July 4, 1776, Benjamin Franklin, along with others who became known as the "Founding Fathers" signed the Declaration of Independence from Great Britain. Representatives of the united colonies met in Philadelphia with representatives of the Six Nations and asked that the Six Nations either ally themselves with the colonies or remain neutral in the coming war for independence.

Unfortunately, after decades of being tricked, swindled, and attacked by the colonialists, members of the Six Nations had little trust in an alliance with the Americans. They were divided as to which side would be most advantageous to support and British agents, working behind the scenes, convinced all but two of the Six Nations-- the Oneida and the Tuscarora--to join the British during the Revolutionary War.

In response, George Washington sent General Sullivan to attack the Iroquois nation. Sullivan burned 40 villages, destroyed 160,000 bushels of corn, and scorched the entire earth. The power of the great League of Six Nations was crushed.

The colonialists won the war, and as feared by many Native American nations, the newly created United States of America began to expand westward. This new nation, based on a system created by the visionary prophet Deganawidah, became the conquering force that transformed the face of North America.

The establishment of this perverted version of a united federation of states required the removal of the native people and a total destruction of their way of life. This belief was incorporated in the very foundation of America. In the Declaration of Independence composed by America's "Founding Fathers," King George of England is blamed for creating a climate that encouraged the in-

digenous people of America to wage war against the European colonialists.

> *He has excited domestic insurrections amongst us, and has
> endeavored to bring on the inhabitants of our frontiers, the merci-
> less Indian Savages, whose known rule of warfare is an undistin-
> guished destruction of all ages, sexes and conditions.*
> *(The Declaration of Independence, July 4th 1776)*

To establish the United States, destroying the "Savage Indian" became a top military priority. This was a task that government troops performed using every available means -- trickery, de-
ceit, violence, murder.   Just like the African, the Native American
was reduced to the status of a non-person in the eyes of the government.

Derogatory words were used to describe the native people
and their culture. They were called "savages," "heathens" and
"cannibals" by the American settlers who encroached on Native
American lands while pushing their European culture further and
further west.

In armed confrontations, when whites attacked native villages, slaughtering men, women and children ruthlessly, the
American press called it a great victory. But when the natives
overpowered the whites in battle, or killed white families in wagon
trains headed west, the press called the attack a "bloody massacre."

By the end of the 1840s, the American West was engulfed
in widespread, full-scale warfare. The philosophy of the European
immigrants was that God had ordained it; it was "Manifest Destiny" that the new United States of America should spread from
shore to shore in North America. The "backward" and "primitive"
native culture must go; the native people must agree to adopt
Christianity as their religion and assimilate into European culture.

Wagon train after wagon train came rolling across the
plains in their covered wagons, fulfilling the ancient Hopi prophecy. When they could, rather than resort to warfare, they established treaties with the natives. However these treaties were often
broken, since the ultimate aim of the white settlers was to totally
remove the natives from the land altogether.

White Settlers Come to Seattle

In the summer of 1850, a group of white explorers encountered Chief Seattle of the Suquamish. The Suquamish were on the shores of Elliot Bay in the midst of a joyful celebration for the coming of the first run of good salmon, their chief food. Seeing the fish come early and in abundance insured that there would be a plentiful quantity of food for the Suquamish for the coming year.

Chief Seattle explained to the white explorers, "This is the reason our hearts are glad today, and so you do not want to take this wild demonstration as warlike...It is meant in the nature of a salute...I am glad to have you come to our country."

Years earlier, in 1839, Chief Seattle had converted to Catholicism under the influence of a Catholic missionary who befriended him during a difficult point in his life -- his wife had died due to complications from childbirth and his people had been greatly reduced in number due to warfare among themselves over the years. He had maintained friendly relations with the whites.

One of the original explorers, Dr. David S. Maynard, became a close friend of the Chief. When the doctor expressed his intention to build a trading post in the area, Chief Seattle recommended a location to him. A year later, a boatload of white immigrants set sail from Portland, Oregon, and on September 28, 1851, it landed on the spot that Chief Seattle had indicated. The following year, white settlers began to pour into the area and a township was established. The city was named Seattle after the Chief who had befriended them.

But there were increasing clashes as the natives tried to hunt and fish in traditional area. In order to extinguish the native claims to the land, the United States government offered the native tribes a treaty. In December 1854, treaty proposals were presented in front of Dr. Maynard's office on Main Street in the town of Seattle. Chief Seattle, saddened that the white man's arrival led to the decline of his people, responded on behalf of the Suquamish and Duwamish peoples. Scott Peterson quotes his powerful historic speech:

"There was a time when our people covered the whole land as the waves of a wind ruffled sea cover its shell paved floor. But that time has long since passed away with the greatness of tribes

almost forgotten.... But let us hope that the hostilities between the red man and his pale face brothers may never return. We have everything to lose and nothing to gain...

The white man's God cannot love his red children or he would protect them. They seem to be orphans and can look nowhere for help. How then can we become brothers?

Your God seems to be partial. He came to the white man. We never saw Him, never even heard His voice. He gave the white man laws but He had no word for His red children whose teeming millions filled this vast continent as the stars fill the firmament. No, we are two distinct races and must ever remain so. There is little common between us. The ashes of our ancestors are sacred and their final resting place is hallowed ground, while you wander away from the tombs of your fathers seemingly without regret.

Your religion was written on tablets of stone by the iron finger of an angry God, lest you might forget it. The red man could never remember nor comprehend it.

Our religion is the traditions of our ancestors, the dreams of our old men, given to them by the Great Spirit, and the visions of our sachems, and is written in the hearts of our people. Day and night cannot dwell together. The red man has ever fled the approach of the white man, as the changing mists on the mountainside flee before the blazing morning sun. However, your proposition seems a just one, and I think my folks will accept it and will retire to the reservation you offer them, and we will dwell apart and in peace, for the words of the great white chief seem to be the voice of nature speaking to my people out of the thick darkness that is fast gathering around them like a dense fog floating inward from a midnight sea." (Native American Prophecies, by Scott Peterson, page 118)

Since the Native American nations had no intention of abandoning their ancient language, culture and religion to adopt the ways of the European, the white settlers and the native people fought battle after battle in what became known as the "Indian Wars." These wars were designed to force Native Americans to surrender their land rights and live in specially reserved areas of land. The natives resisted efforts to remove them from their homes to the "reservations." They knew that these barren tracts of land were only places to whither away and die.

Chapter Five
Prophecies of Doom Fulfilled

5A - Mountain Spirit Returns
By Melody Lightfeather
"The White Mountain Spirit Dance of the great Apache warriors and of the Great Plains warriors and the people of the mountain, discusses an ancient way that is being renewed. In the spirit we see beyond our bodies, on the high mountain into the light."

Chapter Five
Prophecies of Doom Fulfilled

"You have noticed that everything an Indian does is in a circle and that is because the Power of the World always works in circles, and everything tries to be round. In the old days when we were a strong and happy people, all our power came to us from the sacred hoop of the nation, and so long as the hoop was unbroken, the people flourished. The flowering tree was the living center of the hoop and the circle of the four corners nourished it. The east gave peace and light, the south gave warmth, the west gave rain, and the north with its cold and mighty wind gave strength and endurance.

"This knowledge came to us from the outer world with our religion. Everything the Power of the World does is in a circle. The sky is round and I have heard that the earth is round like a ball and so are all the stars. The wind, in its greatest power, whirls. Birds make their nests in circles, for theirs is the same religion as ours. The sun comes forth and goes down again in a circle. The moon does the same, and both are round. Even the seasons form a circle in their changing and always come back to where they were.

"The life of a man is a circle from childhood to childhood, and so it is in everything where power moves. Our teepees were round like the nests of birds, and these were always set in a circle, the nation's hoop, a nest of many nests, where the Great Spirit meant for us to hatch our children."

Black Elk, Holy Man of the Ogalala Sioux

The Cherokee Way

The Cherokee of the Appalachian Mountains were one of the largest Native American tribes in North America. They originally called themselves the Ani-Yun-wiya, meaning the "real or principle people." They are believed to have originally migrated from Mexico up into the eastern area around the Great Lakes, and then later back down into the regions of Tennessee, Alabama,

Georgia and the Carolinas. Eventually the Cherokee were forced into other territories during the European occupation.

Cherokee society consisted of many subgroups that managed to live in relative harmony. John Philip Reid comments on early Cherokee society:

The Cherokees as a nation possessed several discernable characteristics that contributed to both their survival and their vulnerability. Their strength lay in their mountain homeland and in their numbers, for they were generally reckoned one of the largest, if not the largest, of the North American nations, with a population of up to 20,000 men, women, and children; at no time were there fewer than 10,000, and they usually were able to muster about 3,000 warriors when forced to make a stand. Their weakness lay in their divisions, for they were spread throughout 60 independent towns... Their language was subdivided into at least three distinct dialects, and their nation was segregated into five regional groups, often competing against one another, and sometimes, when rival clusters of towns became antagonistic, even competing within themselves. [The five groups were known as the Lower Cherokees, the Valley Cherokees, the Middle Cherokees, the Out Cherokees, and the Overhills.] (The Spirit of American Law, page 7, from John Phillip Reid, A Better Kind of Hatchet: Law, Trade and Diplomacy in the Cherokee Nation During the Early Years of European Contact.)

There was no single leader or person within the Cherokee nation who would be comparable to the American President as it exists in the U.S. today. There was no voting process and there were no politicians in Cherokee society. Instead, leadership was determined according to a consensus of opinion regarding the character of individuals in the society. The people who exhibited the most integrity and high moral principles and would naturally come to assume positions of leadership.

Cherokee headmen did not exert authority; they exercised influence based on the tangible ingredients such as their personalities, the success of prior prophecies, tales told by the conjurers, and the auguries of those whom they sought to sway. For the headmen to employ coercion, even coercion applied through estab-

lished legal institutions or social structures manipulated in pre-dictable ways, would have been a violation of Cherokee constitu-tional premises. (The Spirit of American Law, page 8, from John Phillip Reid, A Better Kind of Hatchet: Law, Trade and Diplo-macy in the Cherokee Nation During the Early Years of European Contact.)

Although the five Cherokee subgroups were not always in absolute harmony, there was a general understanding among each other that they would always be mutually supportive. They func-tioned like a family.

A warrior from the Overhill town of Tennessee, going on a hunt in the Middle settlements, knew that if he stopped in the town of Watuga, he would find fellow clan members to welcome him, men who called him "brother" and identified his interests with theirs. A woman who grew up in the Lower town of Estatoe and who, to escape the dangers of Creek raids, fled to the Out town of Tuckaseegee knew that she need not worry about leaving her fam-ily behind. In Tuckaseegee she would have an extended family, perhaps not the close-knit group of clan kin who formed the social family, but at least a legal group who would protect her rights and avenge wrongs done to her. (The Spirit of American Law, page 9, from John Phillip Reid, A Better Kind of Hatchet: Law, Trade and Diplomacy in the Cherokee Nation During the Early Years of European Contact.)

The Fallen Cherokee Nation

This noble example of a civilized society died hard in the face of the new civilization that emerged with the influx of Euro-pean settlers. White settlers sometimes married Cherokee women in order to acquire the land. The children from these unions tended to lean toward the philosophy of European superiority, as learned from their fathers. Eventually, a color caste system developed within the once homogeneous Cherokee people, exacerbating their minor differences.

Disharmony brought about infighting. Children of white settlers began to see the slave trade as an economic opportunity. They began buying the enslaved Africans, believing as did the

Europeans that owning a slave raised ones social status. This created further division among the Cherokee. Wealthier members of the Cherokee nation would buy tracts of land, and, like Europeans, would purchase black slave labor to work the land.

The Civil War marked a crucial turning point in Cherokee history. Those who had expected that their European parentage and ownership of black slaves would grant them equal status with whites were in for a rude awakening. After the war, both the Union and the Confederacy divided up the Cherokee people, forcing all of them, the lighter skinned and the darker skinned, into other lands. No native person had any rights that a white person was bound to respect.

Lloyd Thompson of the Cherokee Nation, during a 2001 interview, commented on the effects that the post Civil War division had upon the once unified nation:

They both tore up the Cherokee Nation in Oklahoma. That forced my grandparents to move to Louisiana - just to save their own lives. So we lost our alley of recognition. It's hard for us now, those who live in Louisiana, to get recognition from Oklahoma, or from Georgia, or from any other Cherokee, federally recognized, nation. Our Cherokee people have decided that we have had enough of our old ways, we have to reform.

So Cherokees from all over the world - France, England, Germany, Canada, and all across the USA are forming a new Cherokee nation that is independent of Oklahoma and North Carolina. And it's about time we did because you have to recognize all the Cherokees – those with white skin, those with brown skin, and those with black skin.

Up until this time this hasn't been addressed – the Cherokees color and what our people used to be and what our people will be. Our people were brown colored or cinnamon colored – that is not white. The Scots and the Irish gave us their ideas of what our people should be - and they said that slavery was good.

As usual, some people, who had the same color as the slave owners, thought that they were better, because they were myopic. They saw the slaves as something less than they were, when in fact the whites saw all Indians, and the black people who were supposed to be our slaves, as one. (Interview: Lloyd Thompson, Cherokee Nation, South East Cherokee Confederacy)

The initial division along color lines within the Cherokee nation that was created after the Civil War still lingers. The temptation to profit from the slave trade was too strong for some to resist. This great nation, that once referred to itself as "The people of principle," came to have very few principles as they slowly adopted the ways of their oppressors. Angela Y. Walton-Rafi, in her book *Black Indian Genealogy Research*, relates how the Cherokee adopted the barbaric practice of slavery:

> *By the end of the 18th century, slavery was solidly planted in the southeast United States and just as solidly into the life and culture of the five largest tribes. R. Halliburton Jr. in his work, Red Over Black: Black Slavery Among the Cherokee Indians, points out that when regarding black slavery among the Indians, one should not make assumptions about the nature of the slavery practiced among these tribes. He notes that there are perceptions that are inaccurate among Indians, and among non-Indians, such as the belief that Indians were kinder slave masters. Each nation handled slavery differently, just as each nation had its own special relations with the white settlers.*
>
> *Halliburton notes that by the late 1700s the Cherokees began intermarrying with whites, and the mixed blood Indians (Indian and white) became and remained the principle slave owners. These mixed bloods also emerged as the wealthiest of the Indians. With the increase of slaves, Halliburton also points out another significant fact: despite the steady increase in the number of slaves, there were never any abolition societies to emerge in any of the Five Civilized Tribes, nor any expression of discontent with the institution of slavery from the tribes. As a result, slavery became an accepted fact of life especially for wealthy Indians. (Black Indian Genealogy Research, Angela Y. Walton-Raji, page 6, Heritage Books, Inc., Copyright 1993.)*

Self-destructive behaviors continued to creep into many Native nations as they attempted to adjust and compete in the new society established by the invaders. This struggle proved to be in vain.

A Trail of Tears

In 1830, the U.S. government produced the Indian Removal Act. The purpose was simple: to remove Native Americans from any lands that whites should decide they wanted. But of course, because the U.S. was a "civilized nation," there had to be an official decree for such a massive relocation operation.

Among the first to be put out of their native homelands were the Choctaw in 1832. Eventually all of the Five Civilized Tribes were forced to take the "death march" to unfamiliar and uninhabitable lands in Oklahoma and Arkansas. Suffering from starvation in the freezing winter cold, many died along the way. William Loren Katz illustrates the standard procedure for Indian relocation in his description of the Cherokee experience:

For Cherokees it was a murderous "trail of tears." President Martin Van Buren ordered seven thousand soldiers under General Winfield Scott to move a nation of fourteen thousand. Homes were burned, livestock, tools, printing presses, and personal possessions seized and destroyed.

Cherokee men, women, and children, including one thousand six hundred Black Cherokees were prodded westward in midwinter by Federal bayonets. About ten thousand Cherokees survived, but President Van Buren assured Congress that their expulsion "had the happiest effects... The Cherokees have emigrated without apparent reluctance." (Black Indians, by William Loren Katz, page 137)

The Trail of Tears significantly reduced the population among the Five Civilized Tribes. Even after this act of terrorism against the Native population, Native Americans continued to conform more and more to the customs and attitudes prevalent among the European society, and the historical bond between the African and Native American further weakened under the economic reality of slavery.

Between 1830 and 1860 the population of the Four Nations declined sharply, Cherokees by 31 percent, Choctaws by 27 percent, Chickasaws by 18 percent, and the Creeks by 43 percent. At the same time the number of members with white blood increased and so too did the number of slaves each nation held. By 1860 Cherokees had 2,511 slaves, Choctaws 2,344, Creeks 1,532, and Chickasaws 975.

Slavery had become the major economic and political factor in these nations. This meant that their racial thinking was approaching that of the white South. (Black Indians, by William Loren Katz, page 138)

"One Drop Rule" Changes Humans Into Non-Humans

A race based philosophy that divided up humanity on the idea that a percentage of a person's blood could determine their ethnicity was a pseudoscientific idea created to give the institution of slavery a "credible" biological justification. With the African, the white slave master would enforce this "one drop rule."

This meant that if it was determined that a person had any descendents of African origin, that "one drop" qualified them for "nonhuman" status in American society.

But the "one drop rule" was frequently applied to others, including Native Americans, to be included among those "nonhumans" who did not deserve equal treatment. It is indeed quite pathetic to witness, even in these modern times, both African and Native Americans arguing within their respective communities over "racial authenticity."

The Native American community has divisions between the so-called "full bloods" and those who are not. This legitimacy issue is frequently less of a problem if the racial mix is with a "white," but presents more of a problem if the racial mix is with a "black."

Much of this debate stems from the Native American reliance on the financial support of the U.S. government. Those defined as "full bloods" received financial support from the government, while those not defined as "full bloods" received no such support. The government seized the power to define Native American authenticity, promptly classifying people into categories such as "full bloods," "half-bloods," "quarter-bloods," etc.

Those who were not considered "full bloods" were ineligible for financial assistance. Again, this restriction is sometimes overlooked for those with "white" ancestry. This use of racism created sharp divisions along color lines among the Native Ameri-

can people.   It made African ancestry an undesirable thing for Native people. This is an attitude that persists today, an unfortunate
result of U.S. economic and political policy.

Yet another sign that marked the breakup of the African
and Native American alliance was the formation of the "Buffalo
Soldiers." These African American troops, allowed to fight in U.S.
military regiments after the Civil War, were so named by Native
Americans, who found similarity between the kinky hair of the
buffalo and the kinky hair of many of the black troops. They were
also given the name because of their fierceness on the battle field.

The Buffalo Soldiers, black men anxious to prove their
combat skills, attacked the native Americans with the same relent-
lessness as those of the white soldiers. William Loren Katz explains:

*Black troopers, including those with Black Indian ancestry,
operated under orders that often had them viewing Native Americans through the gunsights of their ready carbines. Eleven black
soldiers earned the Congressional Medal of Honor in combat
against Utes, Apaches, and Commanches...*

*In an age that offered black men few decent, manly jobs,
military life appealed to these recruits. Many had served their
country during the Civil War. There is little evidence that these
men disagreed with their government's genocidal policies toward
Native Americans.   And they certainly carried out all orders.
(Black Indians, by William Loren Katz, page 176)*

These black troops, whose own ancestors were removed
from their homelands and brought to America, willingly obeyed
the U.S. government's instructions and helped to remove Native
American's from their homelands.

Even those aware of their own Native American ancestry
would disregard any ties of relationship with mom's, dad's, or
grandma's "extended family." They instead participated in the
government's "Indian Wars" with great pride.

This is a far cry from those days when the African slave
would run to his Native Brothers, seeking shelter from an unjust
slave system; a far cry from the days when the Natives Americans
and West Africans from Mali engaged in Transatlantic trade; a far
cry from when the mighty Natives of Mexico and the African

Egyptians came together to share knowledge of the heavens and earth, and built great pyramids.

Indian Wars

Violence escalated between the U.S. government and Indians during the second half of the 1800s. Some of the major wars included: the Mariposa War in California, 1850-51, with the Milwoks and Yokuts; the Yuma and Mojave Uprising of 1851 in California and Arizona; the Rogue River War in Oregon, 1855-56, with the Takelmas and Tutunis; the Yakima War in Washington, 1855-56, with the Yakimas, Umatillas, Walla Wallas, and Cayuses; and the Paiute War in Nevada, 1860, with the Southern Paiutes.

During the period between 1861 and 1865, the U.S. government enlisted a number of Native American nations to participate in the Civil War. They came from tribes like the Comanche, Kiowas, Mexican Kikapoos, Cherokee, Chickasaw, Choctaws, Creeks, Seminoles, Osagas and Senecas. Most who got involved fought on the side of the Confederacy. After the war, the Union redoubled its efforts to secure North America as part of the U.S.

Additional battles for control of land include the Apache Uprising in Arizona and New Mexico, 1861-63; the Santee and Teton Sioux Uprising of 1862; the Navajo War in New Mexico and Arizona, 1863-64; the Shoshone War of 1863 in Utah and Idaho; the Cheyenne-Arapaho War in Colorado and Kansas, 1864-65; the War for the Bozeman Trail in Wyoming and Montana, 1866-68, with the Cheyenne, Arapaho, and Teton Sioux; Both Hancock's and Sheridan's Campaigns, spanning 1867 to 1869, with Cheyenne, Arapaho, Sioux, Comanche and Kiowas; the Snake War in Oregon and Idaho, 1866-68, with the Yahuskin and Walpapi bands of Northern Paiutes; the Modoc War of 1872 in California; Red River War in Southern Plains, 1874-75, with the Comanche, Kiowas, and Southern Cheyenne; the Sioux Wars for the Black Hills, in South Dakota, Montana, and Wyoming, 1876-81, with the Sioux, Cheyenne and Arapahos; the Bannock War of 1878, in Idaho and Oregon, with the Paiute and the Cayuses; the Sheepeater War of 1879; the Ute War of 1879; and the Apache Wars from 1872 to 1873, again from 1877 to 1880, and yet again from 1881 to 1886.

Besides the wars, the greatest factor in the demise of the

Native American nations was the elimination of the Buffalo. Their meat and their hides were vital sources of food, clothing, and shelter, and their disappearance meant virtual starvation and homelessness for the native people. During the early 1800s, over 40 million roamed the plains. But after the U.S. established a treaty with the Lakota in 1868, the government demanded that the Lakota be confined to a tiny hunting area on the reservation, with little access to the great buffalo herds.

Meanwhile, the government opened up the vast plains of Montana and the Dakotas to white settlers, who recklessly hunted the buffalo to near extinction. This caused the Lakota and the Cheyenne to rally together, and in 1876, they met General Custer and the Seventh Cavalry at the famous Battle of Little Big Horn. The natives won a decisive victory, and General Custer was killed. The military losses in the defeat of General Custer accounted for over one-quarter of the total military deaths in the "Indian Wars" between 1865 and 1891.

The overwhelming defeat at the Battle of Little Big Horn motivated the U.S. government to further increase its efforts to either assimilate the native people or confine them to reservations. The Battle of Little Big is known among native Americans as the "rubbing out of yellow hair." This is referring to General George Armstrong Custard, who was a general in the union army of the Seventh Calvary. There was something else that made history at Little Big Horn: the heroics of the great warrior Crazy Horse.

Additional battles of resistance to land takeovers included the Ute War in Colorado and the Apache Wars in the Southwest, 1872-73, and 1877-80. During the years 1881-86, the legendary Apache chief Geronimo waged his last war of resistance. For nearly a decade, the Apache struggled to retain their freedom, as the U.S. army sought to force them onto the dry, barren San Carlos reservation where they would face a slow degrading death from heat and starvation. By 1886, Geronimo, seventeen fighting men, and their families were being hunted down from both sides of the border by five thousand American troops, thousands of civilian militia, five hundred Apache scouts, and three hundred Mexican volunteers. In 1886, a weary Geronimo finally surrendered to U.S. Brigadier General Nelson A. Miles.

By that time there were 187 reservations, comprising a total of 181,000 square miles of land, intended to house all of 243,000

Native Americans. The whites had hunted the buffalo to near extinction. Gone were the fertile grasslands. Instead, the barren land of the reservation was more like a prison camp than a home.

Just as after the Civil War, the U.S. government had established a Freedman's Bureau to help newly freed slaves to begin a new independent life, at the end of the Indian Wars, the government created the Indian Bureau. It was just as useless, often failing to administer to the basic needs of the native people. With little decent food, poor farming land, and no hunting grounds, the native people began to develop health problems.

Depression and despair caused many to turn to alcohol and with alcoholism came the complete breakdown of the family, the tribe and the nation. By the end of the 1800s, the disruption of Native American civilization was complete.

Crazy Horse

During the Battle of Little Big Horn, there was a fierce Lakota Sioux war chief whose heroics on the battlefield became legendary. His name was Tasunke Witko, also known as Crazy Horse. He was not the first Crazy Horse; he was actually the third generation of men who used that name. He originally had another name but adopted this one around the age of twenty. While still a child, he suffered an accident that put him in a coma for some time. After he awakened, he relayed strange visions experienced that foretold the future:

In it he saw a warrior mounted on a horse that changed colors, riding through hail and lightning, and through the arrows and bullets of enemies, as his own people tried to hold him back. The vision revealed his destiny, giving him a clarity of purpose that few men or women in any culture have had. (Encyclopedia of North American Indians, by Frederick E. Hoxie , pages 137-138)

Crazy Horse also saw that his people had a rough period ahead, but that at the end there would be a light. That rough period that must be passed through had its origins, once again, in the quest for money. There was gold in the land of the Sioux, the sacred Black Hills, which is in present day South Dakota. White prospectors sought to seize the land and claim "ownership." The government made many proposals but the Sioux refused. All subtribes of the Lakota Sioux would ban together to fight for their homeland. The names of the subtribes of the Lakota Sioux were: the Brule, the San Ark, the Two Kettle, the Hunkpapa (Sitting Bull), the Ogalala (Crazy Horse, Black Elk, Red Cloud), the Minnecojou, and the Blackfoot.

The American government had no intention of respectfully asking permission to use the Indian land. Their intent was to remove the Indians and put them somewhere out of the way of the government's nefarious affairs. Author Peter Matthiessen describes their attitude and intentions and the sole reason for both:

(... Commissioner Francis Walker also commented, "There is no question of national dignity... involved in the treatment of savages by a civilized power." He went on to say that the purpose of the reservation system was to reduce "the wild beasts to the condition of the supplicants for charity.") Already, white mountain men and prospectors were passing through the Black Hills without the Indians' consent, and the rumor of plentiful "gold in them thar hills," reported by a military party in 1858, was confirmed in August 1874 by a huge reconnaissance expedition led by a jubilant George Custer. (In the Spirit of Crazy Horse, by Peter Matthiessen, page 9.)

Before his humiliating defeat, which would be known forever as "Custer's Last Stand," General George Custer was already widely known by the Indian population. His unprecedented attack on the Washitaw River Cheyenne made him infamous among the native peoples.

But the greatest fame amongst the Indians, however, was reserved for their own Native American hero, Crazy Horse. He was a young rebel who did not accept the U.S. government's anti-native agenda. He was a believer in the Great Spirit and understood the wisdom of remaining in harmony with nature. This meant that one could not have foolish ideas about personal ownership of the land, for it belonged to all. Anything contrary to that was contrary to the teachings of the Great Spirit, and the culture of the Native American.

The U.S. government requested his presence to discuss ownership rights of the Black Hills, Crazy Horse refused to attend:

5B – Crazy Horse During the Battle of Little Bighorn

This is a Sioux drawing depicting Crazy Horse riding a white spotted horse. Crazy Horse was very respected and well known among his people. Unlike other famous Native Americans, no photo was ever taken of him. (Encyclopedia of North American Indians, Frederick E. Hoxie, page 138)

Crazy Horse, who had had his great vision quest in the Black Hills, sent Little Big Man as a witness for the "wild" Ogalala who refused to come: "One does not sell the land on which the people walk," said Crazy Horse... (In the Spirit of Crazy Horse, by Peter Matthiessen, page 10-11)

The Right to Share the Land

The natives believed that they had a right to their home-land, but not the sole right. Had the U.S. government sought to use the land along side the Indian, there would have been no conflict.

But Crazy Horse, saw this clearly that this was not what the government proposed. He understood, through his visions from the Great Spirit, that the exploitation and misuse of land would continue. He decided to take up arms for his people, expressing his frustration in the following statement:

"We did not ask you white men to come here. The Great Spirit gave us this country as a home. You had yours. We did not interfere with you. The Great Spirit gave us plenty of land to live on, and buffalo, deer, antelope and other game. But you have come here; you are taking my land from me; you are killing off our game, so it is hard for us to live.

Now, you tell us to work for a living, but the Great Spirit did not make us to work, but to live by hunting. You white men can work if you want to. We do not interfere with you, and again you say, why do you not become civilized? We do not want your civili-zation! We would live as our fathers did, and their fathers before them." (In the Spirit of Crazy Horse, by Peter Matthiessen)

Crazy Horse was known for his great abilities as a warrior, stopping Crazy Horse was indeed a difficult thing. He was such a great warrior that even his opponents gave him due respect, recog-nizing his bravery and fighting skills:

I saw before me a man who looked quite young, not over thirty years old, five feet eight inches high, lithe and sinewy, with a scar on the face. The expression of his countenance was one of quiet dignity, but morose, dogged, tenacious, and melancholy. He behaved with stolidity, like a man who realized that he had to give in to Fate, but would do so as sullenly as possible...

All Indians gave him a high reputation for courage and generosity. In advancing upon an enemy, none of his warriors were allowed to pass him. He had made himself hundreds of friends by his charity toward the poor, as it was a point of honor with him never to keep anything for himself, excepting weapons of war. I never heard an Indian mention his name save in terms of respect. In the Custer Massacre, the attack by Reno had first caused a panic among the women and children and some of the warriors started to flee; but Crazy Horse, throwing away his rifle, brained one of the incoming soldiers with his stone war-club, and jumped upon his horse.

Captain John G. Bourke, U.S.A.
(In Memory of Crazy Horse, website,
http://maier1.best.vwh.net/native/crzyop.htm)

Crazy Horse fought in many heroic battles, but in 1877 he was stabbed to death in Nebraska. It is believed Little Big Man, his onetime associate, was the culprit. Years before, Crazy Horse had foreseen his own death in a vision. He saw that it would come about by the hands of his own people. After his death the U.S. government gained the upper hand and eventually relocated the Indians of the sacred Black Hills to some barren lands in the East.

The Congress, in its Christian duty, had set forth to "civilize" the Indian in the same way that the European nations, in this high colonial period, were "civilizing" the nonwhite natives of South America and Africa and Asia, using the same trusty mix of Bibles and bullets." (In the Spirit of Crazy Horse, by Peter Matthiessen, page 8)

Apparently this combination of religious hypocrisy and barbaric violence worked. Those who had set out to dominate the Indian nations eventually achieved their objective, just as they had achieved it among other nations. The spirit of the Native was broken; many eventually adopted European Christianity as a religion.

The destruction of Native Americans culture and way of life caused many to turn to the Great Spirit in hopes that an Indian "Messiah" or "Savior" would come and save them from the hell they were forced to endure.

Chapter Six
In Search of a Savior

6A – Solar Eclipse

Eclipses have long been viewed with great reverence among the nations of the world. They also have had special religious significance in many cultures. In 1889, during a solar eclipse, a Paiute holy man had a vision that the Messiah Jesus had returned.

Chapter Six
In Search of a Savior

Messiah: 1. The Anointed One; the Christ; the name for the promised deliverer of the Hebrews, assumed by Jesus, and given to him by Christians. 2. Loosely, a looked-for liberator of a country or people. (Funk & Wagnals New Comprehensive International Dictionary of English Language.)

The Maasaw or Messiah

Many ancient religions predict the coming of an anointed one to deliver the people from sin and oppression. The Hebrews, suffering under a cruel Pharaoh, were promised by God that a Deliverer would free them from bondage. Moses, born a Hebrew and raised in the Egyptian house of Pharaoh, arose to fulfill that mission. Later in history, the Hebrews, subjugated under Roman rule, were again awaiting a Savior, a Messiah, to set them free, as prophesized in ancient Hebrew scriptures. Jesus is recognized by Christians as the one who fulfilled that prophecy.

Long before Native Americans came in contact with European Christian theology, there existed within Hopi traditions the belief in a Messiah, or in the Hopi language, "Maasaw." According to the Hopi, this individual was sent by the Great Spirit to teach the Hopi the Divine laws under which they were to live.

Where did this belief in the coming of the Maasaw originate? The Maasaw is an ancient Hopi tradition. Long ago, around 1100 A.D., the Maasaw came to the Hopi people of Arizona at a place called Oraibi. He called out to them by tapping on a rock. Only those Hopi who were not preoccupied with vain talk would hear his call and receive the blessings of his teachings. The Maasaw taught the Hopi many things, but according to Thomas E. Mails:

Above all, what Maasaw gave the Hopi at Oraibi was the secret that would enable them to blend with the land and celebrate life. Among other things, it was a way to become natural environ-

mentalists who simply grew up being people who through their manner of life would become one with Mother Earth, and would neither waste nor abuse her. As a natural result of the life-way, they would also live in warm fellowship with one another, and with other human beings and creatures. It was a gentle way for a gentle people, a way to deal effectively with the things that so frequently cause pain in life, and a way to counteract the fulfillments of prophecy. As repeated day by day, month by moth, and year by year, the cycle of things Maasaw taught them to do, peace ruled their hearts. This peace would achieve its greatest value when the closing of the Fourth Cycle of the world came to pass. This was a secret for happiness that was not intended to be a secret, for it was a secret to be shared with all people who truly deserved to hear it. (The Hopi Survival Kit, by Thomas E. Mails, page 57)

The actual description of the Maasaw is very abstract, but something like an apparition. He has been described as having huge sunken black eyes, and a huge sunken black mouth. He had no nose whatsoever. It was a fearsome image, but not an image of a "god" as some may misunderstand. The true role of the Maasaw was not as a deity, but rather a messenger between the Great Spirit and the Hopi people. Thomas E. Mails explains:

While the Maasaw delivered all of this information to the Hopi, he was not the originator. He has been described as a deity, and now and then in a slip of the tongue has been called the Great Spirit. But the Hopi Elders do not confuse him with the Creator. Instead, they know that he servers the Creator, and that his assigned task is to be Guardian of the Earth. (The Hopi Survival Kit, by Thomas E. Mails, page 56)

The Hopi still consider the Maasaw as one who takes an active role in their lives. According to Hopi prophecy, the Maasaw would reappear in the future. Thomas E. Mails said that the Maasaw spoke of returning to the Hopi after a time of great tribulation:

He said we would face many evil obstacles, obstacles which would lessen our spiritual energies and the will to go on, causing us to stray off the path. But, if we reached the end of the path without weakening, we would be rewarded with a good, peaceful and everlasting life. Then Maasaw would be our leader, for He is the First and will be the Last. This is the path our village, Hotevilla, the last remnant of traditional Hopi, has chosen to follow to this day. (The Hopi Survival Kit, by Thomas E. Mails, page 188-189)

This description of the Maasaw greatly resembles the descriptions found in other religions of the coming of God's messengers and messiahs - symbolically as manifestations of God. In the religions of Christianity and Buddhism there are clear examples of men who have been referred to as the physical manifestations of God. God is often given the attribute of being the Alpha and the Omega, or the First and the Last.

It may be that these holy men, being messengers of God, were later on mistakenly elevated to the status of God. The two (God and God's messenger) were associated as one and the same. One example is the arrival of King Abubakari of Mali, seen by the Aztecs as a manifestation of Quetzalcoatl. Quetzalcoatl. was considered by some to be God. Later, this occurred again when Cortez arrived with his armies. Because of the timing and the manner of which he arrived, Cortez was also considered the possible return of Quetzalcoatl.

One can't help but wonder if originally Quetzalcoatl was perhaps just another messenger of God who was later deified. This seems to be a common trend in religion.

The metamorphosis of Native American society from independence to dependency created such a loss of hope that, in frustration, the people began to commit acts of violence against each other. In the case of Crazy Horse, one of his most trusted companions killed him, bringing a tragic end to one of the greatest Indian leaders.

The Hopi, desperate to maintain the sacred teachings of the Great Spirit, felt compelled to take actions to revive the faith of the Native people. Scott Peterson relates one incident in which the Hopi tried to recreate the "Maasaw" and frighten the U.S. military with his presence.

A moment later a more awesome personification appeared: Maasaw, Spirit of Death and Caretaker of the Land. Wearing a

heavy black mask painted with spots, the Maasaw carried a num-
ber of sacred objects, including a liquid-filled medicine bowl.
Stepping closer to the line of soldiers, he dipped a feather into his
bowl, and sprayed each with drops of the elixir. Then, in his most
terrible voice, he ordered the whites to leave at once or hostilities
would commence.

The appearance of the deity did not have quite the effect
the Hopi had been expecting. Brett and his men found the grizzled
old figure mildly ridiculous.   More than a few chuckled and
grinned. Yet the lieutenant was keenly aware of the influence the
comical, masked figure seemed to have over the armed warriors
that surrounded his men. In light of Maasaw's vociferous declara-
tions, and the fact that they were badly outnumbered, Brett wisely
chose to withdraw. Though he warned them that they would surely
be punished for defying the authority of the U.S. government. (Na-
tive American Prophecies, Scott Peterson, page 253-254)

The Hopi's attempt to intimidate the U.S. army by conjur-
ing up a "Maasaw" figure did not have the effect the Hopi desired.
The army had no fear or reverence for the Maasaw. In fact, the
Hopi's unexpected comical display seemed to only produce more
hardships and despair for the Indians.

Although the Hopi elders understood that the Maasaw is
not the Great Spirit and the Great Spirit is not the Maasaw, they
still hoped for some sign from God to show that their prayers for
deliverance were being heard. It may be that another "manifestation of God" will occur with the coming of another Maasaw, or
messenger from the Great Spirit. How will this person be recognized? Will he physically resemble that same Maasaw described
in the Hopi oral traditions? Or will he be recognized by the similarity in spiritual teachings with that early Maasaw?

Wovoka's Spiritual Journey

"Do not tell the white people about this. Jesus is now upon
the earth. He appears like a cloud. The dead are still alive again. I
do not know when they will be here; maybe this Fall or in the
Spring. When the time comes there will be no more sickness and
everyone will be young again. Do not refuse to work for the whites
and do not make any trouble with them until you leave them. When

the Earth shakes [at the coming of the new world] do not be afraid.
It will not hurt you. I want you to dance every six weeks. Make a
feast at the dance and have food that everybody may eat. Then
bathe in the water. That is all. You will receive good words again
from me some time. Do not tell lies." (Wovoka)

The turn of the century was approaching. By this time, the
once great and powerful nations that populated the North American continent were now small and weak and squeezed onto the
small parcels of land known as "reservations."

European immigrants had come by the boatloads, claiming
property, starting families and gradually displacing the native people. The ancient prophecies had come to pass. In a matter of a few
generations, the natives witnessed the catastrophic destruction of
all that they had held sacred. Broken spirited and without hope,
they watched with anger as whites took over their land, disregarded their values and disrespected their way of life. The whites'
attitude of racial superiority spread across the country like a disease, provoking acts of violence and bigotry against those they
called "Indians."

During these times there arose a man from among the Paiute who became known as a prophet, a mystic, and to some, the
Messiah. His name was Wovoka.

Wovoka was born around 1858 in the Mason Valley of
western Nevada near the Walker River, in an oval-shaped hut
known as a "wikiup." The Paiutes had lived in the valley for many
generations before the first white settlers arrived in the 1860s. In
1863, cattle ranchers David, William and George Wilson moved
onto the Paiute's land and, as had become the custom of the whites,
declared it as their own. They considered the Paiute families living
on the land to simply be a part of their holdings.

Wovoka, the oldest of three brothers, was the son of a Paiute holy man named Tävibo. Tävibo was a follower of the Paiute
prophet Wodziwob, originator of a spiritual movement called "The
Ghost Dance." This dance was a prayer ceremony for the resurgence of the Native American people.

During his childhood, Wovoka developed a close friendship with David Wilson's son, Bill. He began working for the Wilson family, as did a number of the Paiutes. He learned how to
brand a calf, pitch hay, clean a stable, and plow the ground. They

gave him jeans to exchange for his rabbit skin clothing.

Bill and Wovoka were about the same age, and their friendship grew into a kind of brotherhood. Wovoka was invited to dine at the Wilson's' table, while the other Paiute ranch hands ate at a crude trough outside in the back. Wovoka's father died when he was about fourteen years old, and shortly after that the Wilson family unofficially adopted Wovoka. They decided that since he was learning how to live in white society, he should have a "white" name. So he was renamed as Jack Wilson.

The Wilsons were devout Christians, and taught Wovoka stories from the Bible. Every night after dinner David Wilson read the Bible to his family, teaching about Jesus Christ, his miracles, his message of peace, and his crucifixion. There in the Wilson household, Wovoka learned the Christian theological teaching that Jesus was sent to earth by God as the savior for all of mankind.

Despite the attempts to integrate Wovoka into white society, the reality of racism slapped him in the face again and again as Bill's teenage friends openly snubbed him. The white girls around their age made it clear that they intended to have nothing to do with Bill's "Indian" brother. As the two boys grew older, they grew farther apart. Scott Peterson notes:

Around the age of seventeen, Wovoka broke off his relationship with the Wilsons. This was a period of soul-searching for the young man who had grown into an imposing figure with a height of six feet and broad, heavy features. At times he felt consumed by an overpowering hatred of the white race. His people's loss of traditional hunting grounds had led to hunger and disorientation. Relocation of much of the tribe into the Walker River and Pyramid Lake reservations left them demoralized. Once dignified braves were reduced to drunks, selling their women to the whites as whores. And then there were the white man's diseases. When he was a boy, two years of epidemics had wiped out about one tenth of the Paiute population. Wovoka's heart ached for the sad state of his fellow natives. (Native American Prophecies, by Scott Peterson, pages 132 & 133.)

Wovoka traveled throughout Nevada, California, Oregon and Washington, working as a farm laborer. He met other native people throughout his travels and discovered that their plight was similar to his own. He returned to Mason Valley and at about the age of twenty, he married a young Paiute woman to whom he gave the name "Mary." Their family grew and eventually they had three daughters and a son.

As the son of Tävibo, the medicine man, Wovoka commanded a certain amount of respect among the Paiute. He had no desire to become a medicine man, but he saw that the spirits of his people needed healing. He searched for ways to renew their faith and hope. The Paiute had become like the walking dead, lifeless, and wandering aimlessly. Wovoka felt their overwhelming pain. It was as though they had fallen into a deep dark bottomless abyss.

The Ghost Dance Movement

In the winter of 1888 an answer to his prayers came through a strange spiritual experience. He had started working for David Wilson again, chopping wood in the mountains at Pine Grove. Soon after he started work, he became ill with a high fever. His wife Mary became alarmed and laid him inside their wikiup where she could try to administer medicines to him. His condition failed to improve and Mary became very afraid he was dying. Then a most unexpected turn of events took place. Author Scott Peterson explains:

Then, on January 1, 1889, while Wovoka was unconscious, one of the most awe-inspiring occurrences of the natural world took place. There was a total eclipse of the sun.

The Paiutes in Mason Valley, in the Walker River and Pyramid Lake reservations, like many Indians throughout the West, were terrified by the sudden "death of the sun." In their religion, the sun is a powerful living being...

For almost an hour the eclipse went on before finally a crescent appeared, then grew and slowly the munificent sun re-emerged, dominant once again. Wovoka lay in a death trance for days after the eclipse and word spread that the holy man was in another world. People gathered around the wikiup. Some of them insisted on testing his seemingly lifeless flesh with fire and a knife, but nothing evoked a response. Wovoka just lay silent and unmoving in a most unusual sleep. Then one day his color slowly began returning to normal. For a long time there was no other outward

change.   Finally, his eyes fluttered open and he spoke in a quiet
voice: "I have been to heaven and talked with God." (Native
American Prophecies, by Scott Peterson)

Wovoka's experience created excitement among the Paiute
community.   Years ago, in 1870, his father, holy man Tävibo, had
prophesied that while all whites would be swallowed up by the
earth, all dead Indians would emerge to enjoy a world free of their
conquerors. Tävibo urged his followers to dance in circles, already
a tradition in the Great Basin area, while singing religious songs.
Tävibo's movement spread to Nevada, California and Oregon.

After his near death experience, Wovoka began to make
similar prophecies. Referring to God as "the Old Man," he declared
that he had been appointed "the Old Man's deputy," and was given
the task to spread God's message of the coming of a Messiah who
would bring a new age of prosperity, spiritual renewal and immortal life to the Native people. Wovoka's prophecies stressed the link
between righteous behavior and imminent salvation. Author Scott
Peterson quotes Wovoka's story:

"When I was in the other world with the Old Man, I saw all
the people who have died.   But they were not sad.   They were
happy while engaged in their old-time occupations and dancing,
gambling and playing ball. It was a pleasant land, level, without
rocks or mountains, green all the time, and rich with an abundance
of game and fish. Everyone was forever young.

"After showing me all of heaven, God told me to go back
to earth and tell His people you must be good and love one an-
other, have no quarreling, and live in peace with the whites; that
you must work, and not lie or steal; and that you must put an end
to the practice of war.

"If you faithfully obey your instructions from on high, you
will at last be reunited with your friends in a renewed world where
there would be no more death or sickness or old age.   First,
though, the earth must die. Indians should not be afraid, however.
For it will come alive again, just like the sun died and came alive
again. In the hour of tribulation, a tremendous earthquake will
shake the ground. Indians must gather on high ground. A mighty
flood shall follow. The water and mud will sweep the white race
and all Indian skeptics away to their deaths. Then the dead Indian

ancestors will return, as will the vanished buffalo and other game,
and everything on earth will once again be an Indian paradise."
(Native American Prophecies, by Scott Peterson, page 137)

Wovoka's revelation awoke a new spiritual fervor among the Paiutes. He told them that in order to hasten the renewal of the earth, the people must perform what became known as "The Ghost Dance" at three-month intervals, for five consecutive days at a time. In this particular dance, each person stood directly behind another, each with one hand on the shoulder of the person ahead, forming a long chain of people that curved into a closed circle.

The dancers were to take a few steps while chanting "Father, I come." Then they were to stop, and while remaining in the circle, they would cry out in grief and name the dead friend or relative for whom they mourned. While crying, moaning and groaning in grief, they took up handfuls of dust at their feet, washed their hands in it and threw it over their heads. Then they raised their eyes to heaven, and, clasping their hands above their head, they stood perfectly still and invoked the Great Spirit to allow them to see and talk to their dead loved ones. After that, they would move rapidly, their bodies swaying, their hands gripping their neighbors hands tightly and moving side to side, their feet making the dust fly, while they chanted again and again, "Father, I come; Mother, I come; Brother, I come..."

They moved as fast as they could and chanted over and over again until, one by one, each began to break from the ring and stagger away. They would fall down on the ground in a trance, where they would lay undisturbed until the dance was over. After the dance stopped, as each person recovered from the trance, they were placed in the center of the ring, where they related to the crowd the visions they had experienced while unconscious.

It was an intense prayer ceremony, which frightened the whites that witnessed it, yet brought a renewed sense of hope among the natives. The Ghost Dance spread throughout much of the West, especially among the more recently defeated tribes and nations of the Great Plains.

Wovoka was not the only one that claimed to have foreseen in a vision a great "resurrection" of the Native American people. Spiritually inclined men from other tribes would also experience visions during this same time.

Black Elk's Vision

Black Elk, of the Ogalala Sioux, was another holy man who had visions of a resurgence of the Native American way of life. During the summer when he was nine years old, Black Elk had a powerful spiritual experience that shaped the direction of his life. In 1872, when Black Elk was nine years old, he had yet to see his first Wasichu, or white man. There were still vast herds of buffalo, and the Indian way of life, Black Elk believed, would last forever. He narrated his story to John G. Neihardt, who later published it in a book entitled *Black Elk Speaks:*

While I was eating, a voice came and said: "It is time; now they are calling you." The voice was so loud and clear that I believed it, and I thought I would just go where it wanted me to go. (Black Elk, "Black Elk Speaks, Being the Life Story of a Holy Man of the Oglala Sioux", page 21)

The next day Black Elk fell gravely ill and lay near death for several days. During that time, as he lay barely breathing, he was experiencing a magnificent vision:

When we had camped again, I was lying in our teepee and my mother and father were sitting beside me. I could see out through the opening, and there two men were coming from the clouds, headfirst like arrows slanting down, and I knew they were the same that I had seen before ... They came clear down to the ground this time and stood a little way off and looked at me and said: Hurry! Come! Your Grandfathers are calling you!
...When I got up to follow, my legs did not hurt me any more and I was very light. I went outside the teepee and yonder where the men with flaming spears were going, a little cloud was coming very fast. It came and stooped and took me and turned back to where it came from, flying fast. And when I looked down I could see my mother and father yonder, and I felt sorry to be leaving them...
Now suddenly there was nothing but a world of cloud, and we three were there alone in the middle of a great white plain with snowy hills and mountains staring at us; and it was very still; but

there were whispers. (Black Elk, "Black Elk Speaks, Being the Life Story of a Holy Man of the Oglala Sioux", pages 21 - 23.)

Black Elk described a magnificent vision of sights, songs, dances, and ceremonies that symbolized events to take place in the near and distant future. He foresaw that his people would experience a time of joy and peace, then later on they would experience a time of war and famine. His vision showed him how all life on earth was interconnected, and all people belonged to one human family.

The vision foretold that he would live to see four generations and would someday be an old man. In his vision he traveled four ascents with his people, which he understood to be the four generations he would know.

At the first ascent, the people camped in a circle. At the center of the circle stood the holy tree. But when they camped at the second ascent Black Elk saw the leaves falling from the sacred tree. At the camp of the third ascent he saw the Black Road of conflict before them. He saw, too, that the nation's hoop was broken, the sacred tree was dying and all its birds were gone. There he saw that "all of the animals and fowls that were the people ran here and there, for each one seemed to have his own little vision that he followed and his own rules; and all over the universe I could hear the winds at war like wild beasts fighting... It was dark and terrible about me, for all the winds of the world were fighting. It was like rapid gunfire and like whirling smoke, and like women and children wailing and like horses screaming all over the world." This third ascent was the time of the generation living in the 1850's. At the fourth ascent a Voice said "Behold this day, for it is yours to make. Now you shall stand upon the center of the earth to see..."

In his vision, Black Elk was shown through symbols and songs that the four races of mankind, the people of the North, South, East, and West, were coming together. He was shown a spiritual rebirth of the Native American nations and a time of peace and harmony on the earth.

I looked ahead and saw the mountains there with rocks and forests on them, and from the mountains flashed all colors upward to the heavens. Then I was standing on the highest mountain of them all, and around about beneath me was the whole hoop of the world. And while I stood there I saw more than I can tell and I understood more than I saw; for I was seeing in a sacred manner the shapes of all things in the spirit, and the shape of all shapes as they must live together like one being. And I saw that the sacred hoop of my people was one of the many hoops that made one circle, wide as daylight and starlight, and in the center grew one mighty flowering tree to shelter all the children of one mother and one father. And I saw that it was holy. (Black Elk, "Black Elk Speaks, Being the Life Story of a Holy Man of the Oglala Sioux", pages 21 - 23.)

Black Elk's vision seemed to reinforce a theme repeated by many prophets and visionaries: that all humanity came from a single male and female and spread across the earth and are all part of the same human family. Mankind split into diverse groups for the purpose of coming back together later to share knowledge with one another. The Holy Quran states in Chapter 49 (Al Hujurat):

Oh mankind, We have created you from a male and a female; and We have made you tribes and subtribes that you may know one another. Verily, the most honorable among you, in the sight of Allah, is the one who is most righteous. Surely, Allah is All Knowing, All Aware. (Holy Quran, Chapter 49, Al Hujurat, Verse 14)

Black Elk recovered from his illness and awoke from his deathlike trance, but it was years before he related his vision to anyone. After several years had passed, it became clear that Black Elk had a special gift, and not only could he foresee future events, he also could heal the sick. By the time he was nineteen, he had become known as a Holy man among the Ogalala.

The Great Spirit Speaks

By the late 1800s, the whites, referred to as "Wasichus" by the Ogalala, had violated most of the treaties they had made with the Native American nations and had forced them onto the reservations. They could no longer hunt the buffalo, or catch the fish, or gather the foods that had built them into strong independent nations. Black Elk relates:

My people looked pitiful. There was a big drought, and the rivers and creeks seemed to be dying. Nothing would grow that the people had planted, and the Wasichus had been sending less cattle and other food than ever before. The Wasichus had slaughtered all the bison and shut us up in pens. It looked as though we might starve to death. We could not eat lies, and there was nothing we could do...

But early that summer when I came back from across the big water (1889) strange news had come from the west and the people had been talking and talking about it...This news said that out yonder in the west at a place near where the great mountains (The Sierras) stand before you come to the big water, there was a sacred man among the Paiutes who had talked to the Great Spirit in a vision, and the Great Spirit had told him how to save the Indian peoples and make the Wasichus disappear and bring back all the bison and the people who were dead and how there would be a new earth...

Wasichus called him Jack Wilson, but his name was Wovoka. He told them that there was another world coming , just like a cloud...

I had a great vision that was to bring the people back into the nation's hoop, and maybe this sacred man had had the same vision and it was going to come true, so that the people would get back on the red road. Maybe I was not meant to do this myself, but if I helped with the power that was given me, the tree might bloom again and the people prosper. This was in my mind all that winter, but I did not know what vision the sacred man out there had seen, and I wished I could talk to him and find out. ("Black Elk Speaks, Being the Life Story of a Holy Man of the Oglala Sioux", pages 230 and 232.)

With the increase of droughts and famines came alcoholism, immorality and depression among his people. The soldiers came to the reservation, exploited the community and abused the women. Black Elk knew that it was time to seek the company of other Indian holy men who were having visions during these times. In the summer of 1890, Black Elk decided to get on his horse and travel to Wounded Knee Creek where another Ghost Dance was to take place.

Mormons and the Messiah Movement

Wovoka had described a spiritual experience of "talking to God" and receiving word that the Messiah, or Jesus the Christ, had come again and was at that moment on the earth. His experience was taken seriously by more than just the people within the Native American community.

Near the turn of the century, many religious groups were expecting the return of Jesus. The Church of Jesus Christ of Latter-Day Saints, known as the "Mormons" believed Native American people to be the Lamanites, descendants of the House of Israel. This Biblical connection caused the Mormons to sit up and take notice when they heard of a prophet among the native people. Scott Peterson explains:

Joseph Smith, the great prophet of the Mormon church... claimed that on September 21, 1823, while in New York, an Angel of God appeared to him and declared he had been chosen to be "an instrument in the hands of God...the preparatory work for the second coming of the Messiah was speedily to commence...I was also told where there were deposited some plates on which were engraven an abridgement of the records of the ancient prophets that had existed on this continent."

Smith went on to explain that "on the morning of the 22nd of September A.D., 1827, the Angel of the Lord delivered the records into my hands. These records were engraven on plates, which had the appearance of gold. Each plate was six inches wide and eight long, and not quite so thick as common tins. They were filled with engravings in Egyptian characters."...

The strange records told how "America in Ancient times had been inhabited by two distinct races of people. The first were called Jaredites...The second race came directly from the city of Jerusalem about six hundred years before Christ. They were principally Israelites of the descendants of Joseph. The Jaredites were destroyed about the time the Israelites came from Jerusalem...The principal nation of the second race fell in battle towards the close of the fourth century. The remnants are the Indians that now inhabit this country."

Joseph Smith translated the full text of the plates, and it

later became known as the *Book of Mormon*. Many Christians consulted Smith regarding the prophecies concerning the second coming of Christ. They were anxious to know the timing of such a return. Smith told them that he had received a revelation while praying very earnestly. He said that God had told him, "Joseph, my son, if thou livest until thou art eighty-five years old, thou shalt see the face of the Son of Man."

The year 1890 would have marked Smith's eighty-fifth birthday, had he lived to see it. However, the controversy surrounding his claims caused Smith to be arrested. He was shot to death in 1844 by an angry mob while being held in jail in Carthage, Illinois. Still, many of his followers, known as the Millennialists, fervently believed that 1890 was the year that Jesus Christ would again walk upon the earth. When a great assembly of Native American tribes met at Walker Lake, Nevada, for a great Ghost Dance ceremony, many Mormons joined them, believing Wovoka to be the fulfillment of Joseph Smith's prophecy.

Hope for the Nations

What began as a renewed hope among the Paiute grew into a spiritual movement of giant proportions. It spread among the Lakota, the Cheyenne, the Shoshones, and many other prominent tribes. The story of Wovoka grew from his vision of the coming of the Messiah, to him actually being the Messiah. The native people called him the "Wanekia." This means "one who makes live."

It was claimed that Wovoka could perform great miracles, and could even make the animals talk. It was said that he came down from Heaven in a cloud. This was a desperate time for the Native American nations. They had witnessed the massive slaughter of the buffalo and realized that their way of life had been destroyed forever. They clung to Wovoka's prediction that God would remove the whites from the face of the earth, bring back the buffalo, resurrect the native people from the dead, and restore them to prosperity. The Ghost Dance had become the last chance of revival for the people. They gathered together in great numbers and danced with frenzy.

When Black Elk arrived at Wounded Knee Creek in the summer of 1890, he saw that many had come to participate in the Ghost Dance:

I was surprised, and could hardly believe what I saw; be-cause so much of my vision seemed to be in it. The dancers, both women and men, were holding hands in a big circle, and in the center of the circle they had a tree painted red with most of its branches cut off and some dead leaves on it. This was exactly like the part of my vision where the holy tree was dying and, and the circle of the men and women holding hands was like the sacred hoop that should have power to make the tree to bloom again...I sat there looking on and feeling sad. It all seemed to be from my great vision somehow and I had done nothing yet to make the tree bloom. (Black Elk Speaks, page 237)

The circle symbolized a united human family - the thing that was needed in order to restore life to the people

Later, when Black Elk joined in the Ghost Dance, he had another vision, an "out of body" spiritual experience in which he saw the return of peace and prosperity to his people:

I must have fallen down, but I felt as though I had fallen off a swing when it was going forward, and I was floating head first through the air...There was a ridge right in front of me, and I thought I was going to run into it, but I went right over it. On the other side of the ridge I could see a beautiful land where many, many people were camping in a great circle. I could see that they were happy and had plenty. Everywhere there were drying racks full of meat. The air was clear and beautiful with living light that was everywhere. All around the circle, feeding on the green, green grass were fat and happy horses; and animals of all kinds were scattered all over the green hills, and singing hunters were return-ing with their meat...

I floated over teepees and began to come down feet first at the center of the hoop where I could see a beautiful tree all green and full of flowers. When I touched the ground, two men were coming toward me, and they wore holy shirts made and painted in a certain way. They came to me and said: "It is not yet time to see your father, who is happy. You have work to do. We will give you something that you shall carry back to your people, and with it they shall come to see their loved ones."

I knew it was the way their holy shirts were made that they

*wanted me to take back. They told me to return at once, and then I
was out in the air again, floating fast as before...*

*Then I fell back into my body, and as I did this I heard
voices all around and above me, and I was sitting on the ground.
Many were crowding around, asking me what vision I had seen.
(Black Elk Speaks, pages 242 and 243)*

Soon after Black Elk relayed his vision, special shirts were
designed, called Ghost Shirts, that were worn during the perform-
ance of the Ghost Dance. These shirts were believed to have mystical powers to repel bullets from white men's guns.

The Messiah Craze

News reports of the Ghost Dance were spreading, as so-
called journalists seized half-bits of information and created sensa-
tionalized stories of "impending hostilities" with native tribes.
Most whites could not recognize the difference between a war
dance and a religious dance, and newspapers ran headlines such as
"Indians Are Dancing" and "Redskins Prepare For War." A story
in the November 29, 1889 edition of the *New York Times* was
headlined, "Rosebuds Ready to Fight" and stated, *"Their war
dance began yesterday morning...The Indians danced in a circle..."*

Whites fearfully began to call Wovoka's movement, "The
Messiah Craze." The Mormon Church was in turmoil. Many believed that Christ had returned to earth as an "Indian" while prominent leaders of the church felt compelled to repudiate the idea.
Still, many Mormons awaited the Millennium when Christ would
usher in a new world. They expected this to take place December
23, 1890, the anniversary of Joseph Smith's birth.

Throughout the year, as the Ghost Dance movement grew
in intensity, the hysteria among whites increased. Rumors spread
of an attack planned by the Lakota, and on November 13, 1890,
President Harrison ordered the secretary of war to assume military
responsibility to prevent an outbreak from the Lakota reservations.

The appearance of military troops at the reservation caused
a panic among the natives, and, fearing the outbreak of violence,
three thousand fled from Rosebud and Pine Ridge to the Badlands.
They were led by Short Bull and Kicking Bear.

Native Americans were enlisted in the armed services to help control the native population. The result was a massacre of natives by natives. Scott Peterson observes:

At daybreak on Monday, December 15, 1890, forty-three Indian police and volunteers led by Lieutenant Bull Head surrounded the two log cabins at Sitting Bull's compound. The old medicine man was found asleep on the floor of the larger cabin. Informed that he was under arrest, he sent one of his wives to the other cabin for some clothes. While dressing, he verbally abused the police. In the meantime, about 150 of his followers congregated outside.

When the police brought him out, Sitting Bull called upon them to rescue him. In response, Catch-the-Bear raised his rifle and shot Lieutenant Bull Head, who, although mortally wounded, immediately killed Sitting Bull. A bloody fight ensued in which six policemen and eight "hostiles," including Sitting Bull's seventeen-year-old son, lost their lives. (Native American Prophecies, by Scott Peterson, page 158.)

Here was another unfortunate prophecy fulfilled. Just as the Hopi elders had warned, "Given his language and his knowledge, our own people will become the instrument by which he will try to rule over us and carve the rest of us into his image."

When Kicking Bear and Short Bull heard of the slaughter of Sitting Bull and the others, they knew that the whites were ready to inflict a grand scale massacre. Chief Sitanka, or "Big Foot," and his followers headed toward the camp at Wounded Knee Creek. The leaders agreed that they should surrender. Big Foot was ill with pneumonia and besides his 106 warriors, there were over 200 women and children.

The Wounded Knee Massacre

The morning of December 1890, Colonel Forsyth and troops from the U.S. Cavalry gathered 470 strong at Wounded Knee. They ordered Big Foot and his people to come out of their teepees and surrender their weapons. What followed was what became known as the "Last Indian War." Yellow Bird, a medicine man, reminded the group that they were wearing their Ghost Shirts and would not be harmed by the soldiers' bullets.

In his book, Scott Peterson describes the scene:

Suddenly, he stooped down and threw a handful of dust in the air. Whether this was a gesture of contempt or a signal to at-tack will never be known. A moment later, though, a young Indian raised a rifle from beneath his blanket and shot at the troops. The soldiers responded with a deadly barrage.

Other warriors pulled concealed revolvers, knives, and war clubs from their belts. A bloody battle ensued. Minutes later, an estimated two hundred Indian men, women and children lay dead or wounded on the frozen ground. Many were blown apart by the cavalry's four Hotchkiss guns that poured in two pound explosive shells at the rate of fifty per minute. Sixty soldiers were also killed or wounded, a fact that enraged many cavalry soldiers...

Barbarously, they hunted down the survivors of the initial encounter. Bodies of women and children were later found par-tially buried in snow up to two miles away. Three days later, a long trench was dug and the frozen corpses of some three hundred Indian men, women and children, stripped of their Ghost Shirts, were thrown in naked and buried without ceremony. (Native American Prophecies, by Scott Peterson.)

In his book *500 Nations, An Illustrated History of North American Indians,* author Alvin M. Josephy, Jr. quotes the report from Thomas H. Tibbles of the Omaha World Herald who had rid-den to Wounded Knee with the 7th Cavalry. He was present during the aftermath of the attack and saw the bodies being examined. Some of the few who had survived were desperately clinging to life.

Tibbles watched in astonishment as the doctors arrived to try to save the living. He described the horrible scene of a badly wounded young women holding on to her baby, trying to give the thirsty child a drink of water. He helped her give the baby a drink, then when he held the cup to the woman's dry, parched lips, she tried to drink, but the water flowed out through a hole in her neck where she had been shot.

Sickened, he went to find a surgeon to help her, and recog-nized an old Civil War surgeon working among the wounded. The

surgeon was badly shaken at the sight. He told Tibbles, "This is
the first time I've seen a lot of women and children shot to pieces.
I can't stand it." (500 Nations, by Alvin M. Josephy, Jr., page 442)

The slaughter of Big Foot's band at Wounded Knee Creek
in 1890 was cruel proof that whites were not about to simply van-
ish. Wovoka was devastated by the cold-blooded killing of families
at Wounded Knee. He believed in the powerful vision he experienced while in a coma, that the Messiah had returned to earth. But
he was disenchanted that the Ghost Dance movement had ended so
tragically, and for years afterward, he wondered how things had
gone so wrong.

In 1892, Wovoka told James Mooney of the Smithsonian
Institution that whites had lied about him. He said he never
claimed to be Jesus. He said that many had disobeyed his instructions, that he never encouraged hostility toward whites. He insisted that his message was one of peace. He also maintained his
claim that he had been to heaven and received divine revelation.

But, the turn of the century came and went, and still there
was no Messiah to bring the people back to their previous glory.
Although the Ghost Dance was still practiced secretly by those
who continued to hope and pray, the religious fervor began to fade.
Wovoka became a disappointed and disillusioned man.

Visitors still came to see him and many still considered him
a holy man. They sent letters and brought gifts. But, soon Wovoka discouraged the visitors and said that he preferred that the
dancing stop. He reclaimed the name Jack Wilson and lived out the
rest of his life with that identity until his death in 1932.

Black Elk, true to his prophetic vision, also lived to be a
very old man. Yet, his childhood vision of a resurrection of his
people did not occur in his lifetime. As an old man, he reflected on
the effects of the Wounded Knee massacre:

When I look back now from this high hill of my old age, I
can still see the butchered women and children lying heaped and
scattered all along the crooked gulch as plain as when I saw them
with eyes still young. And I can see that something else died there
in the bloody mud, and was buried in the blizzard. A people's
dream died there. It was a beautiful dream.
And I, to whom so great a vision was given in my youth, --

you see me now a pitiful old man who has done nothing, for the nation's hoop is broken and scattered. There is no center any longer, and the sacred tree is dead. (Black Elk Speaks, page 270).

It seemed that the prophecies of the coming of a new world would never come to pass. The old Native American ways appeared to be gone forever.

If the white man was the true Elder White Brother, what happened to his half of the sacred Stone Tablet? No, they insist to this day. The true Pahana is still to come.
"Up until this point, there have been a lot of white people," said the Reed and Snake clans' member. "Is this the right white person? Is that the right white person? Most of them nowadays come as lawyers. We know that this person is going to come from the East. So far," he added with a gentle laugh, "we've had lawyers from Utah and Colorado. But no one from the East." (Native American Prophecies, by Scott Peterson, page 252)

It seems that the true Elder White Brother cannot be interpreted as referring to those European immigrants who came to America. Nor does it seem likely that their descendents have, over time, transformed into the true Elder White Brother of the prophecies. It stands to reason that it was not meant to be understood in the context of the complexion of skin tone.

If understood in a metaphorical sense, with white symbolizing purity, it could then be a person of yellow or beige or black or brown or red complexion. Whatever color they that person might be physically, they would have the prophecies of the tablets written on their heart. They would have purity of heart, purity of spirit, and purity of soul. You would recognize these qualities because they would have purity of actions and deeds.

Chapter Seven
The Rise of Gog and Magog

7A – Geronimo (Goyathiay)
The infamous Apache warrior was known for his legendary battles against the US cavalry. He was also recognized as a medicine man among his people. In the photo above he wears the official medicine man headdress. He is a classic symbol of Native American resistance against injustice – representing the last of the major 19th century Native American struggles for liberation. (Encyclopedia of Native North America, page 74)

Chapter Seven
The Rise of Gog and Magog

Soon We will show them Our Signs in the farthest regions of the earth, and among their own people until it becomes manifest to them that it is the truth. Is it not enough that the Lord is Witness over all things? (Holy Quran, Chapter 41 verse 54)

In this Quranic passage God reveals that He and His angels will show signs to people who live far away from that region where the Quran was originally revealed, to show that its message is true and from the Creator. This is followed by an important reminder, posed in the form of a question, that God is aware of all things that have and will take place. Could the prophecy in this Quranic passage possibly be related to the divine visions revealed to Wovoka?

The Master Plan

Wovoka died without having seen the Messiah whose existence he said had been revealed to him during his spiritual experience. The teachings that Wovoka relayed to his people, "Do not tell lies, do not drink alcohol, do not fight with one another," etc. were noble principles. Indeed, these pacifist teachings resembled the teachings of Jesus greatly. This is probably one reason why some came to believe that Wovoka was the return of Jesus and/or a prophet – even though he never specifically claimed to be either. There were, however, many individuals during that time who did make specific claims that they were the Second Coming of Jesus, or a Messiah, or a prophet.

Throughout the 1800s there were great expectations from around the world that such a person would appear. Many of the "major" religions of the world foretold of a Messiah. The Christians awaited the return of Jesus. According to Islamic traditions, Jesus would also return followed shortly after by a "Mahdi." Buddhists were expecting the return of Buddha. All major religions promised the advent of a Divine personage who would usher in a new era of peace for mankind and unite the world under one banner as one human family.

However, the human family during this period was totally disconnected. Native Americans were being persecuted to justify the government's confiscation of their land. Mother Earth and the animal kingdom were under a major attack by the Western powers, as gold, silver and copper mining stripped the land and animals were hunted to near extinction. The prevailing attitude was that nothing was sacred when it came down to the materialistic pursuits of the West. It was a philosophy of greed and not need.

Signs of the Anti-Christ

According to many religious traditions, when the reformer or reformers would come it would be during a specific era when the world would be, as a whole, filled with chaos. The people would be estranged from God and would be morally and spiritually bankrupt. There is a name, in various religious traditions, commonly associated with this time. The Hindus use the name "Kalu Yuga." "The End Tyrant" is the name used in Jewish tradition. In Islam, it is called the "Dajjal." But the most popular name associated with these turbulent "last days" is the term "Anti-Christ."

Although some people believe the Anti-Christ will be one single individual with supernatural like powers, when examining the different religious traditions, the Anti-Christ takes on a much broader definition. There are striking similarities in the above religious traditions with those traditions of the Hopi, and other Native American tribes, relating to that entity that would bring destruction to the Native way of life as well as the whole world.

There is another common term that is used in relation to the "end-times." In the Holy Quran it gives two names to describe a specific group of people:

Until the Gog and Magog people are let through their barrier and they swiftly swarm from every hill. Then will the True Promise draw nigh of fulfillment. Then behold! The eyes of the Unbelievers will fixedly stare in horror: "Ah! Woe to us! We were indeed heedless of this; nay; we truly did wrong!" (The Quran, Abdullah Yusuf Ali translation, Surah 21: Al Anbiya, Verses 95-97)

In both Christian and Islamic traditions the names Gog and

Magog go hand in hand with that of the Anti-Christ or Dajjal. In Christian theology, Gog and Magog are mentioned in the book of Revelations, relating to the time of the Second Coming of Jesus. In Islamic traditions, Gog and Magog are understood to mean wild and lawless tribes who will overcome the barriers of their physical environment - mountains, oceans, etc. - and swarm through the earth. This would be one of the signs of the approaching Divine Judgment and the coming of the Mahdi for the Muslims.

From about 500 AD to 1500 AD, Europe experienced an age of ignorance commonly known as "The Dark Ages." After a thousand years of remaining in this state, European civilization rose and entered a period of enlightenment known as the Renaissance. European nations gradually increased their travel by land and sea. Although they were advancing materially and in the arts and sciences, they were missing an important element from their progression as a people – an element perhaps lost during those turbulent times of "The Dark Ages." They lacked respect for other groups of people and other cultures. They were, according to the behavior they exhibited toward Native American nations, wild and lawless tribes. They followed none of the protocols for civilized conduct between peoples.

There is much resemblance between the wild and lawless tribes known as Gog and Magog and those peoples who emerged onto the world scene after spending a millennium in "The Dark Ages." The Bible records in the New Testament that:

When the thousand years are ended, Satan will be released from his prison and will come out to deceive the nations at the Four Corners of the earth, Gog and Magog, in order to gather them for battle; they are as numerous as the sands of the sea. They marched up over the breadth of the earth and surrounded the camp of the beloved city. And fire came down from heaven and consumed them. (Holy Bible, Revelations, Chapter 20, Verses 7-9.)

This Biblical verse seems to be referring to those nations on the continent of Europe. Some have expanded this interpretation to also include Russia. Some have interpreted Gog to mean Russia. In the Bible it refers to Gog as the "chief prince of Rosh, Meshech and Tubal" (Ezekiel 38:3.) Some believe these names stand for Russia, Moscow and Tobolsk – the two latter being major cities. So Gog and Magog may be those nations in the areas of Russian and Europe.

According to Islamic understanding this is definitely the case. During the late 19th century, in his book *Ayyamus Sulh: Roohani Khazain,* Hazrat Mirza Ghulam Ahmad, of Qadian, India, gave his interpretation:

> *Gog and Magog are a people who would surpass all others in their ability to put fire to various uses and are indeed pioneers in this field. Their very names (Note: in Arabic Yajooj and Majooj are derived from the word ajeej which means fire) indicate that all their inventions, be they ships, trains or other machines, were to be fueled with fire. And they would fight their battles with firearms. They would excel all other nations on the earth in pressing fire into their service. This is why they are called Yajooj and Majooj.*
>
> *Obviously, therefore, they are the European nations who in the science of utilizing fire are so skillful, adept and outstanding that it need not be elaborated upon. They are the same Europeans who have been referred to as Gog and Magog in the old scriptures given to the Israelite prophets. Moscow is even mentioned therein by name, which was the capital of ancient Russia. It was destined that the Promised Messiah would appear in the age of Gog and Magog. (Mirza Ghulam Ahmad, Ayyamus Sulh: Roohani Khazain Vol. 14 p.424)*

Keepers of the Fire

One can't help but notice the striking resemblance between Islam's definition of Gog and Magog as those European nations who have harnessed the energy of fire, and the ancient Hopi traditions that speak of the white brother who was given the sacred knowledge of the fire. The widespread misuse of this knowledge is also clearly spoken of in both traditions.

In Islamic tradition, Gog and Magog and the term Dajjal are two different elements of the same danger. Gog and Magog represent the political element of this danger, the domination of the "western powers;" and the Dajjal represents the religious and cultural element of this danger. According to the traditions of the Holy Prophet of Islam, the Dajjal is described as being blind in his right eye. Written on his forehead would be the word "disbeliever"

(Bukhari and Muslim.) The right eye in Islamic traditions symbolically represents spirituality and the area between the eyes has long been given special spiritual significance in many religions. Perhaps the Bible's warning of "the mark of the beast" on the right hand and forehead symbolically represent thoughts and actions that would be motivated by evil. The materialism and greed that is the driving force behind Western culture is a sign of such evil.

So what then would qualify as the Dajjal, or that religious or cultural belief of Gog and Magog, in this context? Hadhrat Mirza Tahir Ahmad, head of the Ahmadiyya Movement in Islam, explains:

Dajjal is not the name of the Western powers. Dajjal is the name of a power that has an attitude of anti-Christ - but anti-Christ in what sense? In the sense that in name they purport to bow to the will of Jesus Christ, but in reality, in practice they do not pay any homage to the values that were dear to Jesus Christ. This is dajjal, i.e. duplicity. This is an extremely objectionable attitude that has been mentioned in the traditions of the Holy Prophet as dajjal, as a fraud committed against people.

It is possible that some Christians may take offence at what I am about to say. However, if they are realistic and they have a true understanding of the situation, they will not take offence. The situation is exactly as I have stated when we take into consideration the present state of sinfulness and the present state of moving away from Christian values.

Every person who is unprejudiced against the truth would agree that the world of Christianity is moving away from Christian values... What was the teaching of Christ? If someone strikes you on one cheek, turn the other. Compare this with the West's reaction to various situations of threats of aggression. They are more than vengeful. They crush all possible opposition. This is not the Christianity taught by Jesus Christ. Jesus Christ was holy, truly holy...

In short, the behavior of the Christian world is completely opposed to the behavior of Jesus Christ and his true followers. What you find today in this society was not present in the society that Jesus created himself. This is the dajjal, i.e. duplicity. According to the prophecy of the Holy Prophet, the name Jesus Christ would be lauded widely all over the world but the values of

Jesus would be trampled upon. Any such powers must be referred to as dajjal, or, people who deceive the world along with their own people, in the name of Jesus. (Q&A session with Hadhrat Mirza Tahir Ahmad, published in Review of Religions, November 1999)

The irony is that it is the Christian nations who have manifested the Anti-Christ. Somewhere along the line the true philosophy of Jesus was clearly abandoned by those people who would come to represent him to the world. Many, like the Spanish Conquistadors, professed a strong belief in the doctrines of Christianity, yet were completely devoid of all moral goodness. Did these rapists and murderers truly think they were doing "God's work?"

The general lack of respect for other religions and cultures shown by many of the Christian missionaries was apparent in their plan to convert the "savages." In reality, they never made any serious attempt to investigate the Native American spiritual teachings. Had they done so, they would have noticed how much in harmony Native American teachings were with the teachings of Jesus. In their hearts they did not consider the Indians as their brothers, but yet felt it was their religious duty to "save" them from their "pagan" beliefs by making them believe in the "blood of Jesus Christ." The term dajjal (duplicity) and the Native American description of those people who would be "two-hearted," both accurately describe the hypocritical nature of those early Christian missionaries. The Hopi warned their own people against this philosophy of hypocrisy:

The beginning of the new age of the prophecies of tomorrow has begun to unfold before our eyes. It was said that, among Bahanna the people with the Cross will appear in our land. They will be kind and helpful with good hearts. Beware, for they will be the instruments of Bahanna's kingdom and will seduce you into forsaking the laws of our Great Creator. The wicked of our people will join their flock to clear their sins, but this will be in vain. (The Hopi Survival Kit, by Thomas E. Mails, pages 182-183)

This last warning seems clearly to refer to the doctrine of atonement, which is an essential part of the mainstream doctrine of Christianity. Disputes over certain aspects of Christian dogma do not all originate from outside the religion. Within the world of

Christianity there are hot debates over doctrinal beliefs. During the third century council meetings were held concerning doctrines to determine the official beliefs of the Christian Church.

The Council of Nicene in the year 325 was one such council. This Roman council took it upon itself to decide which Gospels should be included and which ones should not. One of those they chose not to include was The Gospel of Barnabas.

Today this book is considered heretical, despite the fact that it was also supposedly written by one of Jesus' disciples, Barnabas, during the same time period that Matthew, Mark, Luke, and John were written. It's understandable why they chose to do away with this Gospel, because it has many passages that are clearly not in harmony with the Roman Christian interpretation - which was heavily based on the teachings of Paul.

In one passage in the Gospel of Barnabas, Jesus prophesizes that after his death his teaching will be corrupted. He reportedly warns against the very belief that later became so central to the teachings of Christianity:

But when God shall take me away from the world, Satan will raise again this accursed sedition, by making the impious believe that I am God and son of God, whence my words and my doctrine shall be contaminated... (The Gospel of Barnabas, edited and translated from the Italian Ms. In the Imperial Library at Vienna by Lonsdale and Laura Ragg, page 122)

Bahanna, the True White Brother?

The term Bahanna, or Pahanna, is commonly used by some Native American nations to refer to "white" people. The Hopi prophecies specifically spoke of the return of the "white brother." It was said that one of the four brothers of the four directions, upon his return, might show signs that he had forgotten the spiritual principles taught by the Great Spirit – principles such as universal brotherhood. It is clear that one of the brothers, the Bahanna, did forget the sacred teachings.

But these terms have deeper meanings than simple descriptions of color. For instance, the Lakota gave the white settlers the name "wasichu," which means "the greedy one" (literally "He who takes the fat.") The term's origins lie not in the description of the physical person, but in the description of the behavior. It came to apply to "whites" in general because a large majority of them who interacted with the Natives Americans exhibited excessive greed.

The Hopi prophecies speak of the return of the "True White Brother" - one who would not be like those "white" people with whom the natives became familiar originally. In this context, it could be literal or metaphorical or maybe even both. It could mean literally some one of white complexion. It could also mean metaphorically one who is pure, righteous, etc. In various cultures and religions of the world the color white symbolically represents these attributes.

Although physical descriptions of certain groups of people are given as signs for the Anti-Christ, the root of the evil of those people would lie in their hearts and minds. In other words, the focus is not what the people look like, but rather the divine principles they do or do not follow. This is because a man's character can only be deduced from his thoughts, which are made manifest through his actions.

In religious prophecies, references to physical characteristics are more or less signs to identify a thing to be understood in a greater context. The prophecies of the Quran also give physical descriptions as signs. These signs possess a deeper meaning. One verse mentions a characteristic commonly associated with people of European descent.

The day when the trumpet will be blown. And on that day We shall gather the sinful together, blue-eyed. (The Holy Quran, Ta Ha, Chapter 20, verse 103)

Commenting on the meaning of this verse, writer and editor Fareed Ahmad, in an article in 1996, stated:

In this verse it is the Arabic word zurqan which primarily translates as 'blue-eyed' and there is no error in this translation, but it also has the second meaning of 'becoming blind or dim sighted (see Lane and Aqrab). There are other Arabic words that describe the blind, words that have been used in other places in the Quran. Therefore the use here of the word zurqan (blue-eyed/becoming blind) is significant...

It further states in verse 104 that those people,

...will talk to one another in a low tone saying that 'You tarried only ten days.'

> *The ten days signifies ten centuries after Hijra and is understood to refer to the European nations in that they remained in a state of dormancy for ten centuries after Hijra, and it was only in the 17th century that they reasserted themselves and started to conquer the world. If we look at the world today then it is easily seen that on the whole the Western nations (which include blue-eyed people) are highly advanced materially, yet spiritual they remain blind and indeed they have created other gods beside the One God in their materialistic pursuits.*
>
> *It should be remembered that the verse does not in any way imply that all blue-eyed people are sinful – it merely states a common characteristic that will be shared by one particular group. To take this verse and insinuate that it is a basis for a racist philosophy would be utterly false and taking it completely out of context. (Notes & Comments, by Fareed Ahmad, Review of Religions: November 1996)*

The term Hijrah (from emigration) refers to the Islamic calendar which began in the year 622 AD, when the Prophet Muhammad first migrated from Mecca to the city of Medina. Ten centuries, or one millennium, after this date would be 1622 AD which is the 17th century.

It is clear that neither Islam, nor Christianity, nor any of the Native American spiritual teachings intend to demonize all Christians or all "white" people. However, when the prophecies of Native Americans, Islam, and Christianity are collectively examined they clearly identify a specific group of people as those who have manifested the "end-times entity" by their actions. It was not the white complexion or the color of the eye, but the philosophy, the evil thoughts and desires of those Europeans who brought with them Anti-Christian values of intolerance and greed.

It was the "white" Europeans, with a corrupted form of Christianity, who came to the Americas and conquered it by force. It was by force that they conquered the eastern regions of South America. And it was by force they conquered the western regions of South America. Even the Indians at the southernmost tip of South America, the Onas and the Yahgans, did not escape. They spread into North America, and subjected every single tribe by force, from the East Coast to the West Coast, to conform to a new government, a new culture, a new religion, and a new way of life. Even the natives at the northernmost tip of Alaska, the Inuit (Eskimos) did not escape.

The Europeans went into the regions of West Africa and colonized it. They set up one of the most barbaric institutions of slavery ever known to man. They brought millions upon millions out of Africa in chains to "the land of the free" and created an environment that forced them into Christianity. They extended their power to the bottom of South Africa, creating a future for its native inhabitants under apartheid.

Christian Europe's colonization continued into the lands of the east, where both China and India came under a heavy influence of British rule. One by one each of the Polynesian Islands and its inhabitants were forced to submit to the West. Even the native people of Hawaii, the most remote island on the planet, would see their homeland trampled underneath the feet of Western exploitation. In Australia, the same scenario that occurred in America was repeated among the Aboriginal people – genocide, disease, and cultural annihilation. And what would the original natives on the island of Tasmania say about their contact with Europeans. Unfortunately, nothing. The Native Tasmanians no longer exist – they were exterminated.

No Nation Exempt

It would be quite erroneous to think that other religions and ethnic groups are exempt from going astray from the teachings of the Great Spirit. Other religions and nations also have prophecies of their own demise – by their own hands. The prophets sent to other nations warned their own followers that this demise would not be the result of external factors. It would be due to their own neglect of their spiritual teachings. The Holy Prophet of Islam told his followers 1400 years ago that:

A time will come when nothing will remain of Islam except its name and nothing will remain of the Quran except its script. Mosques will be full of worshipers, but as far as righteousness is concerned they will be empty and deserted. Their religious leaders will be the worst of creatures under the canopy of the heavens. Evil plots will originate from them and to them will they return. (Mishkat)

Today it is quite clear that within Islamic society there are a number of "fundamentalist" groups whose mission is not to try and spread the message of Islam through reason and argument, exhibiting peace and love; but instead their mission is to terrorize and create mischief throughout the world. In truth, there is nothing fundamentally Islamic about their behavior and it is strange that the term fundamental is so often applied to religious fanatics.

During a 2001 interview, Tall Oak of the Pequot and Wampanoag Nations explained how he documents the fulfillment of prophecy:

When I watch the evening news every night, to me that is documentation of our prophecies. Every night when you watch the news, especially anything that has to deal with the weather, is always at its extreme. The worst forest fires, the worst floods, the worst storms. For as long as they've kept records, they've all been the worst on record. It's no accident. This is documentation of the prophecies being fulfilled.

I have a VCR I bought a few years back... I document all these things every time they're on. I got my VCR ready to go when the news comes on. When I label it on my tape I label it "prophecy."

...It's the Creator speaking to us. That's what is so important about documenting these things as they take place. So every night you hear His voice when you tune in to the news. (Tall Oak Interview 2001)

I was greatly impressed with Tall Oak's meticulous method of documenting this age when so many prophecies are coming to pass. Shortly after this interview was taken at the Schemitzun 2001 Powwow, I saw on the news that night the fulfillment of the Islamic prophecy mentioned by the Prophet Muhammad. I saw on the news a woman in Afghanistan who was shot in the head for not observing the extreme dress code laws imposed by the government. Then they showed another woman who was forced to buy stale bread, which was used as animal feed, just so she could feed

her children. The Taliban of Afghanistan, who began brutally oppressing their women during the 1990s, are a perfect example of
those "religious leaders" who would "be the worst of creatures."
By orders of their "religious police" it is even against the law to fly
a kite!

These extreme beliefs are a result of the neglect and abuse
of the spiritual teachings that were given to their people by the
Creator. The Afghani government might argue that they are correct, yet their interpretation of Islam does not bring peace of mind
to the people of Afghanistan. Other Islamic groups in Afghanistan
have been exposed for their involvement in the drug trade.

All of these Afghani tribes claim to be Muslims yet they
fight among themselves over control of land and territory, differences in ethnicity amongst their people, who should be in power
and have control over illicit trade. The Warlords will declare war
on one another simply if the price is right. As they gun each other
down they yell out *Allahu Akbar! Allahu Akbar!* (God is Great,
God is Great.) This attitude is an example of how the rest of the
Islamic world is also showing signs of decay.

Although many have tried to take on the role of a khalifat,
or spiritual leader, to unite the Muslim community and correct
wrong beliefs and attitudes, the Muslim world can't agree on who
should have such power. Many of them have wound up being assassinated by the very people they had desired to uplift. Many
Muslims, frustrated and misguided, decide to take the law into
their own hands and commit murder in the name of the Creator.

The land of Arabia, where the religion of Islam originated,
is still considered in the minds of many to be the ideal example of
an Islamic society. In reality, however, the prevailing interpretations of Islam in Arabia are not far from those entertained in Afghanistan.

Today Arabia and much of the Muslim world is in turmoil,
with internal warfare violently destroying the lives of the people.
Failure to follow the divine laws have made these nations vulnerable to military subjugation by outside forces. Would the Arabian
government still stand without the military support of the West?
Many Muslims are quick to place all blame on the "Great Satan"
(the United States and Great Britain) but are slow to acknowledge
those "Satans" or erroneous beliefs that have distorted the pristine
teachings of Islam.

Modern vs. Traditional

Native American prophecies also foretold that their demise would not be from the actions of Bahanna alone, but also by the actions of their own people. Thomas E. Mails explains:

The new government order will be established on our land, our own people with short hair will take positions in the government disguised as the ear and tongue for our Nation. They will also be the tools influenced by the Bahanna's kingdom. They will together with the Cross, help fulfill the desire of Bahanna to take over our land by diluting and dissolving our beliefs and traditional culture. (The Hopi Survival Kit, Thomas E. Mails, page 183)

Since the time of the first European settlers there has been an ongoing war within the larger Native American community between those who want to maintain the traditional ways and those who want to assimilate further into modern society. Today among the Hopi there are two factions, the Traditionalists and the Tribal Council, who exist at opposite ends of the polarity. The Traditionalists desire to live off the land like their ancestors in whatever capacity they can, in spite of modernization. The Tribal Council believes that the Hopi people must give up some of their traditions, due to modern circumstances, and fully adopt the ways of modern society. Both groups feel that they represent the best interest of the Hopi people.

The Hopi Tribal Council are like those leaders among the Pequot and other tribes who have built casinos on their reservations in hopes of "modernizing" the Native American community and helping it out financially. The Traditionalists believe that acts such as these are in direct contrast to the teachings of the Great Spirit. They were warned against adopting the ways of the Bahanna, and feel that although there may be some benefit, as a whole it would be to the detriment of the Hopi people. They feel that the overall culture of the Bahanna has not been rooted in higher spiritual principles. Thomas E. Mails explains the Traditionalists' point of view of the Bahanna:

As a whole, they do not have religion. We do not need any of that. We are satisfied with the order of our Great Creator, whose light does not blind us and does not lead us into confusion. Instead His light brightens the road, so that we can absorb its great wisdom and live like humans. While Bahanna are destroying our world by their inventions, they are blinded to such an extent that they do not even know their own origin. (The Hopi Survival Kit, Thomas E. Mails, page 183)

The origin of the white brother is the same origin of the red, the yellow, and the black brother. They are the offspring of Mother Earth and therefore connected to her. As stated earlier, Hopi tradition states that mankind was originally one unified society and that the Great Spirit spread them out into four directions, becoming four colors, to each receive a concentration of sacred knowledge to be learned and later shared with the rest of the human family. Despite the fact that other religious scriptures have clearly alluded to the same thing, it has historically been the tendency for Eurocentric thought to separate itself apart from the human family and the common ancestry shared by all. The bogus theories of scientific racism that were formed during the 19th century only further contributed to delaying the unification mankind.

In his book, *The Hopi Survival Kit*, Thomas E. Mails points out major flaws in Eurocentric thought that have historically contributed to Europeans' inability to unify with the other members of the human family:

Two monumental cultural factors have prevented the European immigrants from recognizing this process of widespread unification: the presumption of racial superiority and the need to conquer and convert. And a recent tendency to discredit all knowledge which does not stand the test of scientific thought. (The Hopi Survival Kit, Thomas E. Mails, page 185)

During the 1960s, a cultural revolution began in "white" society among the young people who had a desire to distance themselves from a world full of racism and materialism. They sought out the wisdom of their Native American brother, and sympathized with the struggle of their African American brother. Today there is much hope that the "white brother" will continue to grow towards understanding his true place in the human family.

Chapter Eight
The Age of the Messiah

8A – Comets

Whether it's a shooting stars, comet, or meteor shower, these types of heavenly events have had special significance in many religious traditions throughout the world. Many times they mark the coming of a great change in a society or the coming of a specific individual. The Gospel of Matthew states that "stars will fall from the sky" to mark the Second Coming of Jesus.

Chapter Eight
The Age of the Messiah

"For many will come in my name, claiming, 'I am the Christ' (or Messiah), and will deceive many." (Matthew 24:5 and also 24:24)

In the New Testament Jesus issues this caution against following false prophets. He states that the appearance of such deceivers will be a sign that marks his return. This means that among a group of individuals claiming to be the Messiah, the true Messiah would also be among them. In chapter 24 of the Book of Matthew Jesus also gives a number of other signs to help identify his Second Coming. Those specific prophetic signs will be mentioned later in conjunction with the prophetic signs of Native American and Islamic traditions, revealing striking similarities.

The Candidacy for Messiah

It cannot be ignored that the time for the coming of the Messiah is well overdue. One should question whether or not this coming may have already occurred. If so we must make an investigation to discover the identities of that person or persons.

First, the question to be explored is whether the Creator will send an independent Messiah to each religion or will there just be one Messiah for the entire world who fulfills the signs for the various religions. If the Creator was to send a different Messiah for each religion, it becomes more difficult to foresee unity among all of mankind, considering the differences we have now.

If it's taken into consideration that, since all Messiahs will be from the same God and therefore will all be "on the same page," it stands to reason that God could just send one messiah. If one Messiah comes, it also stands to reason that he will bring one teaching, resembling and representing the best of the teachings of all religions, for the reformation of the world. It doesn't seem logical that the Messiah would bring a separate reform for each independent religion.

Certain religious groups will argue against a belief that one person will come to unite the world under one religion. Their preference is that only their religion, and their interpretation, is correct and that the only Messiah to return would be specifically for those who share their particular beliefs and no one else. This is an arrogant and selfish belief.

If a universal Messiah did come, many religious groups would quickly label this person as that super human Anti-Christ of their imagination. Although the world has clearly demonstrated that it does not need such an individual to go astray, many still expect a specific person to come and deceive and corrupt the entire world At this point in time, does the Mercy and Justice of God call for a great deceiver or a great reformer?

Let's consider some of those extraordinary individuals who, during their lifetime, were considered to be the Messiah.

Joseph Smith

Born in 1805, he started his unique Christian ministry in 1830 when he was just 25 years old. This church was founded on the belief that he had received revelations from God. These revelations, originally engraved on golden plates, were later condensed into a book that is known as the *Book of Mormon*. This book is considered by his followers to be as equally important as the Bible. On June 27, 1844, Joseph Smith was shot to death by an angry mob. The Mormon Church, officially known as the Church of Latter Day Saints, has always recognized Joseph Smith as a prophet of God in the Biblical sense.

Sayyid `Alí Muhammad Shírází (The Báb)

The origins of the Bahá'í Faith stem from a movement founded by this Iranian man in 1844. Born around 1819, Sayyid `Alí Muhammad Shírází would later call himself, "the Báb," which means "the gate." Those who followed him were called Bábís. In 1848, he wrote a book explaining his teachings and declaring that he was starting a new religious dispensation that abrogated all those that went before it (Judaism, Christianity, Islam, etc.) During that year he was also taken to court, a set up by his opponents. During this trail he announced publicly that he was the Mahdi spoken of in Islamic tradition. His opponents eventually decided to have him executed and in 1850 he was shot to death by firing squad. Many of his followers later joined the Bahá'í Faith.

Mírzá Hausayn `Alí Núrí (Bahá'u'lláh)

According to various writings of the Báb, there was to come after him a messianic figure who would be "Him whom God shall make manifest" - the one foretold by all world religions. Mírzá Hausayn `Alí Núrí was born November 12, 1817 to a wealthy Persian family. While a young man he joined the Bábís. Because he followed the religion of the Báb, he was eventually thrown in jail. While being confined to a dungeon, he had a spiritual experience that became the start of his mission. In April of 1863, he told some of his fellow Bábís that he was that person the Báb had foretold. He would come to be known as Bahá'u'lláh. He is the official founder of the Bahá'í Faith and his followers are known as Bahá'ís. On May 29, 1892 he passed away at the age of 74. Bahá'u'lláh appointed his son, Abdul Baha (May 23, 1844-November 29, 1921) as his successor.

Muhammad Ahmad Ibn Abd Allah

Born in 1844, he is known as "The Divinely Guided One" and "The Mahdi of the Sudan." He officially claimed to be the long awaited Mahdi on June 29, 1881. He said that God had given him the mission of purifying Islam and to fight all those who were against the religion. He would manage to wage a successful "holy war" against British colonization and also Egyptian opposition. He eventually created an Islamic state that extended from regions in Central Africa all the way to the coasts of the Red Sea. In 1885, shortly after conquering the city of Khartoum, he became ill and died. Today, he has a large following known as the Ansaru Allah community.

Cheikh Ahmadou Bamba

Ahmed Ben Mohamen Ben Abib Allah was born in 1852 in the village of Mbacke in the West African country of Senegal. He was considered "spiritually inclined" as a young man and he would eventually attract many people to come and study under him as a teacher. As his following grew it roused the suspicion of the French who had at that time colonized Senegal. Although his Sufi philosophy was one of non-violent resistance, the French believed he was planning a rebellion. Fearing his power they exiled him to

Gabon where he remained from 1895 to 1902. After a short return, the French decided again it was in their best interest to exile him. This time they banished him to the deserts of Mauritania where he remained from 1903 to 1907. The French plot to neutralize Ahmadou Bamba failed, as the people in Mauritania grew to love him. He eventually returned to his homeland of Senegal where he died in 1927. Many great miracles have been attributed to this Sufi Cheikh and various titles have been bestowed upon him such as saint and prophet. Cheikh Ahmadou Bamba was the founder of the Mouride Sufi Islamic Movement.

Haile Selassie

Originally born Ras Tafari in 1892, he would eventually become the Emperor of Ethiopia. He won great popularity due to his determined resistance to the Italian invasion of Ethiopia during 1935 and 1941. It is believed by some that Ethiopia's Imperial Family were the descendents of the son of King Solomon and the Queen of Sheba, who was called Menelik. Haile Selassie and the Imperial Family were Coptic Christians. Although Haile Selassie never publicly claimed to be a prophet or messiah, many would come to believe that he had a divine status. He has been called "the King of Kings" and the "Conquering Lion of Judah." Those who believed in the divinity of Haile Salassie are known as "Rasta-farians."

Noble Drew Ali

Born Timothy Drew on January 8, 1886 in North Carolina. According to some legends, he was the son of ex-slaves and was raised among the Cherokee Indians. In 1923, he moved to Chicago and founded a movement that is today known nationwide as the Moorish Science Temple of America, a movement that incorporates ideas from Islam and Egyptian Freemasonry. Noble Drew Ali taught his followers that they were the descendents of Moroccans who were captured and sold into slavery and also that their genealogy could be traced back directly to Jesus. He also taught that both Native American and African Americans, as well as some other groups, were direct descendents of Canaan and Ham of the Bible. He called these groups the "original Asiatic nations" and believed that the future of all civilization rested on their shoulders. Noble Drew Ali referred to himself as the "second prophet of Islam" and in 1927 wrote the *Circle Seven Koran* – which had information compiled from various religious and esoteric books.

Wallace D. Fard

It has been said that W.D. Fard, also known as Master Fard Muhammad, was born around 1887 in the Arabian city of Mecca. Other sources say he was born in America. Much mystery surrounds the origins of this man who is the founder of a movement that is known as the Nation of Islam. He appeared among the black ghettos of Detroit around 1930 as a peddler of silks. Seeing the poor condition that black people lived in, he actively sought to uplift the community there, discouraging the people against drinking alcohol, smoking and gambling. He taught them that before they were sold into slavery their true religion was Islam. He did not hesitate to condemn the white Christian world for the atrocities committed against those of African descent. During his time in Detroit he proclaimed himself a "prophet of Allah from the Holy City of Mecca." Later on his followers called him "God in Person." Wallace D. Fard vanished from the public eye around 1933.

Elijah Muhammad

Elijah Poole was born on October 7, 1897. He grew up in Georgia and moved to Detroit in 1923. While in Detroit he became acquainted with various Pan-African and Islamic movements, such as the Universal Negro Improvement Association, the Moorish Science Temple, and the Ahmadiyya Movement. He eventually became a follower of W.D. Fard and would become his successor as the head of the Nation of Islam.

Under the leadership of Elijah Muhammad, membership in the Nation of Islam grew nationwide. He continued to teach that Islam was the true religion for African Americans and that the day would soon come when the "white race," as the historic oppressors of the "black race," would have to face the wrath of God. Elijah Muhammad succeeded W.D. Fard as the messenger with the task of resurrecting black people in America. Some of his later followers would consider him a prophet. "The Honorable Elijah Muhammad" passed away in 1973. He was succeeded by his son Wallace Deen Muhammad who took the movement towards a more "traditional" approach to Islam. Minister Louis Farrakhan revived the old Nation of Islam and is currently the supreme head.

Mirza Ghulam Ahmad

He was born in a small town in India in 1835. He spent most of his young life immersed in religious studies. As he grew older his knowledge increased and he became a well respected Islamic teacher. In 1882 he had a number of spiritual experiences and he believed that God had chosen him to reform the religion of Islam. Later he said that the Almighty had proclaimed him to be the Messiah that was spoken of in all world religions, and that he was the Second Coming of Jesus. When Ahmad went public with his claim, he received opposition from Muslims, Christians, and every other religious group in India. Ahmad founded an organization based on his claim called the Ahmadiyya Movement in Islam. His followers are called Ahmadi Muslims. Mirza Ghulam Ahmad died in 1908.

John Alexander Dowie

He was born in Edinburgh Scotland in 1847. While working as a Congregational minister in Melbourne, Australia he became convinced that he had the power of healing. Eventually he established the International Divine Healing Association. In 1888 he came to America and later ended up in Chicago where he founded the Christian Catholic Church around 1896.

In 1901 Dowie claimed to be the Third Coming of the prophet Elijah – the forerunner to the highly anticipated Second Coming of Jesus. Also during that time he founded the city of Zion in northern Illinois. Dowie created the city based on Biblical principles. Alcohol and gambling were strictly prohibited. Even pork was banned in the City of Zion, where all the streets had Biblical names. Dowie died in 1907.

These are just a few of the people during the 1800s who either made specific claims to being divine messengers, or were later given the status of divine messengers by some of their followers. The time period in which all these individuals were born and lived is of great importance, and will be discussed more later in this chapter. But with so many different people fitting the description of Messiah, how can one differentiate between them all?

True vs. False Prophets

Many Native Americans, despite the shaky history they have had with Christianity, have managed to get past this and adopt the Christian faith. Therefore, when examining the issue of true versus false prophets, the Christian perspective must be explored. As stated earlier, the New Testament documents how Jesus warned that many claiming to be him would come in the latter days but that they could not, obviously, all be him. In the same chapter where this verse is (Matthew 24,) another verse also warns:

And many false prophets shall rise, and shall deceive many. (Matthew 24:11)

It is likely that this verse about claimants to prophethood and the other verse about claimants to the Christ are not two different categories; but are actually both referring to one and the same situation. The Bible contains a solution to the problem that arises with the appearance of so many claiming to be from God. The answer lies in the Old Testament in the Book of Deuteronomy. God spoke to Moses concerning this issue. Moses then relayed the message to the children of Israel.

...A prophet who presumes to speak in My name anything I have not commanded him to speak, or a prophet who speaks in the name of other gods, must be put to death.
You may say to yourselves, "How can we know when a message has not been spoken by the Lord?"
When a prophet speaketh in the name of the Lord, if the thing follow not, nor come to pass, that is a thing that which the Lord hath not spoken but the Prophet hath spoken it presumptuously: Thou shalt not be afraid of him. (Deuteronomy 18:20 - 22)

The Quran also relates this story of Moses:

Moses said to them, 'Woe to you, forge not a lie against Allah, Lest He destroy you utterly by some punishment and, surely, he who forges a lie shall perish.' (Chapter 20, Ta Ha, verse 62)

Both the Bible and the Quran state that God will take it

upon Himself to expose and punish those who specifically claimed to be His messengers, but in truth were not. It is important that God should do so because, if not, anyone could make such a claim and mislead people. But it is up to the Creator of the Heavens and the Earth to show signs in that persons favor if they are true, or to do just the opposite if they are false. And as shown above, if they are false, God says that he will severely punish them for their lies.

Duel of the Prophets

There was a very interesting scenario of global proportions that took place between the last two claimants that were mentioned before – Mirza Ghulam Ahmad and John Alexander Dowie. What transpired between them serves as an example in which God appears to have clearly distinguished between two people who both claimed to be His messengers.

Around the year 1902 these two claimants became aware of each other. Although Dowie was in America's Midwest and Ahmad was in northern India, both had established religious publications. Dowie's *Leaves of Healing* paper had subscribers worldwide and Ahmad's *Review of Religions*, established just a year before in 1901, was also gaining popularity.

Dowie had expressed many times in his paper that he believed that a final showdown between Christianity and Islam would take place in the near future. He also believed that his movement, based in Zion, Illinois, would specifically bring about Christianity's victory. On one such occasion he wrote in his *Leaves of Healing* publication that:

One of the greatest systems in the Orient is Mohammedanism... the Mohammedan is taught to look forward to heaven as one vast brothel and harem, where he can find satisfaction in women that are prepared for him as the creatures of lust. Zion will have to wipe out that shocking blot upon humanity. That accursed flag will have to come down from the high towers of Jerusalem.

May God help me to knock at the gate of the Moslem before long! The Moslem will fight. There are hundreds and millions of them. One of the great wars imminent is that between the Cross and the Crescent. But, beloved, there is something stronger than steel. It is the Sword of the Spirit. There is something greater than anger, it is Love. Love subdues the man; it subdues the nation, and will reach the heart... (Leaves of Healing, Volume XIII, page 474)

In 1902 Dowie published a prophecy in his paper that declared that God would destroy all "Mohammedans" in the near future if they did not repent and adopt Christianity. The name "Mohammedans" to refer to Muslims and "Mohammedanism" to refer to the religion of Islam was commonly used by Western society out of ignorance – calling it after its founder like Christianity or Buddhism.

News of this prophecy reached India and came to the attention of Mirza Ghulam Ahmad, who lived in a remote and rural town called Qadian. Ahmad, after becoming more familiar with the opinions of Dowie concerning the fate of Muslims worldwide, gave a response in his own publication that same year. Concerning Dowie he states:

He has repeatedly declared in his paper that his God, Jesus, had told him that all Muslims will be destroyed and not one of them will survive, except those who should acknowledge the son of Mary as their God and Dowie as the apostle of that artificial god... We have a message for Dowie as that he need not be anxious to destroy all Muslims...

There is a very easy way of determining whether Dowie's God is true or our God. That way is that Mr. Dowie need not repeatedly announce his prophecy of the destruction of all Muslims, but should keep me alone in his mind and should pray that of the two of us, the one who is false may die before the other... I am sure that through the adoption of this course a way shall be opened for Mr. Dowie and all the Christians for the recognition of the truth... The only condition is that the death of either of us should not be compassed by human hands... (Review of Religions, Vol. 1 No. 9, p. 348)

News of the challenge reached America and, because Dowie was somewhat of a celebrity, it was widely published in many newspapers throughout the U.S. On March 29, 1903, the *New York Times* editorial read: "The Rival Prophets." The June 25, 1903 edition of the *Baltimore American* had an article entitled "Dowie versus Ghulam." Also during 1903, this event was covered in the *Albany Express* (June 25,) the *Boston Pilot* (June 27,) Chicago's *Inter Ocean* (June 27 and 28,) the *Montana Daily Record* (July 1,) and even the *The London Times* (November 9.)

Dowie did not acknowledge the challenge at first. But because the American news media had brought it to the limelight, and continued to pester him concerning it, Dowie decided to respond. He published the following response later that year:

> *In India, there is a Mohammedan Messiah who keeps on writing to me that Jesus Christ lies buried in Kashmir. People ask me why do I not send him the necessary reply? Do you think that I should answer such gnats and flies? If I were to put my foot on them I would crush them to death. The fact is that I merely give them a chance to fly away and survive. (Leaves of Healing, September 26, 1903) (Republished again on December 27, 1903)*

Shortly after Dowie's September statement Ahmad published another response, which also came to the attention of the American news media. On October 26, 1903 the headline for *The Commercial Advertiser* of New York read: "Dowie Challenged: Indian Messiah Dares Him to Prove His Claims." The following excerpts from the article record the prophecy of Mirza Ghulam Ahmad concerning the future demise of John Alexander Dowie.

> *If the pretender to Elijahship shows his willingness by any direct or indirect means to enter the lists against me, he shall leave the world before my eyes with great sorrow and torment. These two signs are particularly for Europe and America - that they ponder over them and benefit by them. ...*
>
> *If he accepts the challenge within this period and fulfills all its conditions as published by me previously and makes an announcement to that effect in his paper, the world will soon see the end of this contest. I am about seventy years of age, while Dr. Dowie is about fifty-five, and therefore, compared with me, he is a young man still. But since the matter is not to be settled by age, I do not care for this great disparity of years. The whole matter rests in the hand of Him who is the Lord of heaven and earth and Judge over all judges, and He will decide it in favor of the true claimant. (The Commercial Advertiser, New York, October 26, 1903)*

Ahmad claimed that he was given directions by God to engage in this challenge that was also clearly a prediction as to the
fate of Dowie. Ahmad, being a learned Muslim and also a person
who himself dared to make extraordinary claims in the name of
God, was well aware of the various verses of the Quran that warn
that anyone who deceives others claiming they received divine
revelation from God or His angels would provoke His wrath:

*And, had he forged (and attributed) any sayings to Us, We
would surely have seized him by the right hand, and then surely
We would have severed his life-artery. (Chapter 69, Al-Haqqah
(The Reality), verse 45)*

It must be emphasized again that since everyone eventually
dies, the type of death spoken of here would have certain characteristics that must be taken into context given the specific situation.
This death would be accompanied by various circumstances that
would "expose" the one who was lying in God's name and that the
circumstances surrounding their death would appear as if they had
provoked the wrath of God Almighty .

According to Ahmad's prophecy, Dowie's could willingly
accept the challenge directly or indirectly. When Dowie's September response was reprinted in December, it appeared that although he had not openly accepted the challenge, he had not re-
tracted any of his former statements and claims either. According
to Ahmad, only a complete change of attitude and public repen-
tance could avert God's wrath and gain His mercy.

When these exchanges took place in 1903 Dowie was on
top of the world. His Christian Catholic Church had a following of
over a hundred thousand people worldwide. He was a major figure
in the Chicago political scene. His estimated worth was over
twenty million.

With his great wealth he had bought land and established
the city of Zion, Illinois as a Christian utopia. He was healthy, he
had a loving wife and son, and followers who believed in his divine claim and his power to heal the sick. But history records that
John Alexander Dowie would loose all of this.

His life began to take a turn for the worse on October 1st
1905 when he suffered a sever attack of paralysis. Two months

later on December 19th he had a second attack that left him completely incapacitated. Dowie would never walk or stand again and would spend the rest of his life being transported around by his servants on a stretcher.

In an attempt to recuperate, Dowie decided to leave the city of Zion and spend some time on a tropical island. While he was away, a number of his disciples whom he had left in charge stumbled upon some rather disturbing information. A shortage of 2.5 million dollars in Zion accounts led them to a number of questionable "investments." One discovery was made of thirty five thousand dollars worth of expensive gifts given to various female citizens of Zion, further raising suspicions. Around the same time, alcohol was discovered hidden in the basement of Dowie's home.

When Dowie heard the news of his exposure, he returned home hoping to mend the situation. Upon his arrival into Zion, not a single follower came out to receive him or his entourage. The entire population of Zion, had turned against him. His former trusted disciples wanted nothing to do with him. Although he was allowed back into his home, he was completely barred from gaining any access to his million dollar Zion accounts and received a firm social boycott from the Zion community.

Not only was he abandoned by his followers but also by his very own family. His father disowned him. His wife and only son came out together against him and testified that the very man who had prohibited his followers from drinking alcohol was in fact a closet drunkard. The very man who claimed to posses the gift of divine healing was nothing more than a charlatan. Dowie, after loosing everything, eventually went mad.

The outcome of the above confrontation between two men both claiming to be divine messengers of God went in favor of Mirza Ghulam Ahmad, whose prophecy that John Alexander Dowie would "leave the world before my eyes with great sorrow and torment" came true.

Within four years of Ahmad's prediction Dowie, who was in tip top shape, lost everything and died in 1907 crippled and depressed. Ahmad who was eleven years older than Dowie, and had long suffered from a number of illnesses, went on to live another full year before his death in 1908.

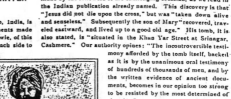

Fulfillment of a Grand Prophecy

Vol. XXVI., No. 25]   THE LITERARY DIGEST   895.

RIVAL MESSIAHS IN A PROPOSED PRAYER DUEL.

MIRZA GHULAM AHMAD, of Qadian, Punjab, India, is "the promised Messiah," according to statements made over his own signature. He has challenged Dr. Dowie, of this country, to a duel, the weapon being prayer and each side to petition the Almighty "that of us two whoever is the liar may perish first." The person who issues this challenge, according to *The Review of Religions* (Gurdaspur, India), is "the Promised Messiah" sent "for the reformation of the world exactly at the time fixed by calculations based on biblical prophecies as the time of the advent of the Messiah," and he has a following of over a hundred thousand members, "rapidly growing." The teaching of this Messiah is that Christ was a mere mortal, a good man, without divinity. Mirza Ghulam Ahmad further declares in the organ already named:

"Dr. Dowie should further bear in mind that this challenge does not proceed from an ordinary Mohammedan. I am the very Messiah, the promised one, for whom he is so anxiously waiting. Between Dr. Dowie's position and mine the difference is this, that Dowie fixes the appearance of the Messiah within the next twenty-five years, while I give him the glad tidings that the Messiah has already appeared. I am that Messiah, and Almighty God has shown numerous signs from earth as well as from heaven in my support. My following, which already claims a hundred thousand souls, is making a rapid progress. The proof that Dr. Dowie furnishes in support of his extravagant claims is the very height of absurdity. He claims to have healed hundreds of sick men. But why did his healing-power fail in the case of his own beloved daughter, where it should have been exercised in the highest degree?"

John Alexander Dowie, writes the Messiah, "claims to have been sent by the son of Mary in his capacity of Godhead, that as his apostle he may draw the whole world to a belief in the despicable dogma of his divinity." The Indian claimant proceeds:

"Whether the God of Mohammedans or the God of Dowie is the true God may be settled without the loss of millions of lives which Dr. Dowie's prediction would involve. That method is that, without threatening the Mohammedan public in general with destruction, he should choose me as his opponent and pray to God that of us two whoever is the liar may perish first. I look upon the son of Mary as a weak human being, altho I recognize him as a prophet of God, while Dr. Dowie takes him for the Lord of Universe. Which of us is right, is the real point at issue. If Dr. Dowie is certain of the divinity of the son of Mary, he should publish the proposed prayer with the signatures of at least one thousand men affixed to it. Upon receiving it, I should address the same prayer to Almighty God and publish it with the signatures of the same number of witnesses. If Dr. Dowie has the courage to accept this challenge, he will thereby open a way for all other Christians to the acceptance of truth. In making this proposal, I have not taken the initiative, but the jealous God has inspired me upon Dr. Dowie's presumptuous prediction that all Mohammedans shall perish."

"An important discovery regarding Jesus Christ" has been

MIRZA GHULAM AHMAD.

He has challenged Dr. Dowie to a prayer duel to the death.

made by the followers of the challenging Messiah, as we read in the Indian publication already named. This discovery is that "Jesus did not die upon the cross," but was "taken down alive and senseless." Subsequently the son of Mary "recovered, traveled eastward, and lived up to a good old age." His tomb, it is also stated, is "situated in the Khan Yar Street at Srinagar, Cashmere." Our authority opines: "The incontrovertible testimony afforded by the tomb itself, backed as it is by the unanimous oral testimony of hundreds of thousands of men, and by the written evidence of ancient documents, becomes in our opinion too strong to be resisted by the most determined of skeptics."

TRANSFORMATION OF THE QUAKER.

QUAKERS, "the people called Friends," have been greatly changed by time, according to Edward Gardner, himself a Quaker, who writes in *The American Friend* (Philadelphia). This transformation, according to him, is one of the significant religious phenomena of the day, and it should not be overlooked by those who would understand the moral forces now at work in this republic. A great future is predicted for the transforming movement. "It will be an aggressive church, not a passive one," he says. "Its work will be constructive as well as preservative." He gives the following details of the Quaker's transformation:

"For a century or more, Friends were known by their peculiar dress. At length it was discovered that simplicity of dress did not mean uniformity, and that the cut of the coat or the shape of the bonnet did not add to the spiritual life of the wearer. The Quaker of to-day is not known by his dress; if he dresses with taste, but not with extravagance, he is, no doubt, conforming more nearly to the spirit of early Quakerism than did his predecessor of a hundred years ago. George Fox himself, it is said, bought his wife a red mantle, and William Penn's dress did not at all conform to the Quaker ideal of a later period.

"Music, painting, and literature are now taking their rightful place among Friends. Congregational singing is recognized as being a part of true worship, and in many places instrumental music is also made a part of the devotional service.

"In the Quaker home of a century ago the sweet influence of song was unknown. The Bible and the writings of early Friends were the only books; no pictures adorned the walls, and Puritan austerity was the rule of life. In the Quaker home of to-day we find music, paintings, and an abundance of books; means of recreation abound, and a daily paper has become almost a necessity."

The Quaker home of 1800 "lacked somewhat in grace," thinks the Friend we are quoting, "in kindly sympathy, and in a broad view of life." Quaker "sternness" may have "repelled some." But there is reason to think that the Quaker home of 1900 has less of these faults. We read further:

"Closer interdenominational fellowship has become very prominent within the last few years. It is very gratifying to know that the Friends have entered heartily into the spirit of it. This agreement on the essentials of Christianity and hearty cooperation in active work gives great encouragement for the future. The sharp contrast between the bitterness of the church-members of one denomination toward those of other denominations in

8B – *Newspaper Report On Prayer Duel*

The above article is one of many that documented the historic prayer duel between the Hazrat Mirza Ghulam Ahmad of India and Dr. Alexander Dowie of Zion Illinois. (Courtesy of The Ahmadiyya Movement in Islam)

On the day John Alexander Dowie died, the *Chicago Evening American* ran an article entitled "Dowie Dies: Unforgiving Wife, Son and Father." In the article it summarizes the rise and fall of the popular American religious icon.

> *When John Alexander Dowie passed away, his death ended the most spectacular and remarkable career that modern times have known. Gigantic success and tragic failures punctuate his life. Here are some of the remarkable works and reversals that marked Dowie's career:*

> > *He built a creed; he was excommunicated.*
> > *He built a city; he was expelled from it.*
> > *He amassed a fortune of millions; he was reduced to virtual poverty.*
> > *He elevated Voliva to a great power; Voliva ruined him.*
> > *He drew about him thousands who worshiped him; he died deserted by all save a handful of the faithful.*
> > *(Chicago Evening American, March 9, 1907)*

The next day the *New York Times* March 10, 1907 edition read "Dowie Dies in the City He Founded: Neither wife nor son, whom he had repulsed, was at his bedside."

Attention again shifted to the mysterious man from India who had foretold the death of the American icon. *The Dunville Gazette* June 7, 1907 read "A Messiah in India." The last report covered by the news on this event was in *The Sunday Boston Herald*, June 23, 1907. It read "Great is Mirza Ghulam Ahmad The Messiah: Foretold Pathetic End of Dowie, and now He Predicts Plague, Floods and Earthquake."

It is interesting that such a highly publicized event, one of obvious religious and historical value, is never spoken of in today's religious and historical circles of America. The American news media during that time found it of value, and confirmed that one of the two claimants was true in all of his predictions.

Chapter Nine
Divine Confirmation

9A – Ghost Dance Shirt

This is one example of the garments worn by people in the Ghost Dance Movement in anticipation of the coming of the Messiah. According to Wovoka's dream, no ornaments were allowed and only simple colors used. The symbols of the moon and stars were common. The above shirt depicts two stars and a crescent. Could these divine instructions also be signs concerning the Messiah?

Chapter Nine
Divine Confirmation

I am the true Messiah who was to come in the last ages: thus has the Almighty spoken to me. I do not claim to be the promised Messiah simply by my own assertion, but Almighty God who made the earth and heaven has borne witness to the truth of my claim... If these are simply my own assertions, and there is no other authority for them, I am a liar. But if Almighty God bears witness to my truth, no one give the lie to me. (Mirza Ghulam Ahmad, Quoted from The Sunday Herald, Boston, June 23, 1907)

The Claim of Mirza Ghulam Ahmad

Mirza Ghulam Ahmad was born February 20, 1835 to a Persian family in the small village of Qadian, India (present day Pakistan.) As a young boy he was very interested in religious studies and exercises. As a Muslim, he was particularly interested in Islamic studies but he also enjoyed studying the other religions prevalent in India during that time, such as Christianity and Hinduism. As he grew older, his devotion to religious learning increased and he became rather aloof towards worldly matters. However, at the frequent requests of his father, and out of respect, he reluctantly involved himself in secular pursuits.

Because of his preoccupation with religious studies, his reputation grew as a learned man of Islamic theology. Around the age of forty Ahmad became more involved in the defense of his faith against growing hostilities from certain religious groups who were attacking the religion of Islam and slandering the name of its founder, the Prophet Muhammad. From Ahmad's perspective, the majority of Muslims during that time did not truly understand the sublime and noble teaching of the Quran. They were not equipped with the knowledge to defend their faith and many held beliefs that rightfully deserved criticism. After he began to write in the defense of Islam, Ahmad quickly became a hero among many Muslims throughout India. He was considered to be one of the most learned scholars of Islam.

In the year of 1882, Ahmad had a series of spiritual experiences. Although he had experienced a number of "true dreams" and visions throughout his adult life and even as a young boy, these experiences became more profound during 1882. In one of his more famous books, *Braheen Ahmadiyya*, he recalls one such experience that occurred that year:

...I saw in a dream that a search was being made for one who should revive the faith. A person appeared before me and pointing to me said (Arabic), "This is a man who loves the Messenger of Allah." His meaning was that the principle condition of this assignment was the love of the Holy Prophet and that I fulfilled that condition. (Braheen Ahmadiyya Volume 4, page 503, footnote 3)(Tadhkirah, page 30)

Dreams have long held great importance in religious traditions. Today, in this very secular world, dreams are regarded as nothing more than the mechanisms of the brain responding to the external input of the physical world. To the spiritually inclined, however, this external input can also come from beyond the physical world when "activated" by the Creator. The Native Americans have always recognized this capacity and looked to dreams for divine guidance.

If the dreamer was successful, he would obtain a vision of a dream spirit who would give him a specific ability or power and show him how to solicit that power through special songs and ritualistic activities.... In dreams, the dreaming soul – that aspect of self that travels in visions away from the body – could contact the dream spirit and receive instructions. Dreams were considered by many native groups to be the most valid means for communicating with the spiritual powers and the primary basis of religious knowledge. (Encyclopedia of North American Indians, edited by Fredrick E. Hoxie, page 170)

Like the spiritual beliefs of the Native Americans, Ahmad regarded the dream state as just one way in which the Creator communicates with His creation and offers guidance. It was this relationship that Ahmad later sought to reestablish between the Creator and all of mankind. Also in the year 1882 he had another dream. In this one he saw the Holy Prophet Muhammad. He recalls:

> *I was occupied in writing something one night and then went to sleep and in my dream saw the Holy Prophet (on whom be peace) and his face was bright like the full moon. He came close to me and I felt as if he wished to embrace me, which he did, and I saw that rays of light proceeding from his countenance had entered into me. I felt these rays were like palpable light and I believed that I was seeing them and not only through my spiritual sight but also with my physical eyes. Thereafter I did not perceive that he had separated himself from me nor did I perceive that he had left me. In those very days the doors of revelation were opened to me and God addressed me and said (Arabic), "Allah bless thee O Ahmad." (Ayena Kamalat-e-Islam, page 550) (Tadhkirah, page 30)*

Ahmad received further revelations that year that led him to conclude that God had chosen him to be the Mujaddid (or Reformer) of Islam for the 14th century of the Hijrah. According to Islamic traditions, God would raise a reformer every century to revive the religion of Islam and help preserve its true teachings. There are various Muslim saints who lived centuries prior to the Islamic 14th century (1800s) who the Muslim world have recognized as Mujaddids. These reformers, however, should not be confused with that special reformer that the Muslim world refers to as the Mahdi.

During March of 1885, Ahmad had another spiritual experience that gave him further insight into the status that God had bestowed on him. He described this revelation in a book entitled *Ishtihar*:

> *The author has been informed that he is the Reformer of the age and that his qualities have a spiritual resemblance to the qualities of Jesus, son of Mary, and that there is a strong affinity between us.*
>
> *I have also been told that following the example of particular Prophets and Messengers, through the blessings of perfect obedience to the best of mankind and the most exalted of all Messengers (on whom be the peace and blessings of Allah) I have been exalted above many of the great saints who have passed away be-*

fore me. (Mirza Tahir Ahmad, Ishtihar Zameemah Surmah Chashm Arya) (Tadhkirah, page 77)

By divine instruction, Ahmad went public. Through a public advertisement he sent out news of his claim to many religious leaders and scholars of different faiths as well as kings and respected leaders. He requested that all seekers after truth come and visit him at his home in Qadian. Then they could assess for themselves his character and wisdom and could perhaps bear witness to heavenly signs shown in his favor.

Many people did come and visit him and came to believe in the truth of his claim. Due to his growing following, an organization was needed and on March 23, 1889, the first initiation ceremony was held commemorating the event. This was the birth of the Ahmadiyya Movement in Islam.

At the very end of 1890, it was clearly revealed to Ahmad that he was that Messiah promised by all religions; including both the Second Coming of Jesus for the Christians and the Mahdi for the Muslims; and that he was the chosen one who would usher in a new era of peace on a worldwide scale and unify all of mankind – and he would do so under the banner of Islam.

Second Comings: Literal or Metaphorical?

There is a reoccurring theme in the traditions of many Native Americans concerning the return of certain individuals. The Incan ruler Pachacuti was expected to return, although he never literally returned. The periodical returns of Quetzalcoatl also seem to have taken place metaphorically with each occurrence. If we examine the traditions of other faiths will we find the same theme?

Many people on earth who are familiar with the Biblical prophecy of the Second Coming of Jesus. Christianity, a popular belief worldwide, is worth examining concerning the debate over literal or metaphorical second comings.

According to the teachings of Christianity, Jesus would return again in the latter days. The manner of his second coming has been interpreted as being literal by the greater percentage of the Christian world. (Also, this literal view is shared by the majority of the Islamic world.) This belief holds that the Jesus that walked the earth 2000 years ago will be the same one who returns. Those who entertain this belief do so because they believe that the Biblical version documented in the New Testament clearly states that Jesus physically ascended. And since Jesus had ascended to heaven, it is inferred and expected that he will someday descend from heaven.

However, there is another story concerning ascension in the New Testament that has been given an entirely different interpretation. The story of this prophet's ascension and return has never been questioned as being anything other than metaphorical.

According to Jewish tradition, God informed the people of Israel that before the advent of their Messiah (Jesus) there would first be a Second Coming of the prophet Elijah. In the Old Testament it states:

Behold, I will send you Elijah the prophet before the coming of the great and dreadful day of the Lord. (Malachi 4:5)

Many of the Jews of Jesus' time believed that Elijah had physically ascended to heaven. The Old Testament describes this ascension of the prophet Elijah while he was in the presence of another by the name of Elisha:

As they were walking along and talking together, suddenly a chariot of fire and horses of fire appeared and separated the two of them, and Elijah went up to heaven in a whirlwind. (2nd Kings 2:11)

Because many of the Jews at that time held the belief that Elijah had literally ascended to heaven in a chariot of fire with flaming horses, they also expected him to descend from heaven in the same way. However, the Bible records that the return of Elijah did not take place in the manner that they anticipated. The Bible states that God revealed to Zacherias, the father of John the Baptist, concerning his newborn son that:

He will go on before the Lord, in the spirit and power of Elijah... (Luke 1:17)

According to the New Testament, God did not support the view of the Jewish majority of that time concerning Elijah's return.

The above verse explains that the manner in which God manifested the return of the prophet Elijah was metaphorical and not literal. It further raises an eyebrow as to whether the Biblical account of Elijah's whirlwind ascension was meant to be taken literally.

Jesus himself supports the idea that the second coming of the prophet Elijah took place metaphorically in the person of John the Baptist.

"But I tell you, Elijah has already come, and they did not recognize him, but have done to him everything they wished. In the same way the Son of Man is going to suffer at their hands." Then the disciples understood that he was talking to them about John the Baptist. (Matthew 17:11) (also in Mark 9:13)

It is interesting that even though God has given this clear example that a literal second coming was not what He had in mind, a majority of the Christians and Muslims, who do not deny that John the Baptist was the Second Coming of the Prophet Elijah, believe without question that the same Jesus of two thousand years ago will return, literally descending from heaven. Jesus it seems, settled this debate long ago when he stated:

For I tell you, you will not see me again until you say, 'Blessed is he who comes in the name of the Lord.' (Matthew 23:39)

When a person comes in the name of another it means that he will act on behalf of that person. So this person Jesus speaks of will recall his teachings and have a similar philosophy, a similar disposition, and a similar mission.

Mirza Ghulam Ahmad claimed to be the Second Coming of Jesus in this capacity. He claimed that just as Jesus was the messiah for the Jews, he was the messiah for the Muslims, and therefore for all of mankind, since Islam's claim is that it was revealed as a universal religion for all of mankind.

Just as Jesus claimed in Matthew 5:17 that he had not come to abolish the law of the Prophet Moses but to fulfill it, Mirza Ghulam Ahmad claimed that he did not come to abolish the law of the Prophet Muhammad, but to fulfill its destiny of finally becoming the religion of every nation and tribe all over the world.

Just as Jesus claimed he was the truth, the way, and the

light, to the people of his time, Mirza Ghulam Ahmad made a similar claim to the people of this age:

> *I am the light of this dark age; he who follows me will be saved from falling into the pit prepared by the Devil for those who walk in darkness. I have been sent by God to lead the people of the world to the true God through peace and humility, and to reassert the reign of morals in Islam. God has provided me with heavenly signs, for the satisfaction of seekers after truth. He has done wonderful things in my support; He has disclosed to me secrets of the unseen and of the future which, according to the holy books, is the sign of a true claimant to divine office, and He has vouchsafed to me holy and pure knowledge. Therefore, the souls which hate truth and are pleased with darkness, have turned against me. But I have decided to be sympathetic towards mankind – as far as I can. So, in this age the greatest sympathy for the Christians is that their attention should be called to the true God, Who is free from such defects as being born and having to suffer death and undergo suffering, the God who made the earliest heavenly bodies spherical in shape and, in His law of nature, set down this point of spiritual guidance that, like a sphere, there is in Him Unity and absence of direction. That is why the things which occupy space have not been made triangular, i.e., the things which God created first such as the earth, the heaven, the sun and the moon, and all the stars, and elements – all are spherical, the spherical nature of which points towards Unity. Therefore there can be no greater sympathy with the Christians than that they should be guided towards the God Whose creations declare Him to be free from the idea of trinity. (Jesus in India, by Mirza Ghulam Ahmad, pages 19-20)*

The circle has always symbolically represented the unity of the Creator in many cultures. It has special significance in many Native American traditions. One Hopi symbol of the sacred hoop shows four different colors, representing the four brothers of mankind, as small circles inside one larger circle.

The various heavenly bodies like the sun and moon and stars, are all common symbols used in many cultures. The shirt worn by the members of the Ghost Dance movement, as shown at the beginning of this chapter, frequently used images of moons and stars. There was a special significance in the way these shirts were made. In Black Elk's vision, he recalled how "two men were coming toward me, and they wore holy shirts made and painted in a certain way." He also commented that, "I knew it was the way their holy shirts were made that they wanted me to take back."

Perhaps these images of moons and stars symbolically represented the belief to be held by those wearing the shirts, a belief in the unity of God and the unity of all mankind. This would end the conflict between them and protect them from spiritual attack. It is a tragedy that those who died at the Wounded Knee Massacre believed that the way the shirts were made would physically protect them from the bullets of the soldiers.

Signs In The Heavens

Astronomers recorded an unusual amount of abnormal activity in the heavens during the latter part of the 1800s. A multitude of comets shot across the heavens, creating a spectacular display in the night sky throughout the second half of the 1800s and early 1900s. The following are some of those awe inspiring comets that appeared during that time.

Great Comet of 1811
This comet could be seen in the skies for 9 months. It is the longest period that a comet has ever been seen with the naked eye. It reached its brightest between September and October. It had bright twin tails, one straight and one that curved. In the famous book *War and Peace*, by Leo Tolstoy, the author makes mention of this comet.

Halley's Comet of 1835
This was able to be seen with the naked eye from September to February, when it slowly began to fade.

Great March Comet of 1843
This comet, when first spotted, was shining brighter than any other comet seen in the previous seven centuries. Its own orbit was 400 years. The tail of the comet extended about 300 million kilometers – the longest ever recorded. Although predominately viewed in the Southern Hemisphere, at the very beginning it was so bright that it could be seen in America and parts of Europe in

full daylight side by side with the sun. Many people of the time thought it to be a sign that Judgment Day was at hand and it caused widespread panic in many areas.

Comet Donati

With an elliptical orbit of 2000 years, this comet was first spotted in August of 1858. It slowly grew brighter and brighter until the end of November of that same year.

Great Comet of 1861

On June 29 this comet came so close to the earth that the earth actually passed through the very end of its tail. It was said to be brighter than any star or planet other than Venus.

Eclipse Comet of 1882

On May 17, this comet was photographed during a total solar eclipse. It was named *Tewfik*, after the ruler of Egypt. It was the first comet ever discovered on the plate of a total solar eclipse.

Morehouse Comet of 1908

Named after American astronomer Daniel W. Morehouse. it showed ongoing variations of its tail from day to day - so much so that it was hard to identify it as the same comet. The tail seemed to break into fragments, almost completely separating it- self from the head at one point.

Halley's Comet of 1910

Halley's Comet returned again shortly after the Daylight Comet. It was the less spectacular of the two. It was viewable to the naked eye from early February to mid July.

Whether it evolved from religious teachings or ancient su- perstitions, the extreme increase in unusual activity in the heavens was a sign for many that something profound was about to happen on the earth. According to many religious traditions, the sudden increase in comets, shooting stars and eclipses were all signs that the earth was about to receive some sort of divine visitation. As the turn of the century approached, religious groups around the world looked toward the heavens and anxiously awaited the com- ing of the Messiah.

Looking to the heavens for signs in Christian tradition has a long history. The specific reference to stars marking the time of the second coming of Christ was also important during the time of the first coming of Christ. In the Gospel of Barnabas, it relays the role of a star in heralding the birth of Jesus. According to the story, three men from the east were guided by a star, perhaps a shooting star, that led them to the Messiah they had been awaiting.

In the reign of Herod, king of Judaea, when Jesus was born, three magi in the parts of the east were observing the stars of heaven. Whereupon appeared to them a star of great brightness, wherefore having concluded among themselves, they came to Judaea, guided by the star, which went before them, and arriving at Jerusalem they asked where was born the King of the Jews. (The Gospel of Barnabas, edited and translated from the Italian Ms. In the Imperial Library at Vienna by Lonsdale and Laura Ragg, p. 6)

The Gospel of Barnabas, although ignored by most Christian clergy, is a dynamic book that further supports the historical reality of Jesus and his teachings. The story of the three men who saw a bright star in the sky as a sign of the Messiah supports other Christian accounts.

Also of religious significance is an event that is described in the book of Mark in the New Testament. In chapter 13 verse 24 it states that "stars shall be falling from heaven" during the time of the Second Coming. This verse seems to be describing the rare event of a meteoric shower.

History records two of the more spectacular meteoric showers took place in the years 1832, and 1833. Other notable showers also occurred in 1866, 1872 and 1885. Many Messianic figures made claims that fell during this era when so many great comets and meteor showers were lighting up the skies. The life span of these individuals in relation to when these heavenly events took place is important. Most of the claimants died before many of the comets had a chance to make their appearance or were born after most of the comets had appeared. Mirza Ghulam Ahmad believed that the heavenly activity that was taking place during these times was related to his claim to being the Messiah. He recalls his experience one night as he witnessed one such event:

On the night between November 27 and 28, 1885 there was such a display of meteors in the sky as I had not witnessed before and so many flames were traversing the skies that there is no other spectacle in the world which can be cited as an illustration. I recall that at that time the revelation (Arabic), "It was not you who let loose but it was Allah Who let loose," was vouchsafed to me repeatedly. This pelting had great affinity to the pelting of the stars in the sky.

This exhibition that occurred on that night was visible all over and was described in great wonder in the papers of Europe, America and Asia. People might have thought that it was purposeless, yet God Almighty knows that the person who watched this spectacle with the greatest attention and derived the greatest delight from it was myself. My eyes continued to be regaled by this spectacle for a long time. This display had started early in the evening and I derived great pleasure from it for it was conveyed to me that this was a sign in my support. (Ayena Kamalat-e-Islam, pages 110-111 footnote)(Tadhkirah, page 82)

Eclipses of the Sun and Moon

Many solar and lunar eclipses also took place during the 19th century. Below are just some of the solar eclipses that occurred during the second half of this century. The Year, month and time (universal) are given. The type of solar eclipse is understood with the letters: P = Partial, A = Annular, T = Total, and H = Hybrid. Latitude and Longitude of the eclipses umbra (shadow) is given to show the duration in minutes and seconds.

1852 Dec 11 03:41 T 35.2N 133.9E 02m05s
1859 Feb 03 01:23 P 62.4S 72.1W
1860 Jul 18 14:26 T 52.5N 20.3W 03m39s
1877 Sep 07 12:49 P 61.2S 91.8W
1879 Jan 22 11:53 A 29.8S   8.5E 03m03s
1880 Jan 11 22:34 T   8.3N 164.1W 02m07s
1881 May 27 23:49 P 68.2N 13.3E
1881 Nov 21 16:31 A 81.2S 114.5W 00m43s
1882 May 17 07:37 T 38.4N 61.6E 01m50s
1888 Aug 07 18:06 P 70.1N 53.0E
1889 Jan 01 21:17 T 36.7N 137.6W 02m17s

1889 Jun 28 09:00   A 9.7S 47.3E 07m22s
1889 Dec 22 12:54   T 12.7S 12.8W 04m18s
1890 Jun 17 09:55   A 36.4N 29.3E 04m09s
1890 Dec 12 03:06   H 52.8S 123.9E 00m28s
1891 Jun 06 16:16   A 74.6N 163.8E 00m06s
1898 Jan 22 07:19   T 9.5N 63.6E 02m21s
1899 Dec 03 00:57   A 86.6S 121.5E 01m01s
1900 May 28 14:54   T 44.8N 46.5W 02m10s
1900 Nov 22 07:20   A 33.1S 64.8E 06m42s

Eclipses historically have held special significance in many religions. For Christianity, the Bible quotes Jesus as prophesizing the eclipsing of the sun and moon, and again the falling of stars, as all signs of his return:

Immediately after the suffering of those days, the sun will be darkened and the moon will not give its light; the stars will fall from heaven and the powers of heaven will be shaken. (Holy Bible, Matthew Chapter 24, Verses 29)

Two thousand years ago, the birth of the Messiah was heralded by the appearance of a bright star in the North, according to the prophecies of that time. The Biblical prophecy above also states that two cosmic events, the eclipsing of the sun and moon, would herald the coming of the Messiah in the latter days.

In the Holy Quran there is a chapter, called The Resurrection, with a very interesting verse:

He asks, When is the Day of the Awakening? But when the sight is dazzled and the moon is eclipsed and the sun and the moon are in conjunction. (Holy Quran, Chapter 75, Al-Qiyamah (The Resurrection), Verse 7)

In the traditions recorded of the Prophet of Islam he also makes mention of the eclipsing of the sun and moon, at specific times, as signs marking the coming of the Mahdi:

As reported by Muhammad bin Ali: The advent of our Mahdi will be marked by two important signs. These signs have never appeared before, not since the creation of the Heaven and the

Earth. One is the eclipse of the moon on the first of the Ramadan, and the other is the eclipse of the sun in the middle of Ramadan, and these two signs have not appeared to mark an event since the creation of the Heaven and Earth. (Sunan of Dar Qutni, by Hafiz Ali ibn Umar al-Dar Qutni, Volume 8)

There are two words in the Arabic language that describe the phases of the moon. These two terms are Hilal and Qamar. In the above hadith the later term, Qamar, is used. It is important to note the difference between these definitions in order to understand the above prophecy. According to one Arabic dictionary:

The Moon is called Qamar after the first three nights and remains Qamar up unto the end of the month. On the first three nights, the moon is called Hilal. (Aqrab ul-Muwarid, vol. II - Arabic Dictionary)

So the prophecy does not state that the moon will be eclipsed during the first night of Ramadan. In reality, this would not even be possible based on the natural cycle of moon. The cosmic laws designed by the Creator of the Universe reveal that in a lunar month, which the Islamic calendar goes by, a lunar eclipse can take place on one of three nights - either the 13th, 14th or 15th night. Taking the scientific laws of nature into account, when the above prophecy refers to "the eclipse of the moon on the first of the Ramadan," it can only refer to that first night of the three nights a lunar eclipse could actually occur on.

The eclipse of the sun would take place in similar fashion, on the middle day of the three possible days (27th, 28th and 29th) a solar eclipse could occur during a lunar month.

... and these two signs have not appeared to mark an event since the creation of the Heaven and Earth.

Eclipses on these dates have occurred before, but here the phrase "to mark an event" is important to note. Jesus' prophecy concerning the eclipses of the sun and moon are not extraordinary in themselves. His return during this time would be the important factor. Likewise, in the above prophecy of the Prophet Muhammad, the dates of the eclipses he specified would have importance during the time of the Mahdi.

It is interesting that the prophecies of both Christianity and Islam about the return of Jesus and the coming of the Mahdi should describe the same event to take place. Is it not fair to speculate that they refer to one and the same person?

History records that this very event of the sun and moon being eclipsed did occur during the intense Messianic times of the late 1800s. Four years after Mirza Ghulam Ahmad made his claim, both the moon and sun were eclipsed during Ramadan - the moon on March 21st 1894 and the sun on April 6th 1894. This was the 13th and 28th days as prophesied.

Not only were both the sun and moon eclipsed over the eastern hemisphere during the month of Ramadan of 1894, visible for all in those regions to see, but the very next year it did the exact same thing in the western hemisphere. In 1895, the moon on the 11th of March, and then the sun on the 26th of March, eclipsed again during the month of Ramadan – which ironically was the 13th night and 28th day of that month back in the eastern hemisphere. (The date of an eclipse can differ in respect to region.)

A Concentration of Dates

Prior to these eclipses spoken of in the Bible and the Quran, another eclipse related to the Second Coming of Jesus had already occurred five years earlier among the Natives of America.

As mentioned in Chapter 5, a total eclipse of the sun took place on January 1 1889. During this event a heavenly vision was experienced by the Paiute holy man Wovoka as he lay at death's door. After regaining consciousness, he relayed that he had been told by the Great Spirit that "Jesus is now upon the earth." It was during this same year, only three months later, that Mirza Ghulam Ahmad founded his movement with the purpose of bringing about a spiritual revolution for the entire world.

Could this movement in someway be related to the visions of Wovoka, Crazy Horse and Black Elk about the resurrection of the Native American people? Could those 250 native men, women and children, who were slaughtered under the command of Colonel Forsyth at the Wounded Knee Massacre in 1890 be the first martyrs to die for believing in the Messiah who had come?

There was a great deal of millennial excitement all over the globe. In Russia another spiritual leader also made predictions that point to this time period. Klaas Epp (1838-1913) was a leader of the Mennonite Brethren in Russia. In 1880, he and some 600 Mennonites migrated to Turkestan in eastern Asia to await the Second Coming. Epp had apparently predicted that Christ would return on March 8, 1889.

Also, as was mentioned earlier, Joseph Smith claimed to have received a revelation that "if thou livest until thou art eighty-five years old, thou shalt see the face of the Son of Man." Had that revelation saw its fulfillment he would have arrived at the year 1890. It was in the year 1890 that Mirza Ghulam Ahmad received divine revelation that clearly told him he was the Second Coming of Jesus that the Christian and Muslim worlds were anticipating.

A Messiah from the East

Black Elk saw that his people would be plagued by famine and sickness and war. They would lose heart and the sacred hoop of his nation would be broken. But then he saw a vision of his own nation being reunited after seven generations and becoming part of the greater hoop of all the nations of the earth.

Then he saw the daybreak star rising in the east, and heard a voice that said: "It shall be a relative to them, and who shall see it shall see much more, for from there comes Wisdom; and those who do not see it shall be dark." Black Elk thought this meant that a great Prophet from the East would bring a message to his people. (Ancient Prophecies of Modern Times, by Bette Stockbauer)

From the Inuit (Eskimos) of northern Alaska, to the Sioux of North American, all the way down to the Inca and Mayans of South America, the prophecies of Native people all speak of the coming of a messiah from the East. Again it must be noted that in anticipation of the coming of Quetzalcoatl, the ancient Mexicans looked to the East. The same was true for the Inca people of Peru concerning the return of Pachacuti. It is interesting that two major religions that originated east of the peoples of America, Christianity and Islam, should also speak of their own messiahs as coming from the east. In reality, one could circle the entire globe again and again looking east, but wisdom dictates that this should not be the case.

Various Islamic traditions also point to the East concerning the coming of their Mahdi. In one such tradition, Abu Hurairah, a companion of the Prophet, tells the story of his education on one of the verses of the Holy Quran:

One day we were sitting with the Holy Prophet when Surah Al-Jumu'ah (Chapter 62) was revealed to him, and in it the words "among others of them who have not yet joined them." I asked the Holy Prophet, "Who are these?" He gave no reply until I asked him thrice. Salman, the Persian, was sitting among us and the Holy Prophet placed his hand on Salman, and said, "Even if faith were to go up to the Pleiades (heavens), a man from these would surely attain it." (Bukhari, 65)

The Holy Prophet was alluding to that person who, in the latter days, would revive the spirit of Islam – the Mahdi. When answering his companion's question, he singled out another one of his companions, who was known to everyone as Salman the Persian. It is understood by this that the Mahdi will also be a person of Persian descent like Salman. The land of Persia is located east of Arabia – hence the Mahdi will come from the east.

In the Bible, Jesus also foretold that his return would occur in the east. In the New Testament, we see the similarity between where the Mahdi will appear and where Jesus (peace be upon him) says he would reappear.

For as lighting that comes from the east is visible even in the west, so will the coming of the Son of Man. (Matthew 24:27)

Jesus made this prophecy while he was in Jerusalem. Therefore it can be inferred that the coming of the Son of Man would be east of this location. This again includes those regions known as Persia. Of the various messiah contenders mentioned earlier, only three came from areas east of Israel; both revered personages of the Bahá'í Faith, The Báb and Bahá'u'lláh; and the founder of the Ahmadiyya Movement in Islam, Mirza Ghulam Ahmad. All three of these individuals came from lands of Persia and were of Persian descent. In the case of Mirza Ghulam Ahmad, the town of Qadian where he was born, was directly east of Jerusalem. (The city of Jerusalem is in present day Israel whose latitude is 31.9129. Present day Pakistan, where the town of Qadian is located, has a latitude of 30.4394.)

The Moment of Truth

The visions of Wovoka and Black Elk placed special emphasis on how the Ghost Dance shirts would be designed. According to *The British Museum Encyclopedia of Native North America* (page 75), the Ghost Dance shirts only used simple colors and no ornaments were added. The shirts most commonly depicted images of moons (including crescents) and stars. Historically, the usage of moons (especially crescents) and stars in various cultures has been traced back to one common heritage.

Another Arabic influence may be found in the coats of arms of medieval Sudan. Most notable of these is the crescent on some Sudanese medieval armor. It is generally represented by one upward sign, but frequently it has three stars connected with it, or the crescent is repeated two or three times. This is a characteristic Muslim emblem. It is also found in medieval Mexico. The crescent accompanied at the bottom by three stars or crescents is found on many Mexican shields. (The Crisis Magazine, "African Explorers of the New World," Harold G. Lawrence)(Islam, Black Nationalism & Slavery, Abid Rashad, page 70)

It has already been established that the Mandinka king of Mali, Abubakari, who was a Muslim, had traveled to the lands of Mexico. The Muslim Sudanese people also used the symbol of the star and crescent as a symbol of their faith.

In Ivan Van Sertima's *They Came Before Columbus*, he further shows the impact of Islam on Central American culture. In his book he displays the images of both Mexican Indian shields with depictions of triple crescents; as well as the use of the crescent among African Islamic civilization.

The crescent moon and star symbols that were depicted on the Ghost Dance Shirts are strikingly similar to the symbol that has become synonymous with the religion of Islam. The Ghost Dance was revealed to the Paiute holy man Wovoka in a vision, the same vision of 1889 in which he was told that Jesus Christ had returned.

9B - Mirza Ghulam Ahmad

The illustration used in US papers was based on this famous photo. It was taken in the late 1800s, long before computer imaging. Some believe it captured an aura of light that surrounded him. Could the True Bahanna of Native prophecy not be referring to one's white complexion, but rather to one's purity of character?

Out of all of the men who arose as prophets and spiritual reformers during the late 1800s, there was one man who fits the prophetic descriptions spoken of in Native American traditions, and those spoken of in other religions, more so than any other claimant in history.

Mirza Ghulam Ahmad's claim to being the Messiah awaited by all world religions was clear. There is no gray area open for interpretation. Either he was true, or he was false. Either he was the Messiah, or he was a liar.

Who is more unjust than he who forges lies against Allah or treats His Signs as lies? Surely, the unjust shall not prosper. (Chapter 6, Al-An'am (The Livestock), verse 22)

Since the time of Ahmad's death in 1908, the Ahmadiyya Movement has experienced rapid growth. Ahmad's prophecy about the success of his movement has proven true. Another prophecy relating to Dowie was that Ahmad's followers would one day inhabitant the city of Zion, Illinois. Today the Ahmadiyya Movement has a sizable community residing there – and the average citizen in Zion has never even heard of John Alexander Dowie.

Some Christians who are aware of his claim have, ironically, labeled him and his movement the Anti-Christ. They do so because he proclaimed that God is unequivocally one and not three, and that the Creator of life and death was not a man who suffered death or experience humiliation at the hands of disbelievers, and that He did not condemn His humble servant to death, but rather, saved him from it.

A majority of the Muslim world also continues to reject his claim, and boldly declare his followers as non-Muslims.

Despite these objections many Muslims, Christians, and people of other faiths have accepted his claim. During the year of 2001, 81 million people pledged their allegiance to the cause of peace as presented by Mirza Ghulam Ahmad. These numbers continue to double each year, as prophesied by the current leader of the Ahmadiyya Movement. They come from the lands of Africa, Asia, Europe, Australia, North and South America and even remote islands in the Pacific. No matter what nation they come from, they believe in the Ahmadiyya Movement's philosophy of "Love for All, Hatred for None."

Chapter Ten
Racial and Religious Persecution

10A – Locomotive Train Fulfills Prophecy
The invention of the locomotive was prophesized by various religions. The Hopi prophecies say that there would be a ribbon built across the land and a bug would crawl upon it. This marked the coming of a great worldwide calamity that would bring widespread destruction to many people.

Chapter Ten
Racial and Religious Persecution

'Harrison will not win this year to be the Great Chief. But he may win next year. If he does...He will not finish his term. He will die in office.' 'No president has ever died in office,' declared a visitor. 'But Harrison will die I tell you. And when he dies you will remember my brother Tecumseh's death. You think that I have lost my powers. I who caused the sun to darken and Red Men to give up firewater. But I tell you Harrison will die. And after him, every Great Chief chosen every 20 years thereafter will die. And when each one dies, let everyone remember the death of our people.' (Tenskwatawa, the Shawnee Prophet)

A Shawnee Prophecy

Tenskwatawa was known as the "Shawnee Prophet." Tenskwatawa was a member of the Shawnee nation. He claimed to have received revelation from the Great Spirit that directed all Native Americans to completely disassociate themselves from "white" society. He was held in great respect as a holy man and predicted an eclipse in 1806.

Tenskwatawa and his brother were both leaders in their community. Tenskwatawa's brother was named Tehcumseh; he was the chief of the mighty Shawnee nation. They believed in the sacredness of the earth and communion with the Great Spirit. They also believed that the land belonged to all Native people and could not be bought and sold by the whites. This of course got them labeled as troublemakers in the eyes of the American government.

In 1811, while Tehcumseh was away, American military forces under General Harrison attacked the Shawnee by their village at the base of the Tippecanoe River, near modern Lafayette, Indiana. Under the leadership of Tenskwatawa, the Shawnee fought back but were defeated. Their village was burned to the ground.

Years earlier, Tehcumseh had realized the American government was determined to take the land. Tehcumseh decided that action had to be taken and that all Native Americans would have to take up arms and fight for their right to live on the land. From 1808 to 1811, Tehcumseh traveled all over Ohio, Michigan, Indiana, and Illinois trying to unite as many Midwestern tribes as he could. But the Battle of Tippecanoe dealt a severe blow to the Pan-Indian political revolution that Tehcumseh had hoped to establish.

After the massacre, Tenskwatawa's reputation was shaken, because he had foretold that the battle would end in victory. Tenskwatawa retreated to meditate, fast and pray. When he returned he prophesied that his brother would die before him. It is also believed that he prophesied a cycle of death for the American presidency. (It is also believed by some that Tehcumseh originally prophesied this and told his brother before his death, who later relayed it.)

It was prophesied that General Harrison would one day become president, and that starting with him, every 20 years the elected U.S. president would die while in office. This prophecy is popularly known as "Tehcumseh's Curse."

Tehcumseh was killed in a battle in 1813, his body skinned and mutilated. Twenty-seven years later the fulfillment of the prophecy began. The same general who had burned down their village, William H. Harrison, was elected America's ninth president in 1840. But just one month after his inauguration, Harrison got pneumonia and died on April 6, 1841. He was the first president ever to die while in office, but not the last.

Twenty years later in 1860 Abraham Lincoln was elected the 16th president. Lincoln completed his four-year term. It seemed at first that he would not fall victim to Tehcumseh's prophecy. However, Lincoln's term in office did not end but continued, as he was reelected in 1864. On April 14, 1865 Lincoln was shot in D.C. at the Ford's Theater by actor John Wilkes Booth.

In 1880, twenty years after Lincoln's election, James A. Garfield was elected president. He was also assassinated. He was shot on July 2, 1881, less than a year after taking office.

In another twenty years, the presidential election again fell on a "zero year" (1900.) This time, William McKinley fell victim to "Tehcumseh's Curse." He died the same year he took office, assassinated by anarchist Leon Czolgosz on September 6, 1901.

In 1920, Warren G. Harding was elected the 29th president.

While on a political tour across the country, Harding, who already suffered from a serious heart condition, died from food poisoning on August 2, 1923.

Franklin D. Roosevelt was the longest-serving president in U.S. history. He was first elected in 1933 and then again in 1936. He was reelected for a third time in 1940. (Today a president is only allowed to serve two terms.) Amazingly, he was elected for a fourth consecutive term in 1944, but apparently died of a cerebral hemorrhage on April 12, 1945. Because of his election in 1940, he falls within the cycle the prophecy.

The prophecy of Tehcumseh found its fulfillment again when President John F. Kennedy was assassinated on November 22, 1963. Again, his election in 1960 fell within the twenty-year cycle.

The only president who ever survived this 160-year long "curse" was Ronald Reagan who was elected in 1980. An assassination attempt was made on his life in March of 1981 but failed. (It is said that although he survived the assassination attempt, he was rendered virtually incapacitated for the rest of his term.)

Assassination attempts have been made on three other presidents: Andrew Jackson, John Tyler and Harry Truman. These all failed. The only presidents who were "successfully" assassinated were those four who fell within the conditions given in Tecumseh's prophecy.

Of all the presidents who died while in office, seven out of eight were those elected in one of the twenty-year cycles of the prophecy. The only other president who died in office was Zachary Taylor in 1850.

Tehcumseh' prophecy was meant to be a constant reminder to those who continue to represent the system that unjustly removed Indians from their native lands and continues to neglect the needs of the original Americans. Nothing prevents the government from rectifying the sad state the Native American community lives in other, than aloofness towards human suffering.

Some believe that the reign of the prophecy ended in 1980 while others anticipate that the prophecy will continue, affecting those elected in 2000, 2020, and beyond. Only time will tell. Perhaps had the past presidential "victims" of the prophecy ever chosen during the last 160 years to do right by the Native Americans, the Great Spirit may have shown them mercy.

The Tribe of Ben Ishmael

After the defeat of Tecumseh's alliance and the end of Native American jurisdiction over this region, the new state of Indiana decreed the establishment of its capital in 1821 at the central point of the state, on the White River. When the surveyors and first officials arrived at this spot, they found the Tribe of Ben Ishmael – and the Ishmaelites did not budge. (Gone to Croatan: Origins of North American Dropout Culture, Hugo P. Leaming, page 21)

For over a century an unusual nomadic tribe consisting of Native Americans, African Americans, and European Americans roamed throughout America's Midwest. This unified group of men and women came together to form a culture that was at great odds with the existing establishment. They are known as the Tribe of Ben Ishmael.

The tribe is named after their founder and patriarch Ben Ishmael (who some believe was an African Fulani ex-slave) and his original family. It first formed shortly after 1785 in Kentucky and migrated towards Ohio during the first decade of the 1800s. The tribe eventually formed a migration route that ran from Illinois through Indiana and into Ohio. They established a "capital" along the Indiana White River under the leadership of the second patriarch, John Ishmael. It was at this location that the city of Indianapolis was later built. Author Hugo P. Leaming notes:

By 1819 the tribe established its capital in the deep woods of the White River, where now stands the city of Indianapolis. The late-nineteenth century state summary of Ishmaelite materials reports: "John Ishmael, then, arrived in this city while yet the Indian was there." The principal Ishmaelite settlements, on opposite banks of the river, were the points from which, much later, grew the two oldest and still existing black neighborhoods of Indianapolis. (Gone to Croatan: Origins of North American Dropout Culture, Hugo P. Leaming, page 20)

It is along the very same White River in Indiana to which Tecumseh and members of the Shawnee nation were once compelled to migrate, long before the Battle of Tippecanoe.

They first settled on Deer Creek, a tributary of the Mad River, and then in 1796 moved to the Great Miami River in western Ohio. In 1797 they moved to the Whitewater River in eastern Indiana, and one year later they settled on the White River, near modern Anderson. Tecumseh remained in this village for seven years, until in 1805 he moved to a new village, near Greenville, Ohio. (Encyclopedia of North American Indians, edited by Fredrick E. Hoxie, page 620)

It is very possible that the tribe of Indians who the Ishmael-ites encountered in 1819 when they settled on the White River were members of the Shawnee nation who had remained behind. It was during Tehcumseh's seven-year stay there that he married, twice, producing one son named Pachetha. It is possible that many Shawnee stayed after Tehcumseh left and eventually joined and merged with the Tribe of Ben Ishmael.

The Ishmaelites, whose membership eventually numbered up to 10,000, consisted of Native Americans, ex-black slaves, and poor whites. Although this large "multi-racial" community was quite unsettling to the American establishment at that time, it was the nomadic lifestyle of the tribe that caused the most conflict be-tween the two vastly different cultures.

In the book, *Gone to Croatan: Origins of North American Dropout Culture*, Hugo P. Leaming describes the philosophy of the nomadic lifestyle:

Hunting cultures often view the land and its animals as common property, or nobody's, or God's. This wealth is privately owned only when in use. Only the insane hunt beyond their hun-ger, for accumulated venison rots. This cultural value may have been reinforced by Native American and African traditions of community ownership or an economy of use. Cultural differences in this respect were central to the conflict between the tribe and the majority society. Fences and title deeds were as immoral to Ish-maelites as was their "thieving" to the majority. (Gone to Croatan: Origins of North American Dropout Culture, Hugo P. Leaming, Ron Sukolsky & James Koehaline, page 25)

So when the newly formed state of Indiana decided to establish its capital along the White River, where the Ishmaelites had settled, conflicts between the two cultures arose. The two cultures remained divided up into the twentieth century, literally with the Ishmaelites on one side of the river and the white settlers on the other. They each considered the other a nuisance and held each other in contempt.

Around the 1840s the conflict intensified. The U.S. government passed "poor laws" allowing members of the Ben Ishmael tribe to be arrested as "paupers" and then sold into slavery – including its white members. These bogus laws, designed solely to break up the tribe and remove them from the land, gave the American government the "right" to even remove the children from their homes.

In 1880, Reverend Oscar C. McCulloch of Indianapolis wrote a manifesto called, "The Tribe of Ishmael," where he suggested a solution to America's Ishmaelite problem. In that manifesto he suggests that the tribe was a biologically degenerate group of people incapable of reform, or assimilation into their society. Because of this, there was then no reason to give them the same rights extended to U.S. citizens.

The Ishmaelites were therefore declared as having no rights, and the law forbade any person to assist the Ishmaelites in any way. Furthermore, efforts increased to legally take away the children of the Ishmaelites. The government charged the Ishmaelites with disobeying the new law of the land, and found new excuses to put the men and women in prisons, and even into mental institutions.

McCulloch's new idea to justify ethnic discrimination based on "science," became very popular throughout the U.S. McCulloch's manifesto of scientific racism spread to other parts of the world with the help of the Eugenics Records Office of the Carnegie Institution.

In 1907 this racist ideology culminated in "The Indiana Plan" - the first compulsory sterilization law in the world. After passing in the House and the Senate it was approved on March 9, 1907 by Governor J. Frank Hanely. It appears on the Indiana laws of 1907 as Chapter 215, on page 377; Burns' Indiana Statutes 1908, sec. 2232. Hugo P. Leaming notes the popularity of "The Indiana Plan":

The proposal in other states was justly called the "Indiana Plan." Adherents of the Progressive movement lent their support to what they considered another social reform, and the law spread to twenty-nine other states between 1907 and 1931. European eugenicists watched America pioneer in this field, and by the early 1930s the Indiana Plan had spread to seven other nations, including Nazi Germany. (Gone to Croatan: Origins of North American Dropout Culture, Hugo P. Leaming, Ron Sukolsky & James Koehaline, page 45)

The practice of genocide was no longer confined to the battlefield. It was now interwoven into the very fabric of the American justice system. The objective of the U.S. government was to destroy the Tribe of Ben Ishmael through forced sterilization. This was the same objective of the government of Nazi Germany when it forced the sterilization of Jews, Gypsies and any other group that didn't fit the category of "Aryan pureblood."

America's First "Nation" of Islam

The spiritual system of the Tribe of Ishmael, not known in detail to outsiders, was not orthodox Christian. Not a single Ishmaelite was ever known to belong to any of the churches of the majority society. (Gone to Croatan: Origins of North American Dropout Culture, Hugo P. Leaming, Ron Sukolsky & James Koehaline, page 27)

An examination into their traditions and customs suggests to some an Islamic influence. First, according to Ishmaelite tradition, the "Ben" was used less like a common name but more like that of a title. So the name "Ben Ishmael," meant "son of Ishmael" as it is used in Hebrew and Arabic terminology. As explained earlier, the prophet Ishmael is the patriarch of the family from which the Prophet Muhammad descended. Furthermore, the founder Ben Ishmael, as mentioned before, is believed by some scholars to have been an African Fulani who was captured and brought to America. The Fulani of West Africa were Muslims (and also one of the few West African tribes who were nomadic.) His name and possible tribal origin suggests an Islamic connection.

Secondly, many customs common in Islam were practiced by the tribe. Some of these practices included complete abstention from alcohol and occasionally a polygamous marriage. A third sign is the naming of certain Midwestern towns:

There are also curious aspects of old Midwest communities located on the Ishmaelite annual migration route. At the northern end is Morocco, Indiana, at the southern end Mahomet, Illinois, and on the last segment, on the way back to Indianapolis, Mecca, Indiana. That three Islamic names appear in Indiana and Illinois is of no great significance in itself, for there are Islamic, ancient Egyptian, Greek, Roman, Hindu, and Chinese place names scattered across the maps of all the American states... But when a community lies on the Ishmaelite route, has an Islamic name and additional historical characteristics that may be related, it is worthy of comment. (Gone to Croatan: Origins of North American Dropout Culture, Hugo P. Leaming, Ron Sukolsky & James Koehaline, page 49)

Mr. Leaming continued, elaborating on the town of Mahomet, Illinois:

Mahomet is the oldest settlement of Champaign County and one of the oldest in this part of Illinois. The origin of the name is unknown and rather enigmatic, considering the negative image of Muhammad in nineteenth-century America. Suggestions to explain the name in local histories have included distinctiveness and ease of spelling, imposition by the Post Office Department without local consultation, adoption from the name of the local Masonic lodge (which would extend to the mystery,) and commemoration of a local Indian chief. The last is the most interesting in the context of this inquiry. In 1870, ten percent of the settlers of Mahomet Township and adjoining townships bore very unusual family names which are difficult to identify as to national origin. Half of these, or five percent of the population, have an "oriental" flavor... Osman, Boormer, and Nebeker are reminiscent of the early and still revered Caliphs of Islam, Osman, Omar and Abu-Bekr... Sherfy suggests Sharrieff, an Islamic holy name; Push is close to Pasha; Gamel is an Islamic name, and Manser suggest the Islamic Mansour... Babb is an Arabic word meaning "gate" (used spiritually by

Bahais); and Hamella and Menealla are constructed like the nu-
merous Islamic names compounded from the word for God, Allah,
such as Nasrallah.

...A historical geography of Champaign County confirms
this identification by signaling out Mahomet and one adjoining
township as having been originally settled by persons of "Mixed
American Southern Extraction." Whatever the phrase is intended
to convey, it is an admirable description of the composition of the
Tribe of Ishmael. (Gone to Croatan: Origins of North American
Dropout Culture, Hugo P. Leaming, Ron Sukolsky & James Koe-
haline, pages 50-51)

The massive suppression of the Ishmaelites by the American government eventually brought a complete halt to the migra-
tory movements of the tribe, forcing them to settle down in various
towns along the way. There are today existing "black" communities in these regions with citizens who descend from these tribes.

It is very clear that from these earlier communities arose
two types of reservations: one, the Indian reservations, and the
other, the Black ghettos. The "Indiana Plan" was just one of many
racist laws that were created to keep these two nations apart.

The Bug and The Donkey

"People came on the East Coast and they went across this
land to the east and they were told in the prophecies that we
should try to remind all the people that would come here of the sa-
credness of all things. If we could do that, then there would be
peace on earth. But if we did not do that, when the roads went
clear from east to west, and when the other races and colors of the
Earth had walked clear across this land, if by that time we had not
come together as a human family, the Great Spirit would grab the
earth with his hand and shake it. (Hopi Representative Lee Brown,
1986 Continental Indigenous Council)

At the 1986 Continental Indigenous Council meeting, Hopi
representative Lee Brown pointed out that racism and segregation
were acts of disobedience to the Divine command to come together
as a human family:

And so if you read the treaty negotiations from Red Jacket of the Six Nations on the East Coast of this land clear to Chief Joseph and Chief Seattle on the West Coast of this land, they all said the same thing. Chief Joseph said, "I accord you the right, and I hope you accord me the right, to live in this land." Always we were trying to live together. But instead of living together, you all know there was separation, there was segregation. They separated the races: they separated the Indians, and they separated the Blacks.

So when they got to the West Coast of this land, the elders that were made aware of these prophecies said they would then begin to build a black ribbon. And on this black ribbon there would move a bug. And when you begin to see this bug moving on the land, that was the sign for the First Shaking of the Earth. (Hopi Representative Lee Brown, 1986 Continental Indigenous Council)

The bug on the black ribbon of the Hopi prophecy accurately describes a train running along the railroad tracks, like a millipede on a thin black ribbon. It also describes the automobile, resembling a beetle, which moves along the roads and highways.

The steam engine locomotive was first invented in the early 1800s in England. Over half a century later, on March 10, 1869, the first transcontinental railroad in the world was completed in America in the state of Utah. By 1900, the railroad was the most popular mode of transportation. The first real automobile appeared in the 1880s, but didn't become widely available to the public until after 1900. In 1908, General Motors was founded. Also that year, Henry Ford began mass-producing the automobile and by 1911 was producing 1,000 gas guzzling cars a day.

The building of the railroad and the automobile was a sign of the terrible prophecy of the coming of the First Shaking of the Earth. Prophecies such as these are often misinterpreted when taken literally. The fact is that those chosen by the Great Spirit, who are given a glimpse into the future, can only describe what they see according to their own reality and experiences. As noted in the traditions of the Prophet Muhammad, he described a prophecy about the Dajjal or Anti-Christ, stating that it would ride a very unusual donkey:

The Dajjal's donkey will travel on water as on land. Trav-

eling on land it will have clouds both in front and behind. (Kanzul'-Ummal, vol VII, p. 267)

The description of this donkey was clearly that of steam ships and the locomotive trains – with the smoke that comes out at its head and trails behind it. In his vision of the future, the Holy Prophet Muhammad could only describe it in terms familiar to his time. Since the common means of transportation during that time was the donkey, he described what he saw in his vision as a donkey – but with unusual characteristics. The vision given to him by the Creator conveyed the exact same message that was given to the Hopi about the bug on the black ribbon. In other traditions of the Holy Prophet, he reportedly says that:

The Dajjal will make his appearance on a white donkey, whose two ears will be seventy yards apart. (Mishkat)

"He will jump about between heaven and earth. (Abu Dawud)

These refer to the airplane, with its wingspan, and how it metaphorically "jumps" into the heavens from one land to another. The Hopi prophecies also clearly describe the airplane in relation to that time of the First Shaking of the earth.

The First Shaking of the Earth would be so violent that this bug would be shaken off the earth into the air and it would begin to move and fly in the air. And by the end of this shaking this bug will be in the air around the world. Behind it would be a trail of dirt and eventually the whole sky of the entire earth would become dirty from these trails of dirt, and this would cause many diseases that would get more and more complicated. So the bug moving on the land, of course it's easy to see now.

In 1908 the Model-T Ford was mass-produced for the first time. So the elders knew the First Shaking of the Earth was about to come about - that's the First World War. In the First World War the airplane came into wide usage for the first time. That was that bug moving into the sky. (Hopi Representative Lee Brown, 1986 Continental Indigenous Council)

World War I, which began in 1914, was the first war in which bombs were dropped from the sky from airplanes. The casualties were unbelievable. The governments of America and Europe wanted to insure that such a global tragedy never happened again. Lee Brown recalled that the Native American elders knew that the First World War, with all of its bloodshed and destruction, had created a great fear in the people.

And so they knew something very important would happen. There would be an attempt to make peace on earth on the West Coast of this land and so the elders began to watch for this. They began to hear that there was going to be a League of Nations in San Francisco so the elders gathered in Arizona around 1920 or so and they wrote a letter to Woodrow Wilson. They asked if the Indian people could be included in the League of Nations. At that time the United States Supreme Court had held that a reservation is a separate and semi-sovereign nation, not a part of the United States but protected by it.

This became a concern because people didn't want the reservations to become more and more separate. They didn't want them to be considered nations. So they did not write back and the Native people were left out of the League of Nations, so that circle was incomplete.

In the League of Nations circle there was a southern door, the yellow people; there was a western door, the black people; there was a northern door, the white people; but the eastern door was not attended. The elders knew that peace would not come on the earth until the circle of humanity is complete, until all the four colors sat in the circle and shared their teachings, then peace would come on earth. (Hopi Representative Lee Brown, 1986 Continental Indigenous Council)

It was not ego that drove the desire of the Hopi desire to be included in the League of Nations. It was a desire to present the prophecies that would help insure a peaceful future for all nations. But the U.S. Supreme Court decided Indian nations were only semi-sovereign and therefore not eligible to participate in a gathering that could gain them global political influence.

The U.S. government did not hesitate to consider the Indian people full citizens, however, when they sent 10,000 Native

American soldiers to die fighting in World War I. Six years after the war ended the U.S. decided to "honor" Indian people with full citizenship, to thank them for their patriotism and right the wrongs that had been done to them. But this proved to be only on paper.

The greatest hoax ever perpetrated upon him was the sup-posed citizenship of 1924 [that] supposedly gave the Indian the same rights enjoyed by other men. The reservation still remains, the agent is still on the job... the Indian Bureau politicians still fat-ten on Indian money and the Indian is still being robbed. (In the Spirit of Crazy Horse, Peter Matthiessen, page 26)

Had the Native Americans been let into the League of Na-tions, the Hopi could have warned American society that it was following a path to total destruction. The League of Nations failed in its mission, because, as Native American prophecies foretold, if any of the four brothers was left out of the circle, world peace would not be achieved.

Race Riots Follow World War

Not only did thousands of Native Americans die in World War I but also thousands of African Americans died fighting for America. After the war ended in 1918, many of the Native and African American soldiers returned home with a much more asser-tive attitude. After putting their lives on the line, they weren't about to tolerate being treated as second-class citizens.

When white men saw the new, fearless black and red men boldly demanding equal rights, they panicked. Repressive meas-ures were quickly enacted to beat the non-whites into submission. Lynch mobs terrorized black neighborhoods. Any minor conflict between a white and black person could ignite a race riot. The hot summer saw so much violence it became known as the "Red Sum-mer."

During the "Red Summer" of 1919 there were more than two dozen race riots. Expanding ghettos, tensions over housing and employment, political convictions and race prejudice, black militance and white demagoguery were among the precipitating factors. By far the bloodiest race riot in Chicago lasted sporadi-

cally for thirteen days.   (Blacks in White America since 1865, Robert C. Twombly, page 202)

Blacks continued to demand economic opportunities and equal justice. Racial tensions increased. Native Americans realized that they had been duped into serving in World War I, and "Indians" would never be recognized as full citizens of America. During this period Native American people, many who had African roots, entered the black community and merged completely. They became part of the "colored" population.

The Ambassador of the Messiah

American foreign and domestic policy reflected the philosophy of white supremacy. During the post World War I era of the 1920s, the U.S. government made it clear that non-white, non-Christian immigrants were not welcome. Politics and religion became intertwined. The government's policy of racial oppression included religious persecution of those who promoted beliefs contradictory to European Christian theology, and its "scientific" support for white racial superiority. Anyone who attempted to change the U.S. social order in this regard was considered dangerous.

On January 24, 1920, as daybreak settled over London's streets, an elderly, light-brown-complexioned man with spectacles boarded the S.S. Haverford bound for America. His dark green and gold turban and his amiable but mysterious manner attracted the attention of several Chinese passengers, to whom he introduced himself as "Mufti Muhammad Sadiq, missionary for the Ahmadiyya Movement in Islam." Each day at sea, several passengers were eager to learn more about this exotic stranger's religion and his plans for a Muslim mission in America. They were mystified by his stories about the life of the Prophet Muhammad and the teachings of the Promised Messiah Ghulam Ahmad... Before the end of the voyage, Sadiq had converted four Chinese men, one American, one Syrian, and one Yugoslavian to Islam. (Islam in the African-American Experience, Richard Brent Turner, pp. 114-115)

Thirteen years after American newspapers had proclaimed an "Indian Messiah" the victor of a widely publicized prayer duel, an ambassador on behalf of that messiah came to the U.S. Mufti Muhammad Sadiq arrived on America's shores on February 15, 1920. He had come with high hopes of spreading the message of Islam to all the good citizens of America, and to inform them of the claim of Mirza Ghulam Ahmad.

But before he could even step foot on American soil, he was met by immigration officials who immediately came on board and took him into custody. The American media, like the *Philadelphia Press*, covered Sadiq's arrival and detention in 1920 with much fan fair and curiosity.

Sadiq was interrogated and accused of coming to America for the sole purpose of teaching polygamy. He explained to them that polygamy in Islam was not a requirement, and that under U.S. law, which made polygamy illegal, it would not then be permissible for a Muslim in American to go against the law of the land. Still, the immigration officials asked him to get on his ship and head back home. Sadiq said he would do no such thing. He was then placed in a detention house in New Jersey where he waited for a court appeal.

Sadiq was on a mission to unite all "races" under one God and one religion. As a companion of the late Mirza Ghulam Ahmad, he knew that Ahmad desired that those people in the western nations should hear of his claim and teachings. Sadiq understood that he had been chosen to bring news of that claim and the teachings of Islam to the people of America. Sadiq was determined to bring the message of universal brotherhood to whomever, wherever. He did not hesitate to put forth these ideals, even as he was being held in the detention house. Richard B. Turner notes:

Many men in the Detention House were impressed with Sadiq's passion and devotion to his multi-racial religion, which offered dramatic changes in name and identity, and they converted. "Under curious circumstances, we got acquainted in the closed walls of the Detention House," Sadiq said of his first convert in America, R.J.H. Rochford. "Watching me praying and reciting the Holy Book, Mr. Rochford inquired of my religion, which I explained to him and I gave him some books to study. Very soon he was convinced of the truth of our religion and being converted was named Hamid." Although Rochford was eventually sent back to England by the immigration authorities, during those weeks of

confinement Sadiq made nineteen other converts to Islam. These
men were from Jamaica, British Guyana, Azores, Poland, Russia,
Germany, Belgium, Portugal, Italy, and France... (Islam in the
African-American Experience, by Richard Brent Turner, pages
114-115)

Sadiq was eventually allowed to stay in the U.S. He had
begun his mission by successfully bringing a group of various nationalities and cultures under one religion. But this multi-cultural
success story with the immigrants of the detention house would not
be so easily achieved outside. After leaving the detention house,
Sadiq was confronted with the deep-rooted racism of American
society, which made many people less receptive to the foreigner
with the foreign religion. Yet, his status as a foreigner also served
as a point of intrigue to others, making them more interested in
what he had to say.

The First Mission House

After traveling to various parts of the country for a few
months, Sadiq eventual settled in Chicago. There on the corner of
4448 S. Wabash he established the very first Ahmadiyya Mission
House in America (a mosque now stands there today.) Although
he still sought to bring Islam to all the people of America, Sadiq
eventually focused his efforts on the downtrodden people of African descent. The longer he lived in America, the more it became
evident that the "land of equality" showed no aspirations towards
achieving this ideal. He perceived the African American community as the descendents of his Muslim brothers in West Africa who
had been unjustly forced to abandon their original religion. After
suffering economic exploitation, they were left in a pitiful state -
economically as well as spiritually.

Sadiq's religious propagation was extremely successful in
the African American community. He sought to build a multi-
racial organization based on Islamic teachings of racial equality.
This emphasis on equality was very appealing to the blacks in
America. Most had experienced extreme segregation, even in the
church, where often blacks and whites could not even worship together in the same building.

After living in America for sometime, Sadiq observed that

whites whom he sought to convert to Islam had difficulty accepting the idea of racial equality. The Ahmadiyya Movement under Mufti Muhammad Sadiq's leadership, condemned discrimination and prejudice. Whites sometimes expressed resentment at the appoint-ment of blacks in leadership positions in Sadiq's organization.

In the 1920's, a young Jamaican by the name of Marcus Mosiah Garvey came to America, inspired by the teachings of self-help espoused by Tuskegee Institute founder Booker T. Washing-ton. He founded the Universal Negro Improvement Association (UNIA) to help black people worldwide to gain economic self-sufficiency. Marcus Garvey's UNIA became known as the first Pan-African movement. Like Paul Cuffe, Marcus Garvey sought to empower the displaced African in America and the colonialized African in Africa. His slogan was "Africa for the Africans, at home and abroad." Whites labeled his organization the "Back to Africa" movement. He espoused an economic philosophy of self-reliance, a political philosophy of separate nationhood, and a reli-gious philosophy that refuted white superiority. Garvey's newspa-pers and pamphlets urging economic self-reliance created a new fervor among the downtrodden and oppressed.

Richard B. Turner notes that many members of the UNIA were attracted by the Ahmadiyya Movement's message. :

Because of the leadership roles that it gave to its black par-ticipants, however, the movement began to attract members of the Universal Negro Improvement Association. Brother Abdullah (James Conwell), a prominent member convert in Chicago, was a Garveyite. There were at least six other Garveyites in the Chicago mission, and they wore their Garvey uniforms to the Ahmadi reli-gious services and meetings. In 1923, Sadiq gave five lectures at the UNIA meetings in Detroit. Eventually he converted forty Garveyites to Islam. (Islam in the African-American an Experi-ence, by Richard Brent Turner, page 127)

Outraged by the way non-white peoples were treated in a so-called "Christian" nation, Mufti Muhammad Sadiq became more vocal in his speeches about the brutal treatment Africans had received under the banner of "Christianity." He urged people of African descent to give due consideration towards Islam, the relig-ion of their ancestors. During the early 1920s there was a great

deal of activity at the Ahmadiyya Mission House in Chicago. In
1921 Sadiq published *The Moslem Sunrise.* He decided that the
cover of this tri-monthly journal would have a depiction of a sunrise over North America – in this case the sun was symbolic for
Islam. The purpose of the journal was to engage in jihad, (popularly known as holy war.) It was the belief of Mirza Ghulam
Ahmad that the real jihad for this age is one of the pen, or a jihad
of words. Sadiq was therefore battling for the minds and hearts of
the American public.

In 1923, Sadiq published this message in his magazine,
The Moslem Sunrise:

*My Dear American Negro... the Christian profiteers
brought you out of your native lands of Africa and in Christianiz-
ing you made you forget the religion and language of your forefathers – which were Islam and Arabic. You have experienced
Christianity for so many years and it has proven to be no good. It
is a failure. Christianity cannot bring real brotherhood to the nations. So, now leave it alone. And join Islam, the real faith of
Universal Brotherhood which at once does away with all distinc-
tions of race, color, and creed. (The Moslem Sunrise, January 2,
1923, page 184)*

Sadiq returned to India at the end of 1923. It has been ru-
mored that he was again asked by American government officials
to leave. Whether that is true or not, Sadiq had been separated
from his wife and children for a number of years. He had come to
America alone to spread the message of Islam and alert its citizens
that the Messiah had come. During his very short stay in the U.S.
he had been extremely busy traveling around and giving lectures.
The impact he made was fitting for someone who considered himself a modern day disciple for the Messiah. Richard Brent Turner
summarizes the impact of Sadiq's Islamic mission to America:

*During his three years in America, Mufti Muhammad Sadiq
converted over seven hundred Americans to Islam. His impact on
American religion during this period, however, cannot be ade-
quately measured by numbers: he provided the first model of multi-
racial community experience for African-American Muslims, and –
the Ahmadiyya community published the first Muslim newspaper*

and the first Quran in English in America... (Islam in the African-American an Experience, by Richard Brent Turner, page 130)

The first English translated Quran had a great impact on the downtrodden black community. Verses in the Quran proclaimed that prophets had been raised up from among all people, refuting the notion of spiritual superiority of any one race over another.

The Quran introduced prophets not mentioned in the Bible, including those from the African continent. Islamic scholars believe that the prophet Luqman, after whom chapter 31 is named, was most likely an Abyssinian or Ethiopian. He has also been identified by some with Aesop, the famous storyteller of Greek legends.

Various Quranic chapters were first translated and printed in *The Moslem Sunrise*. Eventually a completed translation of the Quran was made available to Americans.

The Fruits of Sadiq's Labor

Marcus Garvey's organization attracted those who desired to reject the slave identity America had imposed upon them. As a result of Mufti Muhammad Sadiq's preaching of Islam to members of the UNIA, the religion of Islam came to symbolize a sort of psychological independence from white society. Although Marcus Garvey did not choose an "official" religion for his UNIA, he had praised Islam as an international religion with the potential to connect blacks to their African homeland.

During the 1920s and the 1930s, various Islamic organizations were developed by those who had been influenced by Marcus Garvey's movement.

Despite repressive laws against them, the Ishmaelites, who were at one time 10,000 strong, strived to maintain a culture of independence, as did many Native American nations.

The Ishmaelites helped establish Noble Drew Ali's Moorish Science Temple of America. Noble Drew Ali was said to have been raised among the Cherokee Indians. The organization he founded included teachings from Islamic, Egyptian and Native American traditions. Author Hugo Leaming observes:

10B – The Ambassador Mufti Muhammad Sadiq
(Courtesy of The Ahmadiyya Movement in Islam)

The most valuable testimony to a relationship between the dispersed Ishmaelites and the rise of twentieth-century black nationalism is from an African American wholesale grocer of Chicago, whose work takes him into rural Illinois and Indiana. He has been a devoted student of African American history all his life, but his first loyalty is to Moorish Science. Moorish Science, which was politically associated with the largest black nationalist organization, the Universal Negro Improvement Association (UNIA) led by Marcus Garvey in the 1920s, ... and is the earliest known Islamic organization of the black community in the United States... The well known and larger Nation of Islam, established in 1930, has recognized that Moorish Science was a forerunner of its movement. This adherent of Moorish Science states that when he joined the movement in about 1930, five years after its arrival in Chicago, he met a Mrs. Gallivant, who had joined Moorish Science at Detroit around 1920... She had come from downstate Indiana or Illinois and called herself an Ishmaelite. She spoke of the Tribe of Ishmael as a people who had dwelled downstate, and who after moving north were among the first to assist in the establishment of Moorish Science in the Midwest. (Gone to Croatan: Origins of North American Dropout Culture, Hugo P. Leaming, Ron Sukolsky & James Koehaline, page 47)

The grocer mentioned above was a man named Mr. William Prothro Bey. His company was called United Merchants Exchange. He always requested to be referred to as "Brother Bey." Bey, a name of Moorish origin, was commonly used by members of Noble Drew Ali's Moorish Science Temple of America.

During an interview before his death, Brother Bey recalled that it was in the 1920s when large groups of African American people first became aware of their African and Islamic heritage. He stated that the black community centered around Garvey's movement, which was the largest and most popular black nationalist movement at that time. The UNIA provided a political and economical base for the black community. Because of Mufti Muhammad Sadiq's strong influence in introducing Islam, it also indirectly provided a spiritual base for the UNIA.

By the 1960s there were three major Islamic movements in the Chicago black community: the Ahmadiyya Movement, the Moorish Science Temple, and the Nation of Islam.

The Nation of Islam was another organization that seemed to have its roots in the Garvey movement. Its founder, Elijah Muhammad, who was born Elijah Poole, came to Detroit in 1923 and became a member of Marcus Garvey's UNIA shortly after his arrival. It was during this period that Mufti Muhammad Sadiq gave a series of lectures on Islam to Garvey's followers in Detroit.

When Elijah Poole later became a member of the Black Islamic organization led by W.D. Fard in the 1930s, he was renamed by Fard several times. First Elijah Karriem, then Ghulam Ali, and finally Elijah Muhammad. It is the second name that he adopted that is most intriguing. Author Karl Evanzz notes the strange coincidence of this name:

In 1932, Fard changed Poole's name to Ghulam Ali. In addition to being one of the names of the founder of the Ahmadiyya Movement, Ghulam is a commonly used name in Pakistan... (The Messenger, by Karl Evanzz, page 409)

The influence of Mirza Ghulam Ahmad's Islamic movement, brought to America by Sadiq, would be the most likely reason that could explain how an African American adopted an East Indian name. Also worthy of note is the Quran that was given to Elijah by W.D. Fard.

The first Holy Quran that Fard gave him was in Arabic, and "I couldn't read it. So he got me one in Arabic and English translated by Maulana Muhammad Ali of Pakistan." What he omitted to say was that the translator was, in addition to being from Pakistan, a prominent leader of the Ahmadiyya Movement, which opened its first mosque in Chicago near the site that Fard later chose to establish the NOI's second mosque. (The Messenger, by Karl Evanzz, page 412)

When Elijah became the leader of the Nation of Islam, the elder members of the UNIA sometimes called members of the NOI "Muck-Mucks." This was based on one of the Honorable Elijah's Muhammad's nicknames: Elijah Muckmuck. Among others were similar forms like: Elijah Mukmuhd, Elijah Muhd, and Mohammad Muckmud (*The Messenger*, Karl Evanzz, page 446).

These names were deviations of the correct pronunciation of the name Mahmud, which happened to be the name of Mirza Bashiruddin Mahmud Ahmad, who was the second Khalifa, or spiritual leader, of the Ahmadiyya Movement in Islam. He was the son of the Movement's founder, Mirza Ghulam Ahmad, and it was he who had sent Sadiq to America to spread Islam.

FBI Attacks Political And Religious Dissidents

At the end of World War I, the U.S. Government created the Federal Bureau of Investigations. The FBI, an arm of the justice department, was authorized to investigate and bring to trial any individuals suspected of committing federal crimes or any unlawful activities that could threaten the stability of the country. Under this pretense, the FBI, led by a zealous young Director named J. Edgar Hoover, launched a massive attack on all racial or religious based organizations that challenged the American social order.

The FBI went after Marcus Garvey and the UNIA with a vengeance. In 1925 Garvey was charged with "mail fraud" for sending letters to UNIA members soliciting financial support. He was sentenced to five years in prison, then later pardoned in 1927, and deported back to Jamaica.

Members of his organization were investigated and jailed, and the UNIA, at one time one of the most powerful black organizations in the country, was crushed almost into non-existence.

After Mufti Muhammad Sadiq's abrupt return to India in 1923, many religious leaders came under close government scrutiny. The U.S. Department of Immigration sought to limit new arrivals of Africans, East Indians, Asians and other "non-whites," but welcomed the massive influx of European whites.

North Africans, Arabs and other Middle Eastern immigrants began to identify themselves as "white" on their passports, in order to gain entry to the United States.

Religious leaders that were connected in any way with Garvey's organization were harassed, and in some cases, killed. Just as the government enforced the "Indiana Plan" against the Ishmaelites, many Garveyites and members of various Islamic organizations were arrested, jailed or sent to mental institutions

Reverend Earl Little, the father of internationally known African American Muslim leader Malcolm X, was a dedicated organizer for the UNIA. He was beaten, then thrown in front of a train. The insurance company ruled his death a suicide and refused to pay his family the money from his Life Insurance policy.

Malcolm's mother, Louise Little, worked with Marcus Garvey's publication *The Negro World* with Ahmadiyya Muslim missionary Sheik Ahmad Din. Left widowed and poor, she was forced to accept Welfare. But even under the strain of poverty, she refused to feed her children the pork supplied by the government. Islam forbids the consumption of pork, as does the Jewish faith, and some Christian sects, such as the Seventh Day Adventists. Welfare workers labeled Louis Little "crazy" for refusing food.

Despite pressure from State Welfare workers, she struggled desperately to keep her large family together. In his *Autobiography*, Malcolm described how the government slowly and deliberately tore his family apart:

When the state Welfare people began coming to our house, we would come from school sometimes and find them with our mother, asking a thousand questions. They acted and looked at her, and at us, and around in our house, in a way that had about it the feeling—at least for me—that we were not people. In their eyesight we were just things, that was all...

My mother was, above everything else, a proud woman, and it took its toll on her that she was accepting charity. And her feelings were communicated to us...

She would talk back sharply to the state Welfare people, telling them that she was a grown woman, able to raise her children, that it wasn't necessary for them to keep coming around so much, meddling in our lives. And they didn't like that.

But the monthly Welfare check was their pass. They acted as if they owned us, as if we were their private property. As much as my mother would have like to, she couldn't keep them out. She would get particularly incensed when they began insisting upon drawing us older children aside, one at a time, out on the porch or somewhere, and asking us questions, or telling us things—against our mother and against each other. (The Autobiography of Malcolm X, as told to Alex Haley, pages 15, 16)

State Welfare workers continued to scrutinize Malcolm's family and criticize his mother as she tried to work various jobs to feed her eight children. One by one the children were taken away and sent to foster homes. Louise Little was eventually sent to a mental institution, where she remained for 26 years until Malcolm and his brother Philbert arranged for her release.

Forced poverty, followed by government "Welfare" has historically been used against Native Americans, African Americans and other oppressed people, as a tactic to destroy families and thereby prevent communities from organizing against injustice.

A Message in the Music

The Great Depression that engulfed the country after World War I hit African Americans, Native Americans and immigrants hardest. Jobs were scarce, and organized crime became a means to survive. The FBI became a strong arm of the law, cracking down on gangs and any group it determined was a threat to society. At this time, it was dangerous to openly profess a controversial religious belief such as Islam.

Despite open attacks against all organizations the government deemed "subversive," the multi-racial message of Islam continued to spread. From the first mission house established by Mufti Muhammad Sadiq, Ahmadi Muslim communities spread throughout the U.S. In many cases, African Americans were the primary ambassadors for this message.

...African Americans became prominent missionaries for the Ahmadiyya movement after their conversion. In 1922, The Moslem Sunrise first featured a picture and a short report about a recent black convert, Sheik Ahmad Din (P. Nathaniel Johnson), "a zealous worker for Islam," who had just been appointed missionary in St. Louis, Missouri. Here Ahmad Din led a group of devout Muslims that included blacks, Turks, and a small number of whites. In one of his pictures he wore a fez, which suggests that Din may have been a Freemason or a former member of Noble Drew Ali's Moorish Science Temple movement.

An article about Din in the St. Louis Post Dispatch reports that he had acquired one hundred converts during the first six months of his mission in St. Louis. Another black convert – Brother Omar (William M. Patton) of the Lamarsar Shop – was also cited for his proselytizing efforts in St. Louis, and Sister Noor

(Ophelia Avant) was one of the most enthusiastic black female converts in the St. Louis area. (Islam in the African-American Experience, by Richard Brent Turner, page 126)

Gone were the mass gatherings with fiery preaching that characterized the Garvey movement. For the next three decades, the growth of Islam was more of a subtle revolution. Many first heard its message through a universal language – music.

Jazz musicians have played a significant role in the spread of Islam in America – particularly in the Ahmadiyya Muslim Community. Audiences observed that musicians who had converted to Islam carried themselves with a certain air of independence. They had changed their names to foreign sounding names, they wore a different style of clothing, and the music they played reflected a sound quality never heard before. Some jazz musicians said they were influenced by the rhythms of the poetic Arabic verses of the Holy Quran.

Many African Americans were attracted to Islam after observing and listening to these musicians. They were intrigued by their boldness in adopting non-English names, their polite demeanor, and their abstinence from alcohol and other vices normally associated with the entertainment world.

Islam also attracted people of Native American heritage. One convert who joined the St. Louis Ahmadiyya Muslim community went by the name of Ibrahim Khalil. Ibrahim may have been the first Native American to become an Ahmadi Muslim. Ibrahim was said to be a very private man. What is known about him comes from the oral history of the Ahmadi community in the St. Louis area dating back to the 1930s.

According to Rasheed Ahmad of St. Louis, Ibrahim Khalil was a jazz musician – a saxophonist who played with a band featuring a singer named Ida Cox. He was said to be a very diplomatic individual who was known for always being immaculately dressed in fine suits. While in St. Louis MO, he founded the Pyramid Barbershop, which still exists today on 4338 Oakwood.

Ibrahim Khalil was one of the first professional jazz musicians to become an Ahmadi Muslim, but he would not be the last. During the 1930s, '40s, '50s and '60s other jazz artists would follow in his footsteps. Some of the more famous Ahmadi Muslim jazz artists are: pianist Ahmad Jamal, trumpeter Fard Daleel,

10C – Sheik Ahmad Din (P. Nathaniel Johnson)
(Courtesy of The Ahmadiyya Movement in Islam)

10E – Ibrahim Khalil
(Courtesy of Munir Ahmad of St. Louis Missouri)

saxophonist Charlie Parker, drummers Art Blakely and Talib Daoud, jazz vocalist Aliya Rabia (Dakota Staton,) and Yusef Lateef. Also, John Coltrane's wife Naima, about whom he wrote a famous song entitled *"Naima,"* was an Ahmadi Muslim. Another Ahmadi jazz artist was Sulieman Saud (McCoy Tyner) who was a piano player with John Coltran. Jazz artist named Mustapha Hashim (Kurt Bradford,) who played sax for the Jimmy Lunceford Band in the 1930s and 40s. His band was widely recognized not only in America but also throughout Europe.

Ibrahim was already a Muslim before he came into contact with the Ahmadiyya Muslim community. It is believed that he was originally a member of one of the few Islamic brotherhood societies in America that existed during that time. When he heard about the Ahmadiyya Movement and about the claims of Mirza Ghulam Ahmad, he made a pilgrimage to Chicago to meet with Sufi Mutiur Rahman Bengalee, who was the missionary there during the 1930s. He reportedly accepted shortly afterward and then returned back to St. Louis and became a vital part of its Ahmadiyya community.

According to Ahmadi elder Munir Ahmad, who now owns the Pyramid Barbershop, Ibrahim was originally from Mississippi and his family name before he became a Muslim was Johnson. These last two points suggest that he was perhaps a member of the Choctaw Nation – a majority of whom are located in Mississippi.

Angela Y. Walton-Raji states in her book, *African-American Ancestors Among the Five Civilized Tribes*, that through intermarrying came European surnames into the Choctaw Nation.

> *... this was how European surnames became part of most of the Indigenous tribes. As the Indian women married European men, names such as Ross, Boudinot, Leflore, Johnson were not unusual in Indian communities. (Black Genealogy Research: African-American Ancestors Among the Five Civilized Tribes, by Angela Y. Walton-Raji, page 8)*

Jazz artists like Ibrahim became major ambassadors of the faith of Islam. Their faith had a major influence on their music. These Muslim jazz musicians inspired many with their unique, creative sounds. In addition, some of them also became well versed in Arabic, and became spiritual leaders, authors, and scholars who taught in academic institutions in America and abroad.

Chapter Eleven
A Warning to the United Nations

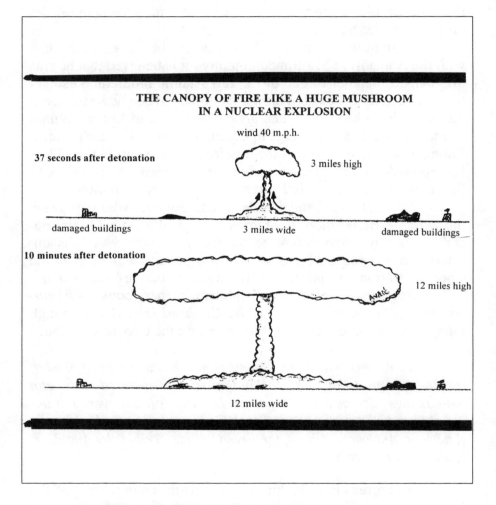

**THE CANOPY OF FIRE LIKE A HUGE MUSHROOM
IN A NUCLEAR EXPLOSION**

wind 40 m.p.h.

37 seconds after detonation   3 miles high

damaged buildings   3 miles wide   damaged buildings

10 minutes after detonation

12 miles high

12 miles wide

11A – The Blast of an Atomic Bomb
Many religious prophecies foretold the coming of the nuclear age. The fulfillment of these prophecies were signs that another great calamity was going to occur and bring destruction to many of the earth's inhabitants. (Picture taken from Revelation, Rationality, Knowledge and Truth, page 614)

Chapter Eleven
A Warning to the United Nations

An incident which shows how strong is the antipathy to-wards Negroes happened only recently in the U.S.A. To quote from "The Times" (London) of May 11th, "There was a hideous outburst of racial feeling at Sherman, Texas, on Friday, during which a Negro was slowly roasted to death, and the Negro quarter of the town wrecked by a mob of white men.

In spite of all the progress in philosophy, ethics and morality which the white man claims for himself, it is curious how some absurd prejudices still cling to him. Himself happening to be fair in complexion, he considers a dark skin, which signifies no more than the effect of certain climatic influences, to be something debasing and degrading. It is a still greater irony that this prejudice should be at its worst in America, the land of equality and freedom… (The Review of Religions Magazine, Vol. XXVIX. June, 1930. No. 6)

White America was still harboring a lot of hatred towards the people of other races, as observed in this 1930 article published in the Ahmadiyya Movement's magazine, *The Review of Religions*.

The few whites who dared to speak out against injustice risked social ostracism. Racism had become an American tradition, so interwoven into the fabric of the culture that it was considered normal. Since European Americans benefited the most from this institution, they waged the greatest resistance against racial equality and universal brotherhood.

The Second Shaking

The failure to bring about true peace only led to the fulfillment of the next set of Hopi prophecies, and the coming of a second World War. The Hopi elders knew that the warnings of their ancient prophecies would be fulfilled.

So they knew things would happen. Things would speed up

a little bit. There would be a cobweb built around the earth, and people would talk across this cobweb. When this talking cobweb, the telephone, was built around the earth, a sign of life would ap-pear in the east, but it would tilt and bring death. It would come with the sun. But the sun itself would rise one day not in the east but in the west. (Hopi Representative Lee Brown, 1986 Continental Indigenous Council)

In the prophecies of the prophet Muhammad, he also stated that one day the sun would rise in the west in the latter days. In Islamic terminology the prophet Muhammad is sometimes called the sun because he brought light to the whole world. In Islam, God is never represented by heavenly objects like the moon or the sun, for He is the power behind them. But the religion of Islam has symbols that are often associated with it. The prophet Muhammad was the living embodiment of Islam in its purest form. So in this sense, the sun was used to represent Islam (although usually it is the crescent moon and star.) It was this prophecy that inspired Mufti Muhammad Sadiq to begin publishing the *Moslem Sunrise.*

According to the Hopi prophecies, even though the sun would at some point rise in the west, it would also rise in the east. This can't be referring to the usual day-to-day rising of the sun in the east. The Hopi understood this metaphorically.

So the elders said when you see the sun rising in the east and you see the sign of life reversed and tilted in the east, you know that the Great Death is to come upon the earth, and now the Great Spirit will grab the earth again in His hand and shake it and this shaking will be worse than the first.

So the sign of life reversed and tilted, we call that the Swas-tika, and the rising sun in the east was the rising sun of Japan. These two symbols are carved in stone in Arizona. When the elders saw these two flags, these were the signs that the earth was to be shaken again. The worse misuse of the Guardianship of the fire is called the "gourd of ashes". They said the gourd of ashes will fall from the air. It will make the people like blades of grass in the prairie fire and things will not grow for many seasons. (Hopi Rep-resentative Lee Brown, 1986 Continental Indigenous Council)

The rise of Nazi Germany, under Adolf Hitler, and Japan

led to World War II and eventually the dropping of the atomic bomb in 1945 – the "gourd of ashes." They said it was the best-kept secret in the history of the United States. The Hopi elders wanted to speak about the "gourd of ashes" back in 1920. They could have warned and foretold it's coming if they could have been allowed to address the League of Nations. Lee Brown recalls:

The elders tried to contact President Roosevelt and ask him not to use the gourd of ashes because it would have a great effect on the earth and eventually cause even greater destruction and the Third Shaking of the Earth, the Third World War.

So they knew after the Second Shaking of the Earth when they saw the gourd of ashes fall from the sky then there would be an attempt to make peace on the other side of this land. And because the peace attempt on the West Coast had failed, they would build a special house on the East Coast of this Turtle Island, and all the nations and peoples of the earth would come to this house and it would be called the House of Mica and it would shine like the mica on the desert shines.

So the elders began to see they were building the United Nations made out of glass that reflects like the mica on the desert so they knew this was the House of Mica and all the peoples of the earth should go to it. So they met and talked about this. (Hopi Representative Lee Brown, 1986 Continental Indigenous Council)

The elders hoped that the horror of the atomic bomb would prompt the leaders of the world to listen to them. They considered writing a letter to the President of the United States, but recalled that their previous attempt had been ignored. They decided that a personal visit may bring better results.

They said that in the 1920's they had written and they had not been responded to, so they said this time we better go to the front door of the House of Mica because things might get a lot worse. So elders representing a number of tribes I believe drove to New York City. When the United Nations opened they went to the front door of the House of Mica and they said these words:

"We represent the indigenous people of North America and we wish to address the nations of the Earth. We're going to give you four days to consider whether or not we will be allowed to

speak." They retreated to one of the Six Nations Reserves in New York State. The Six Nations Reserves are keepers of the Great Law of Peace of the prophet that appeared here in North America, De-ganawidah. And this Law of Peace is still recited, it takes four days between sunrise and noon. Each year an Indian, by memory, must recite it about this time of year. (Hopi Representative Lee Brown, 1986 Continental Indigenous Council)

Like thousands of Muslims who have memorized the entire Quran by heart and recite it during the holy month of Ramadan, the Hopi also commit their sacred teachings to memory, and recite them in a melodic fashion during a special time of the year.

The elders knew the seriousness of their mission. They had to get other nations of the world to hear their prophecies. They had to help world leaders see that some of the prophecies had already been fulfilled. Perhaps then they would understand that unless the nations of the world truly united in brotherhood and followed the laws of justice, there would be no peace. A Third World War would erupt and the earth and its inhabitants would be destroyed.

Four days later they came back and I believe the nations of the earth heard that the Indians had come to the door. And they voted to let the Indians in. They wanted to hear what they had to say. But the United States is one of five nations of the United Nations with a veto power and still they were concerned because this time the Native sovereignty was even stronger. And I believe they vetoed the entrance of the Native people.

So then they knew other things would happen on the Earth, and the United Nations would not bring peace on earth but there would be continuing and deepening confusion. And that the little wars would get worse. So they retreated to the Six Nations Reserve and they talked about this and they said the time is really getting close now, 1949. (Hopi Representative Lee Brown, 1986 Continental Indigenous Council)

Despite the fact that other nations wished to hear from the Native Americans, one nation felt that the other nations of the world didn't need to hear from them – and understandably so. Since the League of Nations visit in 1920, more treaties had been broken and Indian lands were further falling to white developers.

And this trend continued, as noted in the history of the Lakota.

> *By 1942, nearly 1 million of the 2,722,000 acres assigned to Pine Ridge when the reservation was created in 1889 had passed into other hands, and by the 1970s, over 90 percent of reservation lands were owned or leased by white people... (In the Spirit of Crazy Horse, Peter Mattheissen, page 31)*

When the Hopi elders were once again denied an audience with the leaders assembled at the United Nations they decided to assemble their own audiences for the purpose of exposing the prophecies. According to Hopi representative Lee Brown, the elders said, "We're going to divide the United States into four sections and each year we're going to have a gathering. We're going to call these the "White of Peace Gatherings." They began to have these around 1950. They authorized certain men to speak in English for the first time about these prophecies, which had never before been discussed publicly. They knew that it was time to take their message to the masses, and connect with other spiritually minded people who shared their concern about the evil direction in which America and the world was heading.

Will the people of America have to go through a similar ordeal as the people of Japan? It is unfortunate that much of history reveals that mankind, after negating spiritual teachings and becoming accustomed to evil habits, is seldom able to bring himself to break from his evil ways without the assistance of a global catastrophe. During a recent interview, current Supreme Head of the Ahmadiyya Movement in Islam, Mirza Tahir Ahmad, observed that nothing short of another atomic war will touch the hearts of some people:

> *I would like to recount here an interesting conversation I once had with an English businessman while traveling from Dacca to Calcutta... We were exchanging views about matters of religion and although the travel time was very short, we began to agree so quickly that I was surprised.*
>
> *When the journey came to its end, he said, there was one last thing he must say and that is that although he agreed with my philosophy – If I thought that he was going to become a Muslim and change his way of life or that his people were going to do that,*

then I was living in a fool's paradise... I said that I totally agree
with him on that point but added that he would also agree that
there was a phase in the history of Japan similar to our present
phase, before the Second World War, when all the efforts of the
Christian missionaries failed to interest Japan in Christianity, but
once the Second World War broke out the pride of the Japanese
was broken...

It is reported by some Christian scholars that within ten
years, 25% of the Japanese population had converted to Christian-
ity... I pointed out to my fellow traveler that this is what will hap-
pen again to which he responded, light-heartedly, that he would
wait until the Third World War! (Q&A session with Mirza Tahir
Ahmad, published in Review of Religions, April 2002)

It is frightening to think how many people share an attitude
like the English businessman. These are the type of people who
must be "motivated" by either a severe personal tragedy or a
worldwide calamity before they finally do what they already knew
they should do – turn towards God.

Beware the Hotamah – The Atom Bomb

The prophecies in the Holy Quran warn of an impending
nuclear holocaust. In his book *Revelation, Rationality, Knowledge
and Truth*, Mirza Tahir Ahmad states that there are certain verses
in the Holy Quran that clearly speak of tiny insignificant particles
which are described as storehouses of immense energy, as though
the fire of hell was locked in them. He points to Chapter 104, Al
Humaza (The Scandal Monger) which states:

Woe to every backbiter, slanderer, who amasses wealth and
counts it over and over. He imagines that his wealth will make him
immortal. Nay! He shall surely be cast into the "hotamah". And
what should make thee know what the "hotamah" is? Allah's fire as
preserved fuel, which will leap suddenly on to the hearts. It is
locked up in outstretched pillars to be used against them. (The
Holy Quran, Chapter 104, Al Humazah, 2-10.)

Some religious scholars tend to interpret all passages on
future catastrophic events to be in reference to the Day of Judg-

ment, or the Hereafter. However, many prophecies are clearly applicable to the here and now. In his book *Revelation, Rationality, Knowledge and Truth*, Mirza Tahir Ahmad comments on the meaning of this verse and its chapter:

> *This short Quranic Chapter is densely packed with astounding statements which lie far beyond the reach of the people of that age. Strange is it not, to read that the sinful people of a certain description would be cast into the hotamah, which means the tiniest particles, such as we see floating in a beam of light which passes through a poorly lit room.*
>
> *Authentic Arabic lexicons describe hotamah as possessing two root meanings; first hatamah, which means 'to pound' or 'pulverize into extremely small particles', and the second hitmah, which means 'the smallest insignificant particle'. Thus, hitmah is the result obtained by breaking something down to its smallest constituents...*
>
> *As the concept of the atom had not been born fourteen hundred years ago, the nearest substitute to it could only be hotamah which also sounds intriguingly close to atom...*
>
> *Explaining the word hotamah, the Holy Quran speaks of a blazing fire built within it and confined in extended columns...This has only become conceivable in the contemporary age when man has discovered the secret of the atoms and the immense stores of energy which they contain. This is the age when the fire contained in the smallest particles leaps out and engulfs large areas extending to thousands of square miles. Everything that lies within its range is engulfed, man and all. (Revelation, Rationality, Knowledge and Truth, pages 614 and 615)*

The world has been warned, from ancient times to the present, that catastrophes come as a result of mankind's disobedience to divine commands. In the Quran, we are advised to travel throughout the earth and discover those lost civilizations of the past. We are told that nations mightier than those of our present age have been destroyed. Why should we then doubt the prophecies given to our own age, that warn of our destruction unless we change our ways?

Are we, in fact, living in the fourth world? Will a nuclear blast leave all but a few survivors to be the progenitors of a fifth world? Or can we unite the races of man under the banner of peace to save the planet from destruction?

The challenge today, for the spiritually enlightened, is to overcome barriers of race, culture, nationality, and religion and to come together with men and women of understanding who are working to change the direction in which the world is heading. But at times it almost seems like it is the prerogative of man to stray from these ideals. Mirza Tahir Ahmad observes this problematic flaw of human nature:

The enormity of the atomic catastrophe is horrendous, yet little attention is paid by man to investigate and identify the under-lying roots of this evil. The sight of man seldom penetrates beyond the surface he scans. Few among them can introspect themselves to discover the hidden face of their evil intentions. This is a sort of blindness which is specifically related to the crookedness in man. Whenever he himself is responsible for causing suffering and spreading evil around him, he will not identify his own hand behind them. (Revelation, Rationality, Knowledge and Truth, page 620)

Prelude to the Final Calamity

There are specific signs contained in the warnings of the Hopi prophecies that were suppose to take place during the end of this world and before the transition into the next.

One that I used to listen to many times, over and over, was Thomas Banacyca. He is a Hopi man. I believe he is still living. He was authorized to speak in English about what was on the stone tablets and he has dedicated his lifetime to doing this. And they began to tell us at these gatherings, they said, "In your lifetime you're going to see things happen." (Hopi Representative Lee Brown, 1986 Continental Indigenous Council)

These prophecies are similar to prophecies of the Islamic religion. By examining them both, greater certainty is gained that a higher power has indeed informed man of this present age.

In his book *Invitation to Ahmadiyyat*, Mirza Bashiruddin Mahmud Ahmad notes that the Holy Prophet Muhammad foretold:

Women of the time would seem undressed in spite of being dressed. The change has come about in two ways. Firstly, silks and other light fabrics are now produced in large quantities... The cloth manufactured is finer. So the dresses made are thinner. This may satisfy fantastic notions of feminine beauty, but must offend against modesty and sobriety. Secondly, the change has come through fashions which prevail in Europe and America. In these countries women tend more and more to expose parts which it was thought indecent to show in the past. The breasts tend to be exposed... The prophetic descriptions of women's dress, therefore, is true – women today seem undressed even though dressed.

Another change relating to women describes the mode of dressing their hair. According to the descriptions given by the Holy Prophet, women were to coil up their hair so as to produce a hump-like effect on the head. In Europe, women today do not braid their hair as they used to do in the past. Now they keep their hair puffed, giving the impression that something sits neatly on the head. In imitation of European women, women in other parts of the world also dress their hair in the same way... A European fashion is treated with more respect than a message from God. (Invitation to Ahmadiyyat, Mirza Bashiruddin Mahmud Ahmad, pages 99-100)

The ancient Hopi prophecies also tell of a future where the sanctity of women would come down from its sacred pedestal. This sign would act as a warning that other things once held sacred would soon follow in the same footsteps.

Men's clothing will be taken over by women. Women's skirts will be raised above the knee, devaluing the sacred body of the female, indicating that many things will be devalued from the original. (The Hopi Survival Kit, by Thomas E. Mails, pages 187)

Even more shocking, Hopi prophecies tell of a time when the very nature of men and women would be altered completely. Lee Brown recalled how Thomas Banacyca and the other elders described a future time of men turning themselves into women and women turning themselves into men:

"It was strange when they said it in the 1950s and 1960s, but now it seems very clear. But then it was unusual. They said, "You're going to see a time in your life when men are going to become women. The Great Spirit is going to make a man on the earth. He made him a man but this man is going to say, "I know more than the Great Spirit. I'm going to change myself to be a woman." And they will even nurse children. The Great Spirit is going to make the woman on the earth. She's going to say, "I know more than the Great Spirit. I want to be a man. And she will be physically a man." (Hopi Representative Lee Brown, 1986 Continental Indigenous Council)

For the first time, perhaps in the history of mankind, technology has advanced to such a high level that it now allows man to physically affect changes in his own creation, as well as other kinds of creation, like never before. Scientists are able to manipulate biological processes in a few hours what previously took millions upon millions of years to initially form. Lee Brown elaborates on the elder's warnings:

They said, "You're going to see a time in your lifetime when the human beings are going to find the blueprint that makes us." They call that now, DNA, deoxyribonucleic acid. They said, "They're going to cut this blueprint." They call that now, genetic splicing. And they said, "They're going to make new animals upon the earth, and they're going to think these are going to help us. And it's going to seem like they do help us. But maybe the grandchildren and great grandchildren are going to suffer."

I don't know if you heard on the news last night in the United States now they have genetically spliced a new germ, never before released in the environment. They want to release this germ into the cotton fields of the south because they say it will rejuvenate and strengthen the cotton. They had scientists on the CBS Evening News the other night talking about it. One scientist said what the elders said in the 1950's, that this will not harm us. We've put it in a lot of tests. And the other scientist said what the elders also said, no, this has never before been in the environment. We have no idea what it will do. The elders spoke of it long ago. They said it would seem harmless, but it may be able to hurt the great grandchildren. The elders said long ago, "They will release these

*things, they will use them." This is going to be released not too
long from now. (Lee Brown, 1986 Continental Indigenous Council)*

Again we use the Holy Quran as another example to show
that God has warned all of mankind of specific dangers relating to
a specific time in mans' history. The Quran states:

*Satan said: I will assuredly take a fixed portion of Your
servants; And assuredly I will lead them astray and assuredly I
will arouse in them vain desires, and assuredly I will incite them
and they will cut the ears of cattle; and assuredly I will incite them
and they will alter Allah's creation. And he who takes Satan as a
friend besides Allah has certainly suffered a manifest lost. (The
Holy Quran, Chapter 4, Al-Nisa (The Women) verses 119-120)*

In the above verse, one of the methods of physically scar-
ing or branding livestock is mentioned. But immediately following
that it states that "they will alter Allah's creation." This satanic
incitement should not be understood as referring to the act of
branding cattle, although many do find that objectionable. What is
being alluded to is something far more profound – more severe.
Only during this last century has genetic engineering become so
highly advanced and practiced worldwide. During an interview in
London:, Mirza Tahir Ahmad commented on the Quran's warning
against genetic engineering:

*The genetic modification of animal life is a very dangerous
exercise. According to the Holy Quran, this attempt on the part of
man to interfere with the genetic signals within chromosomes, etc.
can produce horrific effects on mankind and whether the experiments are carried out on animals or humans it is the same thing.
To my knowledge they do not have the full command over the outcome of these experiments and the scientists involved in this task
admitted it in so many words. They think that a part of a chromosome can be attached to a part of another chromosome of a female
for instance or from one animal's chromosome to that of another
animal. They believe the result would be as they foresee.
    But the experiments have shown that the results were not
what they had predicted. They were often most unpleasantly surprised. So I am quoting this in favor of a Quranic prophecy that*

*when mankind will try to change human or animal life genetically,
this will be at the behest of Satan, and they will find it to be an extremely dangerous game which will ultimately turn the tables
against humans at large. (Q&A session with Mirza Tahir Ahmad,
London, published in Review of Religions, August 1999)*

Not only did the ancient prophecies of the Hopi speak of a
time when new animals would be created, they also spoke of a day
when animals from the past, those considered extinct, would return.

*The elders talked about this. They said, "You will see new
animals, and even the old animals will come back, animals that
people thought had disappeared. They will find them here and
there. They'll begin to reappear." (Hopi Representative Lee Brown,
1986 Continental Indigenous Council)*

The prophecy about the reappearance of "animals that people thought had disappeared," or, in other words, animals now considered extinct, has been interpreted by some to mean that dinosaurs would come back into existence. If taken metaphorically, the
motion picture industry in films such as *Dinotopia* and the *Jurassic
Park* series have created, through technology and special effects,
extremely realistic and lifelike creations of extinct dinosaurs.

The Hopi also have a prophecy concerning an usual flight
of an eagle. However, when examined within the context of the
modern age, it clearly is a reference to space travel. Lee Brown
explains:

*They said (and I know many of you are from tribes that also
have this prophecy), "You're going to see a time when the eagle
will fly its highest in the night and it will land upon the moon."
Some tribes say the eagle will circle the moon. Some tribes say the
eagle will fly it's highest in the night. "And at that time," they say,
"many of the Native people will be sleeping," which symbolically
means they have lost their teachings. There are some tribes that
say it will be as if they are frozen: they've been through the long
winter. But they say, "When the eagle flies it's highest in the night,
that will be the first light of a new day. That will be the first thaw-
ing of spring." Of course, at the first light of a new day, if you've*

stayed up all night, you notice it's really dark. And the first light, you want to see it, but you can't. It sneaks up on you. You want to see it change but it's dark and then pretty soon it's getting light before you know it.

We're at that time now. The Eagle has landed on the moon, 1969. When that spaceship landed they sent back the message, "The Eagle has landed."

Traditionally, Native people from clear up in the Inuit region, they have shared with us this prophecy, clear down to the Quechuas in South America. They shared with us that they have this prophecy. When they heard those first words, "The Eagle has landed," they knew that was the start of a new time and a new power for Native people." (Hopi Representative Lee Brown, 1986 Continental Indigenous Council)

Even the printing on the U.S. currency has symbolic meanings in the prophecies of the Hopi. Lee Brown explains their interpretation of what the American Eagle depicted on the dollar stands for:

In 1776 when the United States Government printed the dollar, in one claw [of the eagle], if you've ever noticed, there is an olive branch in this claw. They said that represented peace. The Indian elders shared with me in South Dakota that to them that represents the enslavement of black people. In the prophecies of the Six Nations people they say there will be two great uprisings by black people to free themselves. We've seen one about 1964. There will be a second, more violent one to come. (Hopi Representative Lee Brown, 1986 Continental Indigenous Council)

Civil Rights Movement Inspires Native Protests

The Civil Rights Movement organized by blacks during the 1950s and 1960s ended legal racial discrimination. Many other ethnic groups benefited from the removal of racist laws and practices. This gave new inspiration to other oppressed groups in America. The African American call for "Black Power" inspired a similar slogan among Native Americans, who called for "Red Power." In 1968, George Mitchell, Eddie Benton Banai and Dennis Banks founded the American Indian Movement (AIM.) The

AIM was involved in a number of protests. One of the most famous protests is now known as "Wounded Knee II." On February 28, 1973, several hundred Native men and women staged a "sit in" in the area around the historical Wounded Knee site in protest of another treaty that had broken by the U.S. government. This action received a quick response.

... Wounded Knee was surrounded the next day by the FBI, the U.S. Marshal Service, and the BIA police. The most powerful nation in the world had been challenged by a tiny Indian nation that dared to demand restoration of its sovereignty according to the terms of its great treaty. The AIM people who supported it were mostly volunteers from other tribes, and the inter-tribal spirit at Wounded Knee inspired a revival of Indian sovereignty claims all over the continent. (In the Spirit of Crazy Horse, Peter Mattheissen, page 67)

Despite the area's history, the various federal agents on the scene seemed more than willing to bring about another unwarranted massacre, as author Peter Mattheissen:

...A makeshift federal army had been created by the Justice and Defense departments by training civilian law-enforcement officers in paramilitary units and equipping them with armored personnel carriers, automatic weapons, and enough ammunition (133,000 rounds for the M-16 rifles alone) to wipe out every Indian in the Dakotas. The excuse offered for this exercise was the brief detention of a few "hostages," mostly at the white trading post, which has prospered for years from tourists attracted to the site of the 1890 massacre ("Wounded Knee Massacre Historical Site – Mass Burial Grave – Authentic Arts and Crafts – 51 miles")...
(In the Spirit of Crazy Horse, Peter Mattheissen, page 68)

As it turned out, the white "hostages" had been free to leave, and some eventually did. A few others, however, chose not to leave but rather to stay. Other Native Americans who happened to be there when the AIM began its protest, but were not part of the initial occupying party, also chose to stay. One elderly Indian women who stayed recalled that her grandfather, along with his three brothers, were all killed in the original Wounded Knee massacre of 1890. She chose to stay "because I have a wound that was never healed." (*In the Spirit of Crazy Horse*, Peter Mattheissen, page 69).

Just as in 1890, the government overreacted. Fortunately, this time a peaceful end to the stand off was negotiated and no one was killed. The Indian protestors realized that they had taken a very big chance, but were willing to face the consequences.

The elders and chiefs were quite aware of the significance of the brave stand that they were taking on behalf not only of the Oglala but of traditional Indians all over North America and traditional peoples all over the world... The Indians knew that they were risking an angry reprisal from the U.S. government. "Indian people, the smallest number of people in the country, the poorest people in the country, are making a stand here and are ready to die," declared Lorelei Decora of Iowa AIM. (In the Spirit of Crazy Horse, Peter Mattheissen, page 71)

The revolutionary spirit that characterized the African American struggle further inspired Native Americans to continue to fight for their rights.

According to the Native American prophecies, a movement among African Americans to end racial oppression would happen again one day – and would again have a positive impact on the lives of Native Americans. It will bring the world that much closer to reuniting the entire human family, where all races will form a common brotherhood. Regarding the meanings behind the symbols on U. S. currency, Lee Brown stated:

In the other claw are 13 arrows. The founding fathers of the United States said that represents the 13 States. But the elders say that represents the enslavement of the Native people. When the Eagle landed on the moon, they decided to print a special silver dollar to commemorate that. I don't know how many of you noticed it. The original design showed the spaceship landing on the moon but at the last minute it was changed to an actual eagle. And in the eagle's claws is the olive branch, but the arrows are gone. The elders said, "That's our prophecy, we have been released." They said when that Eagle landed on the moon, the powers will begin to come back to us. As an alcoholic person, I feel that one of our

*greatest diseases is alcoholism. Within seven days of the time the
Eagle landed on the moon, the Freedom of Indian Religion Act was
introduced into the United States Congress. The legislation was
introduced in 1969, less than seven days after the Eagle landed on
the moon. Eventually it was passed in November of 1978, signed
by President Carter... These are the physical manifestations of the
spiritual prophecies that we have. (Hopi Representative Lee
Brown, 1986 Continental Indigenous Council)*

Many Native Americans believed that this was the sign that
their people would begin to "wake up." But in order for mankind
to achieve peace, the oppression of all races must end. Native
Americans look at the struggles of African Americans with interest, because, according to their prophecies, the destinies of both
people are intertwined. Lee Brown explained:

*There was one more uprising coming for the black race of
people and then they will be released and this is also going to have
an effect on Native people, a good effect. (Hopi Representative Lee
Brown, 1986 Continental Indigenous Council)*

What will be the nature of this second uprising? The black
revolution of the 1960s was met with overwhelming violence.
Black churches were bombed, killing innocent children. The people who were given the guardianship of the water, were brutally
attacked with water, by those who were given guardianship of the
fire – white firemen and policemen who sprayed hoses on peaceful
protestors. Police dogs were trained to attack black people. Many
people were unjustly arrested and thrown in jail. People were dying and communities were burned to the ground – as if they were
living in hell on earth.

According to Hopi Lee Brown, the next great uprising in
the African American community may even be more intense.

Will blacks be enraged enough to take up arms against the
most powerful military force in the world? Such an armed struggle
would be futile, given the government's proven willingness to
massacre great numbers of people – just consider Wounded Knee.

The real revolution must be a spiritual one. According to
all prophecies, that is the only kind that can succeed.

Chapter Twelve
Can Armageddon Be Stopped?

12A – Earth - A View From Space

Planet Earth is home to human, animal and plant life. The nations of the world are at war and some are threatening to use atomic weapons. Our home could be destroyed by a nuclear holocaust. What will the future bring? Can we save the Earth and its inhabitants? Or will life as we know it be wiped out, paving the way for a few survivors to enter the Fifth World?

Chapter Twelve
Can Armageddon Be Stopped?

"When the Great Leaders in the Glass House refuse to open the door to you when you stand before it that day, do not be discouraged or turn about on the path you walk, but take courage, determination, and be of great rejoicing in your hearts, for on that day the White Race who are on your land with you have cut themselves from you and thereon led themselves to the Greatest Punishment at the Day of Purification. Many shall be destroyed for their sins and evil ways. The Great Spirit has decreed it and no one can stop it, change it, or add anything to it. It shall be fulfilled!" (Hopi Representative Lee Brown, 1986 Continental Indigenous Council)

The news reports of today are grim. More bombings. More shootings. More deaths. No end of war in sight. Nations sit poised with their atomic weapons, ready to render catastrophic destruction. The whole world appears to be flying headlong towards the final conflict known as Armageddon. Can it be stopped?

Prophecy Rock

Just as the prophetic revelations in the Bible and the Quran were recorded centuries ago, the Native American prophecies were also recorded long ago. They are, in fact, etched in stone. Lee Brown of the Hopi tribe described the ancient carvings. He said that near Oraibi, Arizona, there is a petroglyph known as "Prophecy Rock" that symbolizes many Hopi prophecies. Its interpretation is:

The large human figure on the left is the Great Spirit. The bow in his left hand represents his instructions to the Hopi to lay down their weapons. The vertical line to the right of the Great Spirit is a time scale in thousands of years. The point at which the Great Spirit touches the line is the time of his return.

The "life path" established by the Great Spirit divides into the lower, narrow path of continuous Life in harmony with nature and the wide upper road of white men's scientific achievements. The bar between the paths, above the cross, is the coming of white men; the Cross is that of Christianity. The circle below the cross represents the continuous Path of Life.

The four small human figures on the upper road represent, on one level, the past three worlds and the present; on another level, the figures indicate that some of the Hopi will travel the white man's path, having been seduced by its glamour.

The two circles on the lower Path of Life are the "great shaking of the earth" (World Wars One and Two). The swastika in the sun and the Celtic cross represent the two helpers of Pahana, the True White Brother.

The short line that returns to the straight Path of Life is the last chance for people to turn back to nature before the upper road disintegrates and dissipates. The small circle above the Path of Life, after the last chance, is the Great Purification, after which corn will grow in abundance again when the Great Spirit returns. And the Path of Life continues forever...

The Hopi shield in the lower right corner symbolizes the Earth and the Four-Corners area where the Hopi have been reserved. The arms of the cross also represent the four directions in which they migrated according to the instructions of the Great Spirit. The dots represent the four colors of Hopi corn, and the four racial colors of humanity. (Lee Brown, 1986)

According to Prophecy Rock, humanity has one last chance to restore balance to the earth before it is destroyed. What type of energy could literally disintegrate an entire city? Certainly the atomic bomb was incomprehensible to those who foresaw the devastation from its power. The "Great Purification" of the Hopi prophecies can be viewed as a time of great calamity, in which the old wicked world is purged and a new world emerges. This is also foretold in Chapter 101 of the Holy Quran, entitled, Al Qariah (The Great Calamity):

The Day of Noise and Clamor. What is the Day of Noise and Clamor? And what will explain to thee what the Day of Noise and Clamor is? It is a Day whereon men will be like moths, scat-

tered about, and the mountains will be like carded wool. Then, he whose balance of good deeds will be found heavy; will be in a life of good pleasure and satisfaction. But he whose balance of good deeds will be found light will have his home in a bottomless pit. Knowest thou what it is? It is a fire blazing fiercely! (Holy Quran, Chapter 101, Al Qariah, verses 1-12.)

"Noise and clamor" can easily be the sound of explosions. "The mountains will be like carded wool" perhaps is a description of mountains being blown to pieces. And perhaps the "fire blazing fiercely" is another reference to the fire and heat from exploding bombs. Could these collective prophecies be referring to a third World War?

A Third Shaking

Another sign of the times, according to Lee Brown, is that people will perceive that time is appearing to speed up. People on the earth will move faster and faster. As a result, grandchildren will not have time for grandparents. Parents will not have time for children. This will, of course lead to a breakdown in family life. It will seem like time is going faster and faster. The Hopi elders advised that as things speed up, those with understanding should slow down. The faster things go, the slower those with wisdom should go. The speeding up of time is a sign of the coming of the Third Shaking of the Earth. Lee Brown said:

The Great Spirit has been shaking the earth two times: the First and Second World Wars to remind us that we are a human family, to remind us that we should have greeted each other as brothers and sisters. We had a chance after each shaking to come together in a circle that would have brought peace on earth, but we missed that. Tonight they were talking on the news about the sign for the Third Shaking of the Earth. I heard it while sitting in the airport after I missed my plane. They said they're going to build what the elders called the "house in the sky".

In the 1950's they talked about this: they will build a house and throw it in the sky. When you see people living in the sky on a permanent basis, you will know the Great Spirit is about to grab the earth, this time not with one hand, but with both hands. (Hopi Representative Lee Brown, 1986 Continental Indigenous Council)

Satellites have been launched into the sky, great space stations from which activities can be conducted involving everything from international communication to the monitoring of defense systems. Lee Brown stated:

Many of you of Native background may have heard "the spirits will warn you twice, but the third time you stand alone." We've had two warnings, the first two World Wars, but now we stand alone in the third one. As it says in the Baha'i Writings, "there will be no one protected." When this house is in the sky, the Great Spirit is going to shake the Earth a third time and whoever dropped that gourd of ashes, upon them it is going to drop. (Hopi Representative Lee Brown, 1986 Continental Indigenous Council)

This is an ominous prediction for all those who reside in the United States. American historians tend to excuse the dropping of the atomic bomb as a necessary strategy for ending World War II. But could there have been a stronger attempt to negotiate for peace? If the United States had allowed the Native American elders to speak at the first United Nations, perhaps World War II could have been prevented altogether!

After the war, just as the prophecies stated, there was much rebuilding. The American economy was booming. Modern cities with even taller buildings and more paved streets were constructed. Lee Brown noted:

They say at that time there will be villages in this land so great that when you stand in the villages you will not be able to see out, and in the prophecies these are called "villages of stone", or "prairies of stone". And they said the stone will grow up from the ground and you will not be able to see beyond the village. At the center of each and every one of these villages will be Native people, and they will walk as "hollow" shells upon a "prairie of stone". They said, "hollow shells" which means they will have lost any of their traditional understandings; they will be empty within. (Hopi Representative Lee Brown, 1986 Continental Indigenous Council)

The "villages of stone" are obvious references to America's large cities, with their brick skyscrapers blocking the view beyond the next street. The concrete streets and paved lots are the "prairies of stone".

According to the prophecies, after the Eagle lands on the moon, some of the Native people will begin to leave these "prairies of stone" and come home and take up some of the old ways. But many will not. And when the destruction of the cities comes, it will be so complete, it will be as though the cities never existed.

And they said there's going to come a time when in the morning the sun is going to rise and this village of stone will be there, and in the evening there would just be steam coming from the ground. They will be as steam. And in the center of many of those villages of stone when they turn to steam, the Native people will turn to steam also because they never woke up and left the village. (Hopi Representative Lee Brown, 1986 Continental Indigenous Council)

Compare the above prophecy with the following verses in the Bible and the Quran describing a very similar destruction:

When the thousand years are ended, Satan will be released from his prison and will come out to deceive the nations at the Four Corners of the earth, Gog and Magog, in order to gather them for battle; they are as numerous as the sands of the sea. They marched up over the breadth of the earth and surrounded the camp of the beloved city. And fire came down from heaven and consumed them. (Holy Bible, Revelations, Chapter 20, Verses 7-9.)

It was but a single blast and they were extinct. (Holy Quran, Chapter 36, verse 30)

The Biblical description of the "fire from heaven" that would consume, the Quranic description of the "single blast" that would cause extinction, and the "gourd of ashes" of Native American prophecy, imply something like the dropping of an atomic bomb, or perhaps something even more devastating.

Warnings From The Red Prophets

How many times have prophets come to warn the people about the coming of Divine wrath? According to the Bible, God sent many prophets to the progeny of Isaac and Moses, and each time they were ignored. Leaders within the United States government, in their arrogance, refused to listen to the words of the Native American elders out of an arrogant belief that the Native American people have no legitimate religion. Failing to listen to them, they therefore do not see the correlation between the Native American prophecies and those contained in the Book of Revelations in the Bible. They scornfully dismiss the warnings of Indian holy men.

But in the Holy Quran, mankind is instructed to give equal respect to all prophets who have received divine revelation. This means that Native American prophets must be taken as seriously as the prophets of other religions. The Quran commands Muslims:

Affirm; we believe in God and in that which has been revealed to us. And that which was revealed to Abraham, and Ishmael, and Isaac, and Jacob, and his children, And that which was given to all other Prophets from their Lord. We make no discrimination between any of them and to Him do we wholly submit ourselves. (Chapter 2, Al-Baqarah (The Cow), Verse 137)

Only if the people of the time heed their warnings can they be saved from the destruction that they in fact brought upon themselves. Unfortunately, throughout mankind's history, spiritual men who brought warnings of impending doom were laughed at and ignored. The leaders of the day were always powerful and arrogant, and the people were so prosperous they could not fathom losing all of their possessions. They ceased to have any real belief in a divine being Who had the ability to take away in a single instant all that they had amassed. The Holy Quran states:

Then We sent Our Messengers one after the other. Every time there came to a people their Messenger, they treated him as a Liar. So We made them follow one another to destruction. And We made them mere tales of the past. Cursed, then, be the people who believe not! (Chapter 23: Al- Mu'minun (The Believers), Verse 45)

Some religious leaders have taken the Native American prophecies seriously and have tried to share this knowledge with others. In the summer of 1958, a Christian minister named David Young stopped to offer a ride to a Native American elder who was walking along the road. The man accepted with a nod. As they rode along, the elder began to speak of the ancient prophecies. Reverend Young was so fascinated; he recorded the information and circulated it among several Methodist and Presbyterian churches. Some of the prophecies were published in 1963 by Frank Waters in *The Book of the Hopi*. According to David Young, the elder told him:

"I am White Feather, a Hopi of the ancient Bear Clan. In my long life I have traveled through this land, seeking out my brothers, and learning from them many things full of wisdom. I have followed the sacred paths of my people, who inhabit the forests and many lakes in the east, the land of ice and long nights in the north, and the places of holy altars of stone built many years ago by my brothers' fathers in the south. From all these I have heard the stories of the past, and the prophecies of the future." (The Book of the Hopi, by Frank Waters)

White Feather explained that he was growing old and would soon die. His sons had all died. No one was left to pass on the ancient wisdom. The great ceremonies that preserved the history of the origins of the Hopi people and their emergence into the Fourth World had been all but forgotten. He said his people were still awaiting the arrival of Pahanna - the True White Brother, who would bring with him the symbols and the missing piece of that sacred tablet now kept by the elders. The piece was given to him when he left, and when he returned he would have it. This would identify him as the True White Brother. White Feather told the reverend that:

"He will not be like the white men we know now, who are cruel and greedy. We were told of their coming long ago. But still we await Pahana." (The Book of the Hopi, by Frank Waters)

White Feather wished to pass on his knowledge of the prophecies before he died, so that those with spiritual insight could prepare themselves.

"The Fourth World shall end soon, and the Fifth World will begin. This the elders everywhere know. The Signs over many years have been fulfilled, and so few are left.

"This is the First Sign: We are told of the coming of the white-skinned men, like Pahana, but not living like Pahana, men who took the land that was not theirs. And men who struck their enemies with thunder.

"This is the Second Sign: Our lands will see the coming of spinning wheels filled with voices. In his youth, my father saw this prophecy come true with his eyes -- the white men bringing their families in wagons across the prairies."

"This is the Third Sign: A strange beast like a buffalo but with great long horns, will overrun the land in large numbers. These White Feather saw with his eyes -- the coming of the white men's cattle."

"This is the Fourth Sign: The land will be crossed by snakes of iron."

"This is the Fifth Sign: The land shall be criss-crossed by a giant spider's web."

"This is the Sixth sign: The land shall be criss-crossed with rivers of stone that make pictures in the sun."

"This is the Seventh Sign: You will hear of the sea turning black, and many living things dying because of it."

"This is the Eighth Sign: You will see many youth, who wear their hair long like my people, come and join the tribal nations, to learn their ways and wisdom.

"And this is the Ninth and Last Sign: You will hear of a dwelling-place in the heavens, above the earth, that shall fall with a great crash. It will appear as a blue star. Very soon after this, the ceremonies of my people will cease. (The Book of the Hopi, by Frank Waters)

Reverend Young continued to listen in fascination as White Feather told of the prophecies concerning the world's catastrophic ending.

"These are the Signs that great destruction is coming. The world shall rock to and fro. The white man will battle against

other people in other lands - with those who possessed the first light of wisdom. There will be many columns of smoke and fire such as White Feather has seen the white man make in the deserts not far from here. Only those which come will cause disease and a great dying. Many of my people, understanding the prophecies, shall be safe. Those who stay and live in the places of my people also shall be safe. Then there will be much to rebuild.

And soon -- very soon afterward -- Pahana will return. He shall bring with him the dawn of the Fifth World. He shall plant the seeds of his wisdom in their hearts. Even now the seeds are being planted. These shall smooth the way to the Emergence into the Fifth World.

"But White Feather shall not see it. I am old and dying. You, perhaps, will see it. In time, in time..." (The Book of the Hopi, by Frank Waters)

The old Hopi elder fell silent. They had arrived at his destination, and Reverend David Young stopped to let him out of the car. They never met again. Reverend Young died in 1976, so he did not live to see the final fulfillment of this prophecy.

The signs are easily interpreted. The First Sign, men who "strike their enemies with thunder" refers to the Europeans use of guns. The Second Sign refers to the pioneers' covered wagons. The Third Sign speaks of the longhorn cattle. The Fourth Sign describes the railroad. The Fifth Sign is a clear image of electric power and telephone lines. The Sixth Sign describes concrete highways and their mirage producing effects. The Seventh Sign foretells of the pollution of the seas and oceans due to industrial waste and oil spills.

The Eighth Sign tells of the "Hippie Movement" of the 1960s, when many whites grew critical of American policies and values. During this time many sought out Native American communities seeking a life not centered in materialism, and that was in harmony with nature. The Ninth Sign was the U.S. Space Station Skylab, which fell to Earth in 1979. According to Australian eyewitnesses, it appeared to be burning blue.

Lee Brown recalled that a prophecy also declared that when the elders first tried to warn the people at the United Nations, the doors of the "Glass House" would be closed to them. He witnessed the elders' frustration of seeing all of the prophecies fulfilled, yet not being able to touch the hearts of those in positions of national leadership who could avert a world catastrophe. He said:

> ... *this used to bother me when I was a young man. I used to ask the Elders, "Isn't there anything we can do?" And they said, "Well, it's just that way, that if a person does not have the spiritual eyes to see, it's very hard to show them. Or if they don't have the ears to hear, it's very hard to speak with them. We wish that we could go get them all but we can't. It's just that some are not going to wake up. But some will wake up." (Hopi Representative Lee Brown, 1986 Continental Indigenous Council)*

The Unifying Force

When all of mankind, when all of the "four brothers," unify under the universal laws that the Creator gave to every nation, then will the world witness peace flooding over the entire earth like a massive dam breaking under tremendous pressure. That pressure is symbolic of the growing masses of people who are feeling the restlessness of the age. They feel the need for change, for social change, for political change, for environmental change, and for spiritual change.

There are a number of religious groups today who are out to change the world, on all levels. Many are committed to unifying all the "four brothers." Mirza Ghulam Ahmad believed that to achieve this goal, his followers must always disregard differences in cultures and nationalities and strive for unity based on higher spiritual principles. He taught that his followers should show sympathy towards one's fellow man regardless of religion or race.

> *The principle to which we adhere to is that we have kindness at heart for the whole of mankind. If anyone sees the house of a Hindu neighbor on fire and does not come forward to help extinguish the fire, most truly I declare that he does not belong to me. If anyone of my followers, having seen someone attempting to murder a Christian does not endeavor to save him, I most truly declare that he does not belong to us.(Roohani Khazain Vol 12, p 28)*

During a visit to Chicago in 2001 Maulvi A. Wahab Adam, the Ameer (head) of Ghana's Ahmadiyya community, spoke at

Sadiq Mosque, named after the first Ahmadi missionary sent to the U.S., Mufti Muhammad Sadiq. During his lecture, Ameer Wahab Adam stated that the Ahmadiyya Movement was not a new movement, but was the same movement started during the time of the Prophet Muhammad. In the Quran it states:

> *He it is Who sent His Messenger with guidance and the religion of truth, that He may make it prevail over every other religion, even though the idolaters may resent it. (Al-Taubah, verse 33)*

During the time of the Prophet Muhammad, Islam spread to many parts of the globe. It continued to spread after his death, eventually reaching parts of America, but eventually went into decline. As prophesied, Christianity came to dominate the globe. Islamic scholars agree that the time of the final victory of Islam, in its pristine form, would occur in the latter days with the coming of a Messiah. The above Quranic prophecy refers to that time.

The prophecy of the Prophet Muhammad, concerning a reviver of the faith from the lands of Persia, was fulfilled. It is interesting to note that many of the people who are from Persia, when viewed from the superficial eye of race, would be considered "white." Mirza Ghulam Ahmad was of a light complexion, but if he is considered to be the "True White Brother" of the Native American prophecies, should it not be more so because of the purity of his character, rather than the color of his skin?

Mirza Ghulam Ahmad taught his followers that the Prophet Muhammad was the perfect specimen of righteousness whose example all of mankind should emulate. It was revealed to the Prophet Muhammad that God had sent prophets to all the different nations of the earth, but that he was the culmination of all the prophets, for God had sent him as the perfect example to represent the perfect law contained in the Quran.

Furthermore, Mirza Ghulam Ahmad stated that recognition of the prophets of other nations is essential for the future triumph of Islam. Like much of Islam today, all other religions had, over centuries, lost their essence. Fundamentally though, all were originally true and from the same God. Ahmad claimed that he was sent to revive Islam and reestablish it as the summit of the evolution of all the divinely revealed religions. He stated:

Of all the principles to which I have been made to adhere firmly, there is one that has specifically been revealed to me by God Himself. That principle is to desist from declaring false in essence, such religions as have been revealed by God through his prophets and which wide acceptance in certain regions of the world; having survived all challenges, they have become well established and deeply rooted. Having stood the test of time for so long, they have acquired a measure of age and an air of permanence. According to this principle, such religions are essentially true and their founders were most certainly true prophets of God. (Tohfa Qaisariya: Roohani Khasain Vol. 12, page 256)

For this reason, in this book the prophecies of the Native American nations have been approached with absolute respect. They are as legitimate as the prophecies contained in Muslim traditions. They are as legitimate as prophecies contained in the Bible. They are as legitimate as any prophecy of any other major religion of the world. Although America defines itself as a Christian nation, it could gain much insight into its own future by examining the prophecies of the Native American prophets. But if not, then perhaps the warnings in the Book of Revelations will be enough to make America wake up to the reality of God's warnings.

Down Goes Babylon

And in her was found the blood of prophets, and of saints, and of all that were slain upon the earth. (Revelation 18:24)

In 1623, the Dutch arrived in modern day New York. That was the year everything changed for the natives in that area, who had been fishing and farming there for centuries. The Dutch quickly began to settle in the area, which they would come to call New Amsterdam.

Within three years the Dutch had established a sizable community. It was then decided that they would purchase the land from the natives. The Lenape were one of the tribes in that area.

Peter Minuit became the first governor of New Amsterdam in 1626, and he is said to have bought Manhattan Island from the Lenape residents in exchange for 60 Dutch guilders' worth (about

$24) of assorted objects, such as beads and knives. (Destination New York, Linda Tagliaferro, page 33)

This piddling amount of money that was paid for what would later become the hottest property in the world has long been a source of humor in business circles, with the Indians being at the brunt of the joke. However, who the bigger fool was in this scenario is a matter of perspective.

Today, if one person walks up to another standing on a street corner, offering them $1 for the air space around them, the offer would perhaps be accepted. Imagine someone giving you money for something that you know is obviously "common property." However, the person who offered the money believes that the air space on the corner of the street now belongs solely to him. He then decides to place a big plastic bubble on the corner so that no one else can breath the air in that area but him.

Inside his bubble he laughs at how clever he is, and how stupid that person was who sold it to him for just $1. Meanwhile, the people outside the plastic bubble stare curiously, struggling to understand what is going on in the mind of an obvious madman.

The original Native "New Yorkers" did not conceive of the idea of individual land ownership. Perhaps this contributed to the reason why the Dutch were never challenged on their "claim" to Manhattan.

If there was a tribe that could be said to be the owners of the land, it would have more likely been the Wappingers, who were part of the greater Algonquin tribe that lived in an area around present day Yonkers.

While some believe it was the Lenape residents, others believe that the tribe to which the Dutch Governor originally gave money for the island were not even from the local area.

Minuit purchased the island from some unknown Indians who were simply journeying from the west to a summer camping place, probably Long Island, where they could fish and dig for clams. They accepted Minuit's twenty-four dollars' worth of trade goods and went serenely on their way, richer by far than they had been before they camped on Manhattan. (The Colony of New York, by David Goodnough, page 20)

Also during the year of 1626, eleven black slaves were brought to New Amsterdam. These were the first slaves brought to New York. They were put to work for the Dutch West India Co. The European given names of four of them are known. They were: Anthony Portugese, John Francisco, Simon Congo and Paul d'Angola. It is believed that these slaves were the same slaves who later in 1644 petitioned to have themselves and their wives freed. Their petition was accepted and they were even given land grants for the use of farming. The area they were given was in a swampy terrain that is today known as Greenwich Village.

It is also believed that these slaves were involved in the founding of other towns as well. John Francisco was part of an original group of twenty-three persons, predominantly whites, who were given a special government privilege in 1660 to be the founders of the town of Boswyck. Today it is known as Bushwick.

In 1647, under the leadership of governor Peter Stuyvesant, a barrier of wooden posts was built on the north end of the settlement. It became known as "The Wall." It was created to protect the settlers against Indian raids. Today, New York's Wall Street runs along the same boundary line.

In 1658, the Dutch bullied the Native Americans out of another area that they would then name Nieuw Haarlem, after one of their cities in the Netherlands. Later on when the British took over, the residents decided to drop one "a" from the name. Centuries later, Harlem became a cultural center for the African American population.

The British took over New Amsterdam from the Dutch in 1664. It was then renamed New York. The British increased the importation of African slaves and passed a series of oppressive laws that further reduced what little rights slaves could have. In 1706 a new law allowed "Negro, Indian and Mulatto slaves" to be baptized as Christians, although this did not in any way imply that they were free or should be freed. It also stated that any child born of a slave woman is technically a slave under the law – even if the father should be a free black, free Indian, or a white slave owner.

By 1698, there were around 1,100 slaves living on Long Island – half of all the slaves in New York state. New York became the leading slave state of the North, with Long Island having the greatest concentration. Blacks, and also Indians, were both made slaves on Long Island.

It wasn't until the year 1898 that the great city of New York finally reached its present form. That year saw the consolidation of five cities merge to become one. The Bronx, Queens, Brooklyn, Staten Island and Manhattan all became "New York City." These former independent cities were thereafter called "boroughs."

Each of the five boroughs of New York City, that came to be dominated by whites and their slaves, were originally populated by Native American tribes. Author Anne Heinrichs recalls the original tribes that lived in the present day boroughs of New York city.

Some streets in Brooklyn today are the same routes the Indians took between villages. Before Europeans arrived, the Canarsee Indians had settlements in Brooklyn and Staten Island...

Manhattan Indians occupied the northern part of today's Manhattan Island, and the Rockaways lived in Queens. (New York, Anne Heinrichs, page 13)

Today, the city of New York is at the center of world economy. Contrary to popular belief, Washington D.C. is not where all the economic decisions that affect the world are made. The world's most powerful financial institutions, from banks to brokerages to stock exchanges, make their home in New York's financial district, located on both Broad Street and Wall Street.

The headquarters of the United Nations is also located in New York. Here all the nations of the world (excluding the Native Americans of course) come together to discuss world affairs. The city itself is a microcosm of the world. In it live people from all parts of the world. All the nations are gathered in New York.

New York City is also a leading center of art, music and fashion. Its status as the center of American pop culture is only rivaled by Los Angeles. From here, all types of American art, music, and fashion reach the rest of the world.

It is largely due to these characteristics that New York City has frequently been held under the microscope of Biblical prophecy. The city has been accused of being the prophetic manifestation of the city of Babylon mentioned in the Book of Revelations.

And he cried mightily with a strong voice, saying, Babylon the great has fallen, has fallen, and has become the habitation of devils, and the hold of every foul spirit, and a cage of every unclean and hateful bird. For all nations have drunk of the wine of the wrath of her fornication, and the kings of the earth have committed fornication with her, and the merchants of the earth are waxed rich through the abundance of her delicacies. (Revelation 18:2-3)

The implication is that since New York is the center of the capitalist universe, as well as a leading cultural center of the world, it has, through greed and immorality, served as the catalyst for both the economic poverty of many third world countries and the political turmoil of many foreign nations. The influence of American pop culture is also considered to be a huge, and predominantly immoral, influence on the rest of the world. This is a belief that is popular among various Christian groups.

It is suspected that New York City, symbolically representing greater America and the Western nations, is the Babylon of Biblical prophecies. It will be, or perhaps already was, the victim of "divine" wrath.

Therefore shall her plagues come in one day, death, and mourning, and famine; and she shall be utterly burned with fire: for strong is the Lord God who judged her.

And the kings of the earth, who have committed fornication and lived deliciously with her, shall bewail her, and lament for her, when they shall see the smoke of her burning.

Standing far off for the fear of her torment, saying, Alas, alas that great city Babylon, that mighty city! In one hour is thy judgment come. (Revelation 18:8 -10)

Even the most skeptical person cannot help but notice the eerie similarities that the above verses have with the terrorist attacks that took place on September 11, 2001. The city of New York, as well as the entire world, was dealt a massive blow when both of the towers of the World Trade Center were completely destroyed – in a very short period of time.

For in one hour so great riches is come to naught. And every shipmaster, and all the company of ships, and sailors, and as many as trade by sea, stood far off. And cried when they saw the smoke of her burning, saying, What city is like unto this great city! And they cast dust on their heads, and cried, weeping and wailing, saying, Alas, alas, that great city, wherein were made rich all that had ships in the sea by reason of her costliness! For in one hour is she made desolate. (Revelation 18:17-19)

The first airplane hit the north tower of the World Trade Center at 8:45 a.m. and at 10:28 a.m. it collapsed. The south tower was the second to be hit, but the first to collapse. It was hit at 9:03 a.m. and it collapsed at 10:05 a.m. All the nations and all of their leaders across the world witnessed this event. They saw the smoke from the aftermath burning for days afterwards.

All types of industries were directly affected by the collapse of the twin towers. Many had offices in the towers including: American Bureau of Shipping, Zim-American Israeli Shipping Co., China Chamber of Commerce Inc., AT&T Corporation, Baltic Oil Corporation, Dow Jones & Company Inc., and Fireman's Fund Insurance. Various financial corporations from all around the globe, who worked out of the towers, fell victim to the attacks. Foreign banks like the Bank of Taiwan and Banco LatinoAmericano de Exportaciones. Investment firms like EuroBrokers Inc. and Oppenheimer Funds Inc., Computer service companies like Sun Microsystems Inc. and The Beast.Com. These are just a few of hundreds of companies that conducted their business there.

According to the Book of Revelation, Babylon is a city of industrial commerce where many things would be bought and sold:

The merchandise of gold, and silver, and precious stones, and of pearls, and fine linen, and purple, and silk, and scarlet, and all thyine wood, and all manner vessels of ivory, and all manner vessels of most precious wood, and brass, and iron, and marble. And cinnamon, and odors, and ointments, and frankincense, and wine, and oil, and fine flour, and wheat, and beasts, and sheep, and horses, and chariots, and slaves, and souls of men. (Revelation 18:12-13)

The largest stock exchange in the world is the New York Stock Exchange. It is located on Wall Street but also had offices in the World Trade Center. It is interesting to note that every single item mentioned in the above Biblical verses has been bought and sold on the New York Stock exchange, including slaves.

New York's Stock Exchange origins date back to 1792, when brokers stood under a buttonwood tree along Wall Street transacting stock sales. Slavery in New York wasn't abolished until 1827 (although there were a few exceptions to the rule that continued until 1841.) So for several decades the business of buying and selling human beings would have been conducted in the same area New York's financial district exists today. Slavery was a billion-dollar industry. Although New York had banned slavery relatively early, during the height of the abolitionist movement, most of New York's power brokers were vehemently opposed to ending slavery in the South. They had established successful trade with the South, whose primary source of wealth came from slave labor.

Clearly New York City has a shameful past. But the real question to be asked is: Does this have anything to do with it being the Babylon mentioned in the Bible? Does this somehow relate to what took place on September 11, 2001? Or is it all just an ironic coincidence of completely unrelated events?

It is not considered politically correct to ask such questions. But if we desire to be spiritually correct, we must be willing to ponder these questions under the light of religious prophecy.

The fact is that, since many prophecies are subject to interpretation, in the case of Revelation chapter 18, a person could throw up a number of rationale objections. For instance, it took 62 minutes for the south tower to collapse; the north tower took even longer at one hour and 43 minutes. Revelations states that Babylon was destroyed "in one hour," therefore a person may find reason to doubt any connection between the chapter and the events on September 11. Furthermore, some verses seem to imply that after Babylon falls there will be no more business transactions taking place whatsoever.

And the merchants of the earth shall weep and mourn over her; for no man buyeth their merchandise any more: (Revelation 18:11)

Although there were plenty of merchants shedding tears that day; their loss wasn't permanent. Although the towers were no more, the New York Stock Exchange and Wall Street survived.

When reading the chapter, it does seem to give the impression that all of Babylon, the entire city or nation, would be destroyed. But besides the towers and a few surrounding buildings, all of New York City still stands. The rest of America is also alive and kicking – with all western nations supporting it 100 percent.

So what is the appropriate response? A sigh of relief? Should we take comfort in knowing that, since all of New York wasn't destroyed, it could not therefore be related to the Babylon of the Bible? The purpose here is not to prove whether New York or America is Babylon, or to justify a terrorist attack; the purpose to raise awareness of this prophecy. Perhaps the events of 9/11 should be taken as some sort of wake-up call from God.

Unfortunately, even if all of New York City was destroyed, there would still exist plenty of people who would not recognize any Biblical similarities. Even though an estimated 80% of the money that passes through New York City's banking systems can be tied to the drug trade, people will hesitate to say that God would ever condemn this great city, home of the U.N. and various world banks. Despite the tremendous increase in natural disasters – hurricanes, tornadoes, earthquakes – cities like New York, Los Angeles, and others will not stop their immoral and unjust practices.

Great nations may be given sign after sign by the Creator, but each time these signs are disregarded as coincidences.

The people of Pompeii Italy may serve as an example to those who choose to ignore "warning signs." In 62 AD this Roman city was struck by a massive earthquake that destroyed much of the city. After this event the people did nothing to change their ways and proceeded to rebuild the city. 15 years later at roughly 12 pm on August 24, 79 AD, Mount Vesuvius erupted in southern Italy just southeast of Naples. Pompeii, in close proximity to the volcano, was completely destroyed.

Modern archaeologists have uncovered the ruins of Pompeii and discovered many people who were buried alive by the ash. But what they learned about the culture in Pompeii was quite astonishing – an abundance of brothels, and pornographic images found in homes and in public arenas. It has been determined that Pompeii, a Roman city, was heavily engaged in the institution of slavery. Today, the city of Pompeii and the fate of its citizens is a popular tourist attraction.

12B – A Victim of the Destruction of Pompeii

The legendary eruption of Mount Vesuvius in Pompeii, Italy in the year 79 AD caused hot molten lava to rain down upon the people. The lava cooled, encasing their bodies in hard rock, Over time, the bodies disintegrated, leaving a hollow stone. When archaeologists poured liquid plaster into the rock, it hardened into the shape of the body that had been trapped within. Archeologists discovered bodies in many different positions, indicating that the rain of hot lava from the sky caught most people totally by surprise. The body of the individual above is on display in Pompeii for all tourists to see. It is a reminder of that tragic event - and perhaps a warning to future generations. (Photo courtesy of Michael and Phyllis Ward)

Conclusion:
The Vision Quest

13A – Sally White Eagle

In her quest to learn about her Native American heritage, Najma Rafat came to learn about her grandmother Sally White Eagle. Sally White Eagle was a member of the Choctaw tribe. Her descendents, including Sister Najma and her son Nafi, journeyed to the Gathering of Nations out of respect for their ancestors and also for all those who died as part of the Ghost Dance Movement. This led to us being instrumental in discovering some of the additional information that will be discussed in the conclusion. (Photo courtesy of the Rafat family.)

Conclusion:
The Vision Quest

I wish to give due respect and honor to all women. Women have played the most crucial role during my journey to write this book. They have been instrumental in bringing much information to light and have offered me spiritual support. In many traditions like those of the Native Americans, women are the keepers of the sacred traditions. They are the ones who teach the children and secure the future of a nation.

This fact reminded me of something my beloved Prophet Muhammad, may God bestow His choicest blessings upon him, once said. He said that "Heaven lies at the feet of thy mother." What he meant is that the teachings that a mother gives her children at an early age, the principles she instills in them, will guide them through the rest of their lives. It will determine whether they will be spiritual individuals who give praise to the Creator or of those who create total chaos.

Women have suffered just as much, if not more, from the widespread departure from the spiritual laws given to mankind from the Creator. From the Trail of Tears, to the slave trade, to the Wounded Knee Massacre, to the Black Civil Rights Movement, women have lost their lives along side men.

The reality is that we are all, men and women, imprisoned by the same evil force - the greed that produces unspeakable cruelty against ones fellow man. The racism that has been allowed to rule the land of America is ungodly. It crushes the spirit and kills the soul. Laws that force individuals onto poor, barren strips of land, or into raggedy, unsafe buildings are ungodly laws.

It is not only the whites who have been guilty of racism and discrimination. Many times immigrants from other ethnic groups and nationalities look at the poor and oppressed of America with scorn. They believe the media images that have been projected around the world -- images of savages, criminals, alcoholics, drug addicts, and just plain lazy, good-for-nothing, low life people who live off of welfare and handouts.

Immigrants, who are ignorant of America's history of brutality and murder inflicted on these oppressed groups, look at them with disdain and conclude that whatever hardships the people are suffering, they must have brought it upon themselves. These immigrants, arriving in America with money and education, are afforded opportunities that have long been denied to the Native inhabitants and denied to those of African ancestry. From Wounded Knee to Watts, the list of atrocities goes on and on. Gunned down. Beaten to death. Burned alive.

And yet, despite the horror of the past, despite the cruelty of the present, the oppressed struggle to obey the Divine command to strive toward brotherhood. Despite the broken promises, the violated treaties, the unenforced Civil Rights laws, despite the deception, oppressed people continue to pray, sing songs of praise to God and to worship. Sometimes faith is the only thing oppressed people have left. And from that faith, sometimes miracles happen.

When the weight of oppression has broken the spirit of a people, they sometimes fall prey to destructive habits to escape the pain of their suffering. Alcoholism and drug abuse run rampant among people that have lost all hope. It is often these people through whom God manifests His miracle of spiritual healing.

Sganyadaiyo, or Handsome Lake, was a holy man of the Iroquois Nation. He was born in 1735 in the area where New York State is today. Early in his life he began to develop a drinking habit. As he got older it only increased. He ended up moving in with his brother Cornplanter. While his brother Cornplanter was out negotiating for peace with the governments of the thirteen states, Handsome Lake was wasting away from a disease that had become a great plague among the Indian people, alcoholism.

On June 15, 1799, Cornplanter, summoned urgently to his house, was told that his brother was dying. The unconscious Handsome Lake – in at least one account he was taken by his family for dead and dressed for burial – awakened some four hours later and began to recount three visions he had had while he lay sick. In the first, he had been visited by three messengers, he said, handsome men dressed alike and carrying pronged blueberry saplings as canes, who at first prescribed medicine to cure him of his illness. He pledged to the messengers that, should he be allowed to walk on the earth again, he would repent of his sins. (Encyclo-

pedia of North American Indians, Edited by Frederick E. Hoxie, page 230.)

This man, whose alcoholism had driven him to the lowest depths of existence, was giving a new life by the Creator. While on what appeared to be his death bead, Handsome Lake experienced three profound visions that changed his life drastically. In his third vision the Creator revealed to him a new code of conduct he was to live by. This is known as the Code of Handsome Lake.

This new code included, among other things, complete abstention from alcohol and an emphasis on honoring marriage and family. He eventually rose to become a great spiritual teacher. So respected did Handsome Lake become that he was even requested by other nations, like the Onondaga, to come and share his spiritual knowledge with them.

Handsome Lake is an example that no matter how dark our pasts may be, we can still overcome, with God's Grace, and rise to spiritually levels where we reflect the light of the divine.

Bringing The Doors Together

The discovery of the existence of the Dogon Door and its connection to an ancient door kept by the Hopi was the beginning of a spiritual journey for me. In an interview with my friend, Dogon priestess Gilda Hamilton, I inquired more about the door. She told me of her experiences in Mali, West Africa. She mentioned that the Dogon priest had given her the door to bring back to America. It was specifically instructed that it be brought back to the Midwest. I recalled hearing some similar prophecies about events to take place in the Midwest. In an interview with religious scholar Muzafar Ahmad Zafar, he stated that Mirza Ghulam Ahmad had prophesized that something would occur in America"s Midwest that would have a tremendous impact and be of great spiritual importance.

These similar prophecies peaked my interest, needless to say. Gilda said that it was important that the Dogon Door come to the Midwest because there it could reconnect with the true Dogon. She told me that they said true Dogon would eventually be contacting her. I told her that I hadn't ever heard of any Dogon being sold into slavery in America. She told me that "Dogon" in general refers to the keepers of the prophecy and the people of God. The Dogon of Mali were the literal keepers of the door. She also said that they claimed to be the descendents of the early teachers who taught Joseph and of those original Essenes and Nazarenes - or the people of Jesus.

I inquired of her what it was that she thought I should be doing with this information. She said that according to what the Dogon priests said would happen, it would be a natural process and someone would eventually contact her. She told me that I was the only one who contacted her. The Dogon understood the prophecy and the connection between different nations of people – including the spiritual quest of the Native Americans. According to the Native Americans and the Dogon, all the doors were one day to come together. When that occurred there would be a new spiritual awakening.

I told sister Gilda that my understanding was that the Messiah had already come and that any prophecies related to the modern times, would relate to the coming of that Messiah. She told me that that's exactly why it was up to me to accept this spiritual quest and seek out this information and make the connections – and bring the doors back together and other prophecies. I told her I didn't think I was the one to do that because my position was just as a writer and researcher.

She paused for a moment and then explained that every man and woman has a spiritual journey and from everything that has happened, she spiritually felt that I was the one who must accept this spiritual journey. What really impacted me was that she then said that if I didn't accept this journey I was nothing more than a piece of meat.

She said the only thing that makes us all different from one another are the things we do in life. If this could be so important to a people that they would be willing to send one of their sacred objects to a different country for the mission, and if all of her spiritual understanding tells her that I'm the person that's supposed to accomplish the mission, how could I just refuse?

Once I accepted the task and began researching for this book, Allah blessed me with meeting many people who would give me inspiration while on my journey. One such individual was my sister in faith, Najma Rafat, who on several occasions offered me valuable information.

Sister Najma's grandmother was known as Sally White Eagle. Her and her son Nafi's personal quest to learn more about their family history represents a growing interest among many African Americans. Frequently this quest reveals Native American roots. Because of this, there is a rekindling of brotherhood and sisterhood between these two nations.

Another young brother named Micah Tair, who became part of the Black Indian Society research team, also came to learn more about his own Native American ancestry. The Black Indian Society was formed to help African Americans learn more about their native ancestry. Brother Micah recalls why he joined the Black Indian Society:

I became a member of the Black Indian Society because of the historical relationship in my own family between Africans and Native Americans. My African ancestors were slaves in this country. It also happens that my Indian ancestors were also slaves. Some of my Blackfoot Indian relatives were slaves.

My great-great grandmother, known as "Grandma Man," was a full-blooded Cherokee – and also a slave. While a young woman, she was raped by her slave master. Shortly after it was over, she managed to kill him and escape. But a reminder of the whole horrible event remained, as she was pregnant. Some might take it as a curse, but my grandmother followed higher spiritual principles, and bore the child and raised him, my great grandfather Golden Smith. Had she not been so strong in her principles, neither me nor my family would be here today. Her prayers are our blessings. Through her I feel a connection in my mind and heart to all of my Native American sisters and brothers. (Micah Tair, Interview 2002)

The Gathering Of Nations

Despite the hardships and ridicule, the Native American culture continues to be rejuvenated. Each year, a celebration is held, a family reunion of sorts in which all tribes come together. It is a celebration of life called *The Gathering of Nations* founded by Derek and Dr. Lita Mathews. It is a tribute to the Ghost Dance Movement. At this great Powwow they remember the great prophecies that tell of when the nations gather together, all the races of man, in one unbroken circle, that only then will peace be restored to the land. They dance, they sing, they share the ancient wisdom of the elders, and they strengthen the bonds of brotherhood and sisterhood among each other.

The circle is widening, to include not just the Native American nations, but the nations of the world. There are many who are having dreams that tell them this is a special period in which we are living. Now is time for the family to come together.

In the year 2000 William Skip Johnson of Top Artist Inc. introduced me to Melody Lightfeather and her husband Gerald Watson. They were intrigued by my research on Native American history and religious belief. I told her about the Dogon Door, and asked her about the Hopi sacred tablets. I also inquired about the Ghost Dance Movement, or Messiah Movement, which led up to the Wounded Knee Massacre. She asked me if I had had any spiritual experiences and I told her about a dream I had:

AILING HOLY MAN DREAM
In this dream, I saw a Native American holy man lying on a cold, concrete slab. He was dressed in a loincloth. The flesh on his chest was completely rotten. A voice told me to go and lay my hands on his chest, but I hesitated, unwilling to touch him. Again the voice commanded me to go, and I slowly walked toward the holy man and stretched out my hands. I laid my hands upon his chest and immediately the rotten flesh was completely healed. He looked up at me and said, "See, that was all I needed to heal me, just a simple touch."

She told me the significance of this dream and encouraged me to continue in my research. Eventually I went to the *Gathering of Nations* Powwow in Albuquerque, New Mexico, where I met many other native people who became my friends and gave me interviews that we used in this book. Many were reluctant to mention their names for fear of reprisal by certain political forces that still hold great influence in Native American communities.

On my way to visit the sacred lands, at the Hidden Valley of the Picuris Old Pueblo, I was told stories of how the early Spaniards would throw Native people off the mountains trying to force the people to tell them where the gold was. (There was no gold.) In these mountains there were caves where eagles would nest and the Indian people would lower their children into these caves to hide them from the Spanish so that the children would not be killed. The legend goes that the children would cry out in terror as they waited in the dark caves for parents, who sometimes had been murdered and therefore never returned. It seems that the winds still carry the cries of the children.

One shudders to think how many times scenarios like these occurred. It is no different than the Inca who first encountered the Spanish and then fled for their lives into the Andes.

Umm Shariq relates that she heard the Holy Prophet say: "People will fly into the mountains for shelter against the Anti-Christ." (The Sahih of Muslim by Hafiz Abu'l Husain Muslim ibn Hajjaj al-Qashiri)

After listening to so many stories like these and going to the sacred lands and offering prayers to the Creator I felt compelled to write this book in honor of those men, women and children whose lives were lost, simply because they dared to pray for deliverance from oppression. The Wounded Knee Massacre was particularly horrifying to me, because I could see that here was a people who had faith in God and they were shot to death because they believed in a Messiah.

The Dream State

One day, while watching a television documentary on Australia, I saw an interview with an Australian Aborigine. He was painting a traditional Aborigine mural and was talking about what is known as the "Dream State." For thousands of years the Australian Aborigines have relied on the "dream state" for guidance. It is their link to the Creator.

The elder began talking about how he knew that he was nearing the end of his life. He was not sad however, in fact he looked at death as a close companion. Although he was materially poor, without the luxuries that many of us are accustomed to, he said he felt that he was wealthy. He had been given all that he needed by the Creator. He was completely content with living a very naturalistic lifestyle. He did have one regret however, which when he spoke of it, made him break down and cry. He was deeply concerned that the Aborigine youth would have no knowledge of the dream state because most of them have pursued a western lifestyle centered around materialism. Along with the western way of life there frequently develops a belief that the spiritual experiences of the prophets and other religious people are nothing more than the mere delusions of madmen.

I was very moved by the Aborigine elder's tears. I silently vowed to him that I would try to become his voice so the youth would not forget about the dream state.

Long before I began working on this book, I was listening to a talk given by the current spiritual head of the Ahmadiyya Movement, Mirza Tahir Ahmad. In the speech he relayed a dream he had. In his dream he and a companion were swimming across a wide river. Although he made it across he saw that his companion did not and had to turn back.

The very night after hearing this statement I had a dream where I saw myself swimming across a river. When I made it to the other side I saw Mirza Tahir Ahmad. He grabbed my hand and pulled me out of the water and stated, "I see you made it to the other side."

I feel it is important to mention this experience in the context of this book because I know there are many people who are familiar with these types of experiences and value them. Many Native American people give as much consideration, if not more, to dreams and visions as any other experience.

Such religious experiences are vital to those who seek the truth. I am aware of people all over the world who had powerful dreams and visions that led them to believe in the truth of Mirza Ghulam Ahmad's claim to Messiah. I believe that people in every corner of the earth, regardless of what they believe, have had, are having, and will have, religious experiences that will guide them to this truth. There is indeed a Creator who communicates with his servants. Mirza Tahir Ahmad states:

> *Continuity of Divine revelation is indispensable for supporting a profound unshakeable belief in God which cannot be attained with the help of rational investigation alone. Hence, revelation must play a major role in strengthening belief in the existence of an Omniscient, Omnipotent God.*
>
> *Revelation is not confined solely to the office of prophet-*

hood. It is simply a means of communion between God and man. It is a universally excepted experience; to deny it is to deny the testimony of millions of people from all ages, all over the world. (Revelation, Rationality, Knowledge and Truth, page 715)

Revelation, true dreams and visions also offer guidance in one's affairs. While writing this book I had a number of dreams that gave me a deeper understanding into this mission I was on.

EAGLE DREAM

In this dream state I felt that I was lifted up by the Great Master's hand into the heavens, cradled like a mother's baby. As my eyes focused, I realized that I had been lifted up to where the ozone layer was, and I was extremely overwhelmed by this. My eyes felt normal when focusing but my body felt as light as air. I could see this massive hole in the ozone layer, as a result of all the carbon monoxide and pollution and poisons created by modern society. I felt my heart began to beat faster at the realization that we were destroying the ozone. I shouted, "Oh my God, look what they have done to the heavens by their actions."

After that this sweet gentle voice, with all the power of the Creator of the heavens and the earth, spoke to me close in my right ear. It said, "It is not their actions that created the problem with the ozone. It is their thoughts and their minds that created a problem with the ozone. By the time you act upon something it is too late. So tell them they must change the way they think." Then the hand was suddenly removed from underneath me and I began to fall back to the earth, but I wasn't afraid.

Then I felt a cool wetness and I realized I fell into a river. When I hit the water I descended to the bottom and then transformed into this beautiful fish, a Red Stock-Eyed Salmon. I realized I was hungry so I swam to the top of the river and jumped out to eat these fireflies that were hovering above the water.

As I danced and frolicked in this feast of fireflies, this strong voice again spoke. "When man eats according to the natural order of things it eliminates the physical, mental and emotional illnesses and diseases of today. When the fish eat the fireflies and we eat the fish our bodies build up an immune system that is more powerful than what can be reproduced in a laboratory." Although I heard the message loud and clear I was enjoying the feast so much I just wanted to keep jumping out for more.

But after this when I jumped I didn't catch any fireflies but instead I sprouted wings and became an eagle and ascended up into the heaven. I was transported back many, many moons to the time before the Europeans came to this land that is now called America. I was soaring high. The air had the smell of perfume, so clean and fresh. I could see the land below from the sky. It was like paradise on earth. I didn't want to stop soaring. Looking down at the river again I felt thirsty so I flew down to get a drink. The water was so sweet. I thought to myself that we really have no idea what pure fresh water really tastes like. It's really good!

BUFFALO VISION

It was early morning and I was sitting on the edge of my bed in my room. I was awake and my eyes were wide open. I began to hear what sounded like stampeding. when I looked and began to focus I saw a herd of maybe a thousand buffalo charging at me. At first I thought I should run but then I thought "Wait, I'm in my bedroom. Surely this is an illusion."

Then the Buffalo communicated to me, "Don't listen with your ears, listen with your heart. We lived for thousands of years with our Native Brother. We were willing to supply all their needs including food, clothes, tools and many instruments for their survival. We were happy with our arrangement with our Native Brother and we had grown to be a hundred million strong. See, the Natives ate our meat but when they died they would return to the earth and there would be beautiful green grass that would grow and we would eat the grass. We were all part of the circle of life. But when our White Brother came, we could not understand how he could just kill us thousands and thousands at a time. We thought that these people must really be hungry. But then we realized that they just wanted us for our skins as trophies.

"They would call us dumb animals because we wouldn't run from them. But the Great Creator created us and he gave man dominion over the earth to act responsibly and only take what they need. And if we had sought to hide, they would have only pursued us to kill us. So I ask them this question: Who was the dumb animal? The one who acts according to the natural order of things or the one who kills one hundred million of us?

"So go and tell my story. Little did they know that when

they killed our Indian Brothers and us they were killing themselves - and loosing their souls.

"So, go and tell the story of the buffalo. And we know that you will tell our story truthfully because the Indian Brothers called you, the African people, the people of the buffalo."

GREAT CHIEFS DREAM

In this dream I saw great chiefs riding on horses on what I understood was the Trail of Tears. They appeared much larger then what they would have been in reality. They were elaborately dressed in garments with feathers. It seemed that they went on for miles and miles, there were so many of them. I could hear them singing their songs and the rhythm of drums. Everything seemed like it was going in slow motion as they moved toward me. The head chief at the front said to me, "I represent all the great chiefs and when we sing our songs and dance this is how we give thanks to the Creator. But then when our White Brother came they did not understand. They attacked us and called us uncivilized. But the great Prophet Solomon wrote the Song of Songs, didn't they under- stand that our songs were sung for the Great Creator? So who is the savage, the one who oppresses or the one who sings the songs to the Creator?"

Today, the songs and ceremonies of the Native people are mocked in so many ways, whether in old movies which show "In- dians" with their feathers and painted faces or at sports games where "mascots" dress up in Native American garb and imitate the dance motions as a form of entertainment for the spectators.

The truly Godly people do not scorn, ridicule or condemn the forms of worship of other people.

I understood that what was needed to revive the spirit of the Native people was for someone to touch their hearts, and give them a message of hope. That was my task.

Ancestors From The Stars?

Along this amazing journey, one of the more intriguing things I learned about the Native people is their matter-of-fact atti- tude towards the existence of intelligent life on other worlds. In many of their traditions they tell how the early Natives had encountered aliens long ago and that during a significant portion of their history they actually maintained an ongoing relationship with alien beings.

Nancy Red Star, of the Abenaki/Cherokee Nation, gave me much insight into the Native American perspective on the issue of extraterrestrials. She is the author of numerous books including *Star Ancestors* and her most recent work *Legend of the Star Ancestors*. Her last name, Red Star, is in reference to the star of Sirius and a special connection that her people have with it.

The Hopi people also have a connection with Sirius. They call it the "Blue Star Kachina." Some of the Hopi believe that alien beings from a planet around Sirius visited Earth long ago. They are called Kachinas, Little People, and Star People. In some of the Hopi traditions, the Kachina came to save some of their people during the destruction of one of the previous worlds.

Just as the Hopi and the Dogon share a common tradition concerning sacred tablets, they also share traditions that involve the star Sirius. The Dogon of West Africa believe that some of their ancestors came from a planet around Sirius.

Did interplanetary meetings actually take place? Verses in the Quran seem to indicate that such a possibility could have taken place. In chapter 42, verse 30, of the Quran it states:

And among His Signs is the creation of the heavens and the earth, and of whatever living creatures He has spread forth in both and He has the power to gather them together when He will so please. (The Holy Quran, Chapter 42, Al Shura, verse 30.)

This verse, stating the existence of living creatures in both "the heavens and the earth" and God's power to "gather them together" implies that some sort of meeting between worlds will take place in the future. However, it does not rule out that such a meeting may have taken place in the past.

The star Sirius is in the constellation of Canis Majoris (Big Dog,) which is here in the Milky Way Galaxy. Due to its prominence in the constellation it is also called the "Dog Star." Of all the stars in the night sky, Sirius is the brightest of them all. It glows blue in the night sky but is believed to have appeared red thousands of years ago. This shining star is also headed directly towards the Earth at thousands of miles per hour. But before you get concerned, know that it is 8.7 light years away (51 trillion miles!) Like millions of other heavenly bodies, the polarized energies emitted from Sirius also rains down upon the earth.

Besides the Hopi and the Dogon, Sirius had symbolic meanings in many other ancient traditions as well. In Zoroastrian tradition it stood for the spirit of wisdom. The ancient Arabs worshipped Sirius, believing it could bring good or bad luck to them.

What I found most interesting, however, is the relationship that Sirius had with the ancient Egyptians (from whom the Dogon also claim to descend.) As many people are already aware, the Ancient Egyptians had great knowledge in the realm of astronomy. This knowledge had a great impact on their culture.

The pyramids of Giza were designed and arranged to symbolize the stars in the constellation of Orion's Belt. (Note: other pyramid sites in the world, like in Mexico, have the same arrangement. Also, the Pyramid of the Sun of Teotihuacan in Mexico is said to be the same size as the Great Pyramid of Giza. The Burma Tibetan Pyramid, known as The Pyramid of Gathering, is said to be the same size as the Khufu Pyramid of Egypt.)

It has also been determined that many of the Egyptian temples of worship, like the Temple of Isis at Denerah, were designed in order to allow the light of Sirius to reach their innermost chambers. For exactly what reason is not yet known.

According to some of the ancient texts, the Egyptians made use of special "star medicines" that were believed to absorb the energy that was emitted from Sirius. Just as the chlorophyll contained in plants photosynthesizes energy from the light of the sun, the ancient Egyptians believed that some plants were able to photosynthesize the light of Sirius.

It's reported that these plants were found in the area between the Nile and the Red Sea, known as the "Divine Lands." By taking these "star medicines" the Egyptians believed that it could cause a transformation in human cells, similar to how certain plants effect metamorphosis in caterpillars. The Egyptians used these "star medicines" for the purpose of spiritual advancement.

Whether these "star medicines" actually worked I cannot say. (The Dogon of Mali claim to have knowledge of the formulas for some of these "star medicines.") I found it quite shocking later when I realized that there is a chapter in the Quran that appears to show a connection between stars and plants.

There is a chapter in the Quran entitled Al-Najm (from which Najma, my Muslim friend's name, is based.) The Arabic term *najm* is commonly translated as meaning "star." At the very beginning of that chapter it reads:

> *By the star when it falls...* *(The Holy Quran, Chapter 53, Al Najm, (The Star) verse 2.)*

Strangely, Arabic lexicons reveal that the word *najm* has two main, seemingly unrelated, meanings. The other meaning that the word *najm* has is "stemless plant." One meaning refers to stars and the other refers to plants. Why should this be so? In light of information that has emerged on certain ancient Egyptians practices, one can't help but wonder if it is somehow related.

Furthermore, in the very same chapter, and nowhere else in the Quran, it makes mention of the Creator's status by stating:

> *... He is the Lord of Sirius.* *(The Holy Quran, Chapter 53, Al Najm, (The Star) verse 50.)*

This verse was revealed to the Prophet Muhammad after he witnessed some of his fellow Arabs worshipping Sirius. The Prophet wondered why the Arabs would worship a star and not Almighty God who created the star.

A Living Legacy

The Native American people today are no longer willing to let their history be defined by the Europeans, who had reduced them in their history books to uncivilized and savage people.

Like African Americans, this incorrect history has had a negative impact on the psychology of the Native American people for generations. From the many dialogues I have had with native people I realize that their psychological wounds run just as deep as African Americans. In my first book *Slavery: The African American Psychic Trauma* I tried to help heal the wounds of African Americans. It is my hope that this book may, in some small way, help heal some of the deep wounds of my native brothers and sisters. Perhaps there is a need for a book called *Colonialization: The Native American Psychic Trauma.*

Today a new reality for the Native American people is surfacing. We find an example of this in the story of a woman known as Empress Verdiacee "Tiara" Washitaw-Turner Goston El-Bey.

Empress Verdiacee is a descendent of the great Washitaw Empress Ayimarieeyah Washitaw–Tunica, who reigned during the second half of the 1700s. Empress Verdiacee claims that the Washitaw are descended from the ancient Olmec of Mexico.

Furthermore, the Washitaw are also said to be descended from those original migrants who came to America from the lost continent of Atlantis (by way of the Olmec.) Modern archeology has already proven that part of her claim is valid. In a book compiling various documents and articles called *Return of the Ancient Ones*, published by the Washitaw Publishing Company, it's noted that:

...when the tomb of the Emperial Empress, Ayimarieeyah, was discovered in 1955 and carbon dated by the Smithsonian Institute, it was affirmed that the Washitaw–Tunica Muurs were descendents of the ancient mound builders (the Olmecs). The truth was verified when a commission sanctioned by the State of Louisiana, the United Nations and the United States examined the ancient remains at Poverty Point where many ancient earthen mounds were constructed. The Washitaw–Tunica Muurs (the Olmecs) are the true and original proprietors of all the Americas. (Return of the Ancient Ones, Washitaw Publishing Company)

The name "Muurs" used above is another way of spelling "Moors." So it should also be understood that the Washitaw claim a Moorish heritage as well.

The Washitaw established itself as a Sovereign independent nation and seceded from the Union of 1781 and in 1789 seceded from the Northern two-thirds of the so-called State of Louisiana. The Washitaw Nation also holds the Spanish de Bourban land grants for East and West Florida, as these lands were included in the original Louisiana (1713); and this land claim was affirmed by the French, the Spanish and the British authorities at his time. The protection of the land rights and sovereignty of the Washitaw were also reaffirmed resulting from the Treaties of Paris (1763 and 1783) and the Treaty of San Lorenzo/Pinckney Treaty (1795).

The Washitaw are a good example of the constant evolution and blending of various cultures over thousands of years. They are descended from the Olmec who resided in Mexico. The Olmec were visited by West African Muslims who were also called Moors. Thousands of years prior to that they had been visited by ancient Egyptians. And many thousands of years prior to that the Washitaw's state that the ancestors of the Olmec migrated from a continent that today is called Atlantis.

Whenever people migrate, they bring with them the history from their past. When they intermarry with the indigenous people, the two cultures blend together, creating a unique culture that combines the histories of both people. Western historians often refuse to acknowledge the highly developed culture and civilization of the people who preceded Europeans on the American continent

Today the Washitaw, like so many Native American tribes, are struggling to preserve their legacy as original owners of the land. The Washitaw land represents about one third of the United States. Empress Verdiacee is one of many indigenous people who are trying to reclaim their land. Her specific claim is that a large area, beginning but not ending with Louisiana, was originally part of the great Washitaw Empire. This territory was claimed, illegally by the French, and later sold to the United States of America. This illegal transaction is popularly known as the "Louisiana Purchase." The only land that the French had the right to sell was the City of New Orleans.

The Washitaw have produced many documents in support of this claim. All information has been compiled into a booklet entitled, *Return of the Ancient Ones*, which can be acquired from the Washitaw Publishing Company (P.O. Box 1509, Columbia via: USA Postal Zone 71418).

Empress Verdiacee's dedication and hard work is a testament to other indigenous people. The Washitaw land claim verifies the legitimacy of other Native American treaties. All treaties should be honored and the nations should be compensated. Perhaps other indigenous nations can find justice in the World Court.

In 1993 the Cherokee nation invited the Washitaw nation to come together to discuss their struggles and promote intertribal unity. This affair was in remembrance of the 1843 International Indian Council, where many tribes made peace with one another and began to work together to survive in those fast changing times.

Historically, Native American nations have had difficulty getting recognition from the United Nations. But twice during the 1990s the Washitaw were recognized by the U.N. when they visited the U.N. offices in Geneva, Switzerland. An article included in *Return of the Ancient Ones* notes that:

... a Washitaw Delegation traveled to the United Nations at Geneva, Switzerland, in 1993 and filed charges against the U.S. for acts of genocide against its people. At the same time the Washitaw also sent a bill to the U.S. for 80 quadrillion dollars in gold representing the back rent owed on the land stolen in the name of Louisiana plus the Floridas. In 1996, a Washitaw Delegation journeyed back to Geneva to attend an Indigenous People's Conference. The Washitaw received its Sovereign Nation status on this occasion. (U.N. Indigenous Nation #215) (Return of the Ancient Ones, Washitaw Publishing Company)

The 1993 and 1996 Washitaw visits to the U.N. represent movement in the right direction towards bringing all four brothers back into the sacred hoop. The fact that this Washitaw delegation could actually file charges against the U.S. says a lot. Could they have done that at the U.N. offices in New York or would they just have had their entry vetoed like the earlier Hopi delegations?

Apparently, the Washitaw had to travel all the way to Switzerland just to be heard. Nevertheless, it is one step closer towards one day when the Native American nations will be fully allowed into the world community in the "official capacity" that the United Nations represents.

The United Nations has acknowledged the Washitaw as the "oldest indigenous nation of Earth." The Washitaw are the remnants of the Ancient Ones (Uaxashaktun) of Muu (Amurru). (Return of the Ancient Ones, Washitaw Publishing Company)

The fact that the United Nations in Geneva, Switzerland also officially recognized this group of indigenous people from America as the "oldest indigenous nation of earth" shows that the history of the Native American nations, as understood and told by many of them, is beginning to be acknowledged.

As Native Americans cleanse their history of the largely

CHEROKEE NATION

P.O. Box 948 · Tahlequah, Okla. 74465 · (918) 456-0671

Wilma P. Mankiller
Principal Chief

John A. Ketcher
Deputy Chief

July 30, 1993

Empress Verdiacee Tiari Washitaw-Turner Ghoston
Nation Wishitaw Of DUG DAH MOUND WAH
Columbia
P.O. Box 1509
VIA US Postal Zip 71418

Dear Empress Ghoston:

No greater or more opportune time has existed in our history than the present to come together and deliver our messages collectively to the rest of mankind.

We are currently organizing a very special event as a forum for this purpose. Scheduled for September 1993, the event commemorates the 150th Anniversary of an 1843 International Indian Council that was organized by the Principal Chief of the Cherokees.

The original 1843 International Indian Council took place here in Tahlequah, Oklahoma. Eighteen (18) Tribes from throughout the Western Hemisphere, two-hundred eighteen (218) Delegates and over four-thousand (4,000) attendees joined together to renew friendships and peace between our nations and adopt international resolutions.

Our effort to organize this event once again among our Native Peoples is a message of paramount importance to non-Indian peoples throughout the world and not merely a side note to contemporary history of interest only to ourselves and to scholars.

Our cultures, governments, medicine and religion have provided the best foundations for modern society in law, civil rights, human relations and survival far in advance of Indoeuropean culture.

Together as sovereign nations, we will have the opportunity during this event to record and discuss with distinguished panelists global issues like ethnocide, genocide, reclaiming our lands, and protection of our languages and cultures.

13B – Letter From the Cherokee Nation
The following was a letter sent in 1993 from the Cherokee Nation of Tahlequah, Oklahoma to the Washitaw Empress Verdiacee. It calls for a new camaraderie between Native American tribes in order to uplift their people.

The closing of the 1843-1993 International Indian Council will be marked by the signing of two (2) proclamations; a proclamation will be adopted and presented to the United Nations and world communities in this "Year Of Indigenous Peoples," calling on them to recognize and acknowledge the contributions and importance of Indian Nations in the world family. And finally, a new proclamation of Friendship and Peace among the tribes attending the event will be promulgated.

Leaders and delegates from every Indian Nation are being called upon to join us in order to share our cultures, renew friendships and recreate the spirit and tradition of the original 1843 International Indian Council.

You are invited to send a delegation which includes: tribal government representatives, a tribal translator and a cultural representative in the areas of traditional dance, songs or arts.

Your presence as a representative of a great and sovereign Indian Nation is important and will honor us. I look forward to welcoming you to the 1843-1993 International Indian Council.

Sincerely,

Cherokee Nation
1843-1993 International Indian Council
Events.

P.S. Additional information on the 1843-1993 International Indian Council is enclosed.

13C – Letter From the Cherokee Nation (page 2)

biased European versions, this will additionally result in the cleansing within their culture of many "western" evils like racism which has severely infected their community.

During a conversation with one Native American sister, she spoke with great pain in her voice. The words of this beautiful sister were louder than a drum. The sister did not want her name mentioned because she was afraid that her statement might invite certain officials who hold power to harass her once she returned to the reservation. She is not a radical or revolutionary activist, she is a normal everyday American Indian woman who works for a community based organization. Still, her thoughts reflect those of many other Native Americans as well:

"What hurts me as much or more than anything that we've talked about, and all the other things that we could talk about, is the fact that they degree your blood now. They have since the beginning, since they tried to move everybody and tried to get rid of all of us. They have it in paper at the Smithsonian where they talk about, "well, if we can't kill them all then we'll just quantum them out of existence." So what they do is they divide you up into eighths, sixteenths, whatever. It's forced halves, eighths, sixteenths, thirty-seconds, sixty-fourths - thinning your bloodline.

"So if your parents intermarry, which all of us have to do now because our nations our so small, sooner or later the government then gets to say "Oh, you don't have enough blood now." Makes no difference who your relatives are or how you were raised or nothing – all those things that are important... And it doesn't matter if we recognize each other, which is what should count. None of that counts anymore." (Anonymous Interview, Gathering of Nations Powwow 2001)

The sister also told me some of her experiences that were deeply personal. On a number of occasions we had to pause the interview because she was so overcome with emotion.

The practice of defining her people by the superficial concept of race was particularly troubling for her. It so happens that this sister was very light complexioned, even by Native American standards. Without knowing her one might believe she was "white." But, throughout her life she was ostracized by the white community. Again this is largely due to the concept of race brought by the Europeans, enforced in the "one drop rule," and continued to this day among the Native American community in an official government capacity. The sister explains:

"Your BIA card gives you your quarters and quantum. BIA is Bureau of Indian Affairs. So the government does this. The federal government decides who's Indian and who's not.

"It was decided in Lincoln's time, when you guys (African Americans) were freed, that they could no longer do that. They used to grade slaves as octoroons and quadroons and mulattos, etc. It was decreed in law that no longer was this applicable because you were a human being and not a livestock anymore. But they still do it to Indians to this day. They even sold Indians as slaves 50 years after the Emancipation Proclamation when all the black people were free!" (Anonymous Interview, Gathering of Nations Powwow 2001)

The insistence of the federal government to require Native Americans to carry BIA cards does not help maintain tribal unity. There is a planned strategy to keep Native Americans as a whole from coming together. The issue of color is one such tactic.

Just as the sister mentioned above resembles a white person, the Washitaw Empress Verdiacee resembles a person who is black. This is because she has African ancestry.

The Empress Verdiacee and members of the Washitaw nation kept written records such as the original land grants, deeds and treaties. Other historical documents exist, enabling the United Nations to verify the truth of the Washitaw land claims. The Reports from the Lewis and Clark Expedition of 1804-1806 document the historical presence of the Ouachita-Tunica (Washitaw) at the request of the President of the United States.

In 1973 the Division of State Lands, a section of the Department of Natural Resources for the State of Louisiana, published a work entitled *History of Land Titles in the State of Louisiana* in an issue of the *Louisiana Historical Society* periodical. In it they discuss the "...historical interest in determining the very first owner of that certain tract of land..." In that document the Native American presence in the area of Louisiana is acknowledged in reference to the "debate" over who the land belonged to originally – the French, the Spanish, or the Indian.

THE RETURN OF THE LAND

DIVISION OF ADMINISTRATION
STATE LAND OFFICE

BUDDY ROEMER
GOVERNOR

DENNIS ETNE
COMMISSIONER

January 8, 1992

Verdiacee Goston
Empress of the Washitaw
P.O. Box 1051
Columbia, La. 71418

Re: Maison Rouge Grant
     1848 Tax Adjudications
     Ouachita Parish, La.

Dear Ms. Goston:

On January 8, 1992, you requested that cancellations be issued
relative to adjudications for unpaid property taxes for the year
1848 in Ouachita Parish, Louisiana, in the names of:

Daniel W. Coxe	10,000 Acres	Maison Rouge Grant
Wycoff & Harrison	16,000 Acres	Maison Rouge Grant
G. V. Turner	10,000 Acres	Maison Rouge Grant
C. G. Fershey	2,800 Acres	Maison Rouge Grant
Suc. Henry Turner	1,928 Acres	Maison Rouge Grant
Henry Turner	5,519 Acres	Maison Rouge Grant
Sarah Tyler	5,600 Acres	Maison Rouge Grant
Coff & Harrison	16,000 Acres	Maison Rouge Grant
Eliza Quitman	1,036 Acres	Maison Rouge Grant

Total   68,883 Acres

Article X, Section 20 of the Louisiana Constitution of 1921
states:

> Whenever any immovable property shall have
> been forfeited or adjudicated to the State for
> the nonpayment of taxes due prior to January
> 1st, 1880, and the State shall not have sold or
> disposed of same, nor dispossessed the tax
> debtor, or his heirs, successors or assigns,
> prior to the adoption of this Constitution, it
> shall be conclusively presumed that such
> forfeiture or adjudication was irregular and
> null, or that the property has been redeemed;

STATE LAND OFFICE • P.O. BOX 44124 • BATON ROUGE, LOUISIANA 70804-4124
AN EQUAL OPPORTUNITY EMPLOYER

13D – Return of the Land

*The above is an official document from the State of Louisiana. It is a response
to Empress Verdiacee acknowledging 68,883 acres of land for unpaid property
taxes since the year 1843. (Return of the Ancient Ones, page 443)*

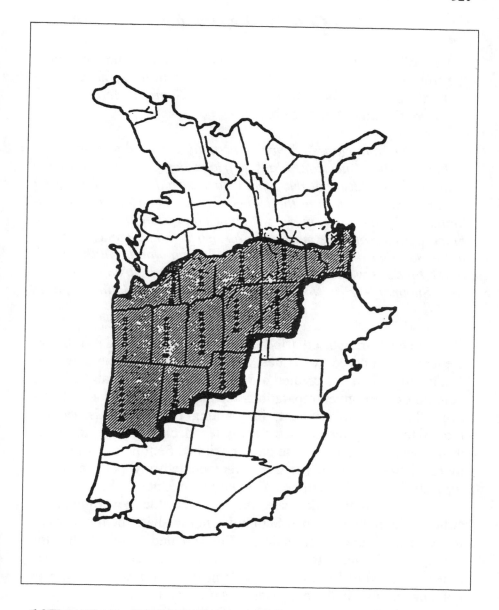

13E – Map of the Washitaw Empire

The Washitaw Nation claims the shaded area above was part of their original empire that was taken from them unjustly. This vast territory was sold by France to the U.S. for $15 million in 1803 and subsequently doubled the size of America. This was known as the "Louisiana Purchase." Could America's Midwest be the center of a new spiritual awakening for the Native American people? (Return of the Ancient Ones, page 218)

A Case For Reparations

Whether they are related to the African or the European, the truth is that most Native American tribes of today have multi-cultural roots. In her book *A Powwow Summer Across North America*, Dr. Lita Mathews observes:

The Narragansett Tribe is actually a tri-cultural mixture: Indian (Native American, black (African descent) and European (Anglo). This culture or tribe and its ancestral heritage dates back to early colonial times in the United States. The Narragansett Indian blood lines are so mixed with black and white that true Indian blood consists of little more than ancestral family names. This is not to say that they do not posses any Indian blood, but the purity of the blood is weak. Nevertheless, their spirit is strong. (A Powwow Summer Across North America, by Dr. Lita Mathews, pages 86-87)

The Narragansett tribe, like the Seminole and Washitaw, are part of hundreds of tribes who have a multicultural legacy. American racism has created a conflict within these nations. The Seminoles were given reparations for the loss of their land. However, the U.S. Government, in granting reparations, issued the money to the lighter skinned Seminoles, declaring these to be the most "pure blooded." Those darker skinned Seminoles, who had a more distinct African heritage, were denied any portion of the reparations. The Government declared them "non-Indian."

To further exacerbate the conflict, the government instructed the lighter skinned Seminoles not to share the money with the darker skinned Seminoles. This created a racial division among a multiracial, multicultural people that had originally been allies. The word "Seminole" itself means "run-away." This was not a name of an indigenous Native American nation.

African Americans who are fighting for reparations should also remember not to fall into the same trap of color and class divisions. The struggle of all people should be recognized, and all claims for reparations should be honored.

If all of those African American elected officials who are actively seeking reparations for slavery were to rally around the Empress and the Washitaw nation, they could create a strong case for the U.S. Government and the World Court to seriously examine. When African Americans and Native Americans recognize their common ancestry, they can present a unified case for reparations and achieve victory.

The Washitaw submitted a tax bill to U.S. Government, for an $80 quadrillion dollars in gold, representing the back rent owed on the land stolen in the name of Louisiana and Florida. The Government would not be able to pay this bill without becoming bankrupt, but it is a legitimate claim. Therefore, the government should negotiate an amount of back rent it can pay, and it should continue to pay taxes on the land to the Washitaw nation.

The Washitaw, a legitimate multi-racial sovereign nation in the U.S., would be able to use this money to rebuild impoverished areas and eliminate many of the problems of poor health, crime, insufficient education and other social ills that stem from lack of financial resources.

World Peace or Final Destruction

The United States is at a crossroads in history. According to Native prophecies, these are the times when a major change will take place, and the world as we know it will cease to exist.

Newspaper headlines tell the story of a collapsing economy and a country plagued by natural disasters – droughts, fires, floods. There are wars abroad and conflict at home. The family has disintegrated and the country has plunged into a moral decline.

Now is the time for those who foresaw the coming of a Messiah, a spiritual healer and a reformer, to come together. Let us all recognize that the solution to our collective plight is a spiritual solution. We must become one nation, one world, under God. Let the red, the black, the yellow and the white seek out common ground and convene with those who desire to save our world from the designs of madmen.

If we are successful, peace will reign. If we fail, the prophesies of the Native Americans, and of the Bible and the Quran, are very clear: The world will witness the battle of Armageddon - the final conflict between good and evil. America, the world's future is in your hands. Either we share what we have or we lose it all in an atomic blast. Where do you stand?

SPIRIT WOMAN

by Sultan A Latif (Flying Eagle)
(Dedicated to the memory of Sister Melody Lightfeather)

Oh Spirit Woman, fly high like a bird in the sky.
I saw your spirit reflecting the truth of who you are.
When Indian women would come to you
And had major challenges they could not resolve
You would look at them and reassure them
The Creator had not forgotten them
You would tell them to hold fast to their faith.
Sometimes poor people wanted something
They couldn't afford because they had no money.
Still you would let them have your artwork
Without reservations.
Your mission was not just to be creative,
And to be an artist,
But also to touch the hearts of people.
Oh, Spirit Woman, fly high!
I saw you when the white women would come
And they would want to purchase your art.
They had unlimited credit cards and finances
As they engaged themselves with you.
What they received was far more
Than what they could buy with their credit cards.
I saw their hearts change and their faces smile
And maybe for the first time they became human beings.
I saw them raising their standards
From "I have all the money in the world,"
To "I am part of the world."
I witnessed this because of your presence.
Oh Spirit Woman, fly high like a bird in the sky.
I saw you when black women came to you.

Sometimes they would be apprehensive.
They would say, "Oh this is a Native American Woman.
She looks something like us.
But where is she really coming from?"
Then you opened your arms
And reached out and embraced them like a sister.
I heard your words, Oh Spirit Woman.
You said, "Without your people, my people,
We would not have survived.
The blood that runs in your veins also runs in mine.
We are sisters indeed."
I saw tears in their eyes
They were so moved
By your love and compassion.
Oh Spirit Woman,
I see you flying high like a bird in the sky
You have truly expressed love for all mankind.
In your quest to show the devastation
Heaped upon your people by the invaders.
You still showed everyone love and compassion.
Oh Spirit Woman,
You are flying high like a bird in the sky.
Sadly, our friendship was a short one,
My heart feels as if our relationship lasted an eternity.
Death came like a thief in the night.
The lesson to be learned here is
When death comes, no one knows the time or the hour.
Your demise tore my heart as if you were my blood sister.
I know the prayers we offered at the Kiva were answered.
The Indian Holy Man told you we must finish this book,
He said this book is for our children and our future.
I hope that I've done justice to When Nations Gather.
We pray to God that he will bless you where ever you are
Oh Spirit Women, fly high like a bird in the sky,
We will miss you dearly.

LESSON PLAN

These activities are designed to be used as written assignments and classroom discussions after the completion of each Chapter.

Introduction
1) Describe the differences between communal ownership of land and private ownership of land. How did these differing cultural practices create a conflict between Native American and European immigrants?
2) List some of the negative stereotypes of Native Americans as portrayed in films or old American history books.

Chapter 1: The Beginning or the End
1) Describe the difference between the linear concept of time and the circular concept of time.
2) According to Native American spiritual beliefs, how many times has the human population been destroyed? Why?

Chapter 2: The Descendants of Atlantis
1) List some of the signs that indicate the existence of the lost continent of Atlantis.
2) List some of the signs that indicate extensive communication between the ancient Egyptians and the inhabitants of America.

Chapter 3: The Spanish Empire Expands
1) What was Columbus' promise to King Ferdinand and Queen Isabella when he borrowed money to sail to westward to the Indies?
2) Describe the differences between the arrival of African explorers and the arrival of European explorers to the Americas. What kind of relationships did each group establish with the native people?

Chapter 4: The Invasion of North America
1) How was the Seminole nation created?
2) Describe the form of government created by Deganawida. What ideas did Benjamin Franklin borrow from him?

Chapter 5: Prophecies of Doom Fulfilled
1) What was the "Trail of Tears" and why was it so called?
2) Describe the "One Drop" rule and how it determined racial classification.

LESSON PLAN

Chapter 6: In Search of a Savior
1) Describe the similarities in Wovoka's spiritual experience and Black Elk's spiritual experience.
2) Why did the Mormons believe that the Messiah would come from among the Native American people?

Chapter 7: The Rise of Gog and Magog
1) According to Biblical prophecy, what are the signs of the Anti-Christ?
2) According to Hopi prophecy, what are the characteristics of the True White Brother?

Chapter 8: The Age of the Messiah
1) List some of the people who were thought to be the modern day Messiah.
2) What was the challenge issued by Mirza Ghulam Ahmad to Alexander Dowie?

Chapter 9: Divine Confirmation
1) List some of the prophets of the past who were expected to return to earth.
2) List some of the dates of solar eclipses and comets.

Chapter 10: Racial and Religious Persecution
1) To what modes of transportation did the bug and the donkey refer?
2) How did the FBI under J. Edgar Hoover treat political and religious dissidents in the 1920s, 30s and 40s?

Chapter 11: A Warning to the United Nations
1) To what does the Hopi prophecy that God would "shake the earth" refer?
2) How did the Civil Rights movement affect Native Americans' fight for justice?

Chapter 12: Can Armageddon Be Stopped?
1) What is the prophecy of the "Third Shaking of the Earth?"
2) List the similarities between the city of New York and the city of Babylon as mentioned in the Book of Revelation.

Conclusion:
1) What do the Dogon and the Hopi people believe about the planet Sirius?
2) What portion of the U.S is owned by the Washitaw nation?

Bibliography

We are sincerely grateful to all the outstanding authors and speakers listed below. Their works and speeches provided an excellent source of information for this book. We highly recommend their books for those who wish to do further research.

Books and Speeches

Ahmad, Mirza Ghulam, *Jesus in India*, Islam International Publications Limited, United Kingdom, 1989.

Ahmad, Mirza Ghulam, *Tadhkirah*, Islam International Publications Limited, United Kingdom, 1980.

Ahmad, Hazrat Mirza BashirudDin Mahmud, *Invitation to Ahmadiyyat*, Islam International Publications Limited, United Kingdom, 1997.

Ahmad, Mirza Tahir, *Revelation, Rationality, Knowledge and Truth*, Islam International Publications Limited, United Kingdom, 1998.

Banyacya, Thomas, *United Nations Address*, 1992.

Boyce, William D., *Illustrated Africa, North Tropical and South*, Rand McNally & Company, 1925.

Brown, Lee, *Speech*, Continental Indigenous Council, 1986.

Emaciyapi, Ehanamani (Dr. A.C. Ross), *Mitakuye Oyasin "We are all related"*, Wiconi Waste, Denver, CO, 1989.

Evanzz, Karl, *The Messenger: The Rise and Fall of Elijah Muhammad*, Vintage Books, New York, NY 1999.

Brother G, *Shades of Memnon: The Africa Hero of the Trojan War and the Keys to Ancient World Civilization*, Seker Nefer Press, 1999.

Josephy Jr., Alvin M., *500 Nations, An Illustrated History of North American Indians*, Alfred A. Knopf, Inc., Pathways Productions, Inc., 1994.

Gilbert, Adrian G. and Cotterell, Maurice, *The Mayan Prophesies*, Element Books Inc. 1995.

Goodnough, David, *The Colony of New York*.

Haley, Alex, *Autobiography of Malcolm X*, Ballantine Books, New York, NY, 1973.

Heinrichs, Anne, *New York*.

Hoxie, Fredrick E., *Encyclopedia of North American Indians*, Haughton Mifflin Company, Boston New York, 1996.

Jackson, John G., *Introduction to African Civilizations*, The Citadel Press, Seraucus, NJ, 1980.

James, Peter and Thorpe, Nick, *Ancient Mysteries*, Ballantine Books, New York, NY, 1999.

Katz, William Loren, *Black Indians: A Hidden Heritage*, Aladdin Paperbacks, New York, NY, 1997.

Khan, Anwer Mahmood, *Fulfillment of Prophecy: Hazrat Ahmad's Challenge to John Alexander Dowie*, 2000.

Leaming, Hugo P., *Gone to Croatan: Origins of North American Dropout Culture*, edited by Ron Sukolsky & James Koehaline, Autonomedia/AK Press, New York, Edinborough, 1993.

Mails, Thomas E., *The Hopi Survival Kit*, Penguin Books, New York, NY, 1997.

Mathews, Dr. Lita, *A Powwow Summer Across North America*, A Gathering of Nations Publishing, Albuquerque, NM, 2000.

Matthiessen, Peter, *In the Spirit of Crazy Horse*, Viking Press, New York, NY, 1983.

Muhammad,, Amir Nashad Ali, *Muslims in America: Seven Centuries of History (1312-2000)*, Amana Publications, Beltville, MD, 2001.

Muller, Robert A., and Oberlander, Theodore M., *Physical Geography Today, Portrait of A Planet*, Random House, New York, NY, 1978.

Neihardt, John G., *Black Elk Speaks, Being the Life Story of a Holy Man of the Oglala Sioux*, University of Nebraska Press, 1989.

Peterson, Scott, *Native American Prophecies*, Paragon House, St. Paul, MN, 1999.

Quick, Abdullah Hakim, *Deeper Roots, Muslims in the Caribbean Before Columbus to the Present*, The Association of Islamic Communities in the Caribbean and Latin America, Toronto, Ontario.

Ragg, Lonsdale and Laura, *The Gospel of Barnabas*, edited and translated from the Italian Ms. In the Imperial Library at Vienna.

Rashad, Adib, Islam, *Black Nationalism & Slavery*, Printers Inc. Beltsville, MD, 1995.

Reid, John Phillip, "The Spirit of American Law," *A Better Kind of Hatchet: Law, Trade and Diplomacy in the Cherokee Nation During the Early Years of European Contact.* University Park: The Pennsylvania State University Press, 1976.

Savilla, Elmer M., *Along The Trail, The Story of One Little "Indian."* Published.

Tagliaferro, Linda, *Destination New York*

Turner, Richard Brent, *Islam in the African-American Experience*, Indiana University Press, Bloomington Indianapolis, 1997.

Twombly, Robert C., *Blacks in White America Since 1865*, David McKay company, Inc. 1971.

Van Sertima, Ivan, *They Came Before Columbus*, Random House, Inc., New York, NY, 1976.

Walton – Raji, Angela Y., *Black Indian Genealogy Research: African American Ancestors Among the Five Civilized Tribes*, Heritage Books, Inc., Bowie, MD, 1993.

Waters, Frank, *The Book of the Hopi.*

Return of the Ancient Ones, Washitaw Publishing Company (P.O. Box 1509, Columbia via: USA Postal Zone 71418).

Religious Scriptures and Reference Books

Aqrab ul-Muwarid, vol. II - Arabic Dictionary

Funk & Wagnalls New Comprehensive International Dictionary of the English Language, Deluxe Reference Edition, Publishers International Press, Newark New Jersey, 1982.

The Original African Heritage Study Bible, King James Version General Edition, Reverend Cain Hope Felder Ph.D., The James C. Winston Publishing Company, Nashville, TN, 1993.

Holy Quran, Arabic Text English Translation with Commentary, Ahmadiyya Movement in Islam, London Mosque, London, England, 1981

The Holy Quran, Abdullah Yusuf Ali translation, Published in Pakistan.

Selected Saying of the Holy Prophet of Islam, Islam International Publication, Ltd. 1997

Selected Sayings of the Promised Messiah, Islam International Publication, Ltd. 1997

The Declaration of Independence, July 4th 1776.

Newspapers Magazines, Media

Mahir Abdal-Razzaaq El, "Digging for the Red Roots," *Message Magazine* July 1996.

Ritter, Jim, *Chicago Sun-Times*, December 10, 2000, page 34A

Techqua Ikachi, Issue #3

Review of Religions, November 1996.

Review of Religions, November 1999.

Review of Religions, April 2002.

The Commercial Advertiser, October 26, 1903.

Leaves of Healing, September 26, 1903.

Chicago Evening American, March 9, 1907.

The Sunday Herald, Boston, June 23, 1907.

The Moslem Sunrise, January 2, 1923.

"Timeline of Muslim Exploration of the Americas, 1178 CE Muslim Explore America?" *The Islamic Bulletin*, P.O. Box 410186, San Francisco, CA 94141-018-6415-552-8831, Fax 415-552-4737, info@islamic-bulletin.org

In Memory of Crazy Horse,
http://maier1.best.vwh.net/native/crzyop.htm

Flood on Superstitious Mountain, Native American Lore, 1996 StoneE Productions, www.ilhawaii.net/~stony/lore72.html

Conquistadors Miniseries, *The Learning Channel*, 2001

Also Recommended

Ghost Wolf, Robert, *Last Cry: Native American Prophecies: Tales of the End Times*, Grail Publishing, Sante Fe, NM, 1997

King Hassan II. *The Story of The African Moors from Morocco in America*, Royal Communique1996, The Greater Metro Atlanta-Based Moorish International Divine Movement, Post Office Box 288, Stone Mountain, Georgia 30086-2088.

Salahuddin, Abu Bakr Ben Ishmael, *Saving the Savior*, Jammu Press, 2001.

Latif, Sultan A. and Naimah, *Slavery: The African American Psychic Trauma*, Latif Communications Group Inc., 1994.

Red Star, Nancy, *Star Ancestors*, Destiny Books, Rochester, Vermont, 2000.

INDEX

334